TOMMY REMEMBERED

[AND OTHERS]

P.N. JACKSON

 www.trafford.com

North America & international
toll-free: 1 888 232 4444 (USA & Canada)
fax: 812 355 4082

I visited my local Hospital today, it is called the Wharfedale General Hospital. I was there for a routine blood test. I arrived late hoping that it would not be too busy. I was in luck, there was only one elderly lady just leaving. "Please come in Mr. Jackson," said a young lady. In I went. She tried to take a blood sample from my right arm but as this can be a problem, and it was, she said she would take one from my left arm. As she did so, she said, "Be careful Mr. Jackson, there is a drop of blood on your arm, don't mark yourself." She then put a plaster over the wound.

"Thank you, what is your name?" "Marie," she replied. "Well, Marie, that drop of blood reminds me of when I was studying to be an embalmer. Although wearing gloves, I had a habit of wiping my hands down my sides. One day I got such a whack across my hand, I never did it again." "You're an embalmer then?" said Marie. "Yes," I replied. "What do you do then?" So I explained the procedure. "Are you sure there is no one waiting?" "There Is nobody waiting, you are the last patient." I talked; Marie listened. We travelled together sixty years or more back in time. "Well, Marie! I will have to make tracks, my family will wonder where I have got to." "I think you should write a book," said Marie. "What me!" I replied. "Yes, you. Why not?" she said. "Why not?" I replied, "I can't tell you the last time I wrote a letter. I am a lousy writer. I always print instead of writing, I can forget things in the time it takes to cross a room, and I do not have the time." "I think you should make time," said Marie. "I will think about it," says I.

I have enjoyed a nice meal with my wife and son, they have gone into the lounge to read or watch T.V. I settle into my chair and gently rock to and fro. The fire is glowing, bathing the room in a soft red light. As I sit gently rocking to and fro, I close my eyes, and I start to think back in time. Good Lord! I have recalled my first memory. I cannot believe it.

I sit and remember my parents when they were young. Here is Tommy, a very young Tommy with a shock of hair that stands up-wards and forwards (When he can find a comb, he wears it fringe-

like.), bright eyed, a grin that exposes two small buck teeth, a grey
"V"-necked jersey which always seems to have a hole in it near his
right hand trouser pocket. Although we always wore garters, for
some reason his left sock was always round his ankle.

Memories are jostling with each other. Some clear; some con-
fused- too many to handle. I open my eyes. I think maybe, just
maybe, I could have a go at it. I rouse myself and get an "A4-
lined." folder and find a pen. As I sit down to write, my wife
comes into the room and asks me what I am doing. "I am going
to write a book." "What about?" she asks. "About Tommy and
me." "But you can't remember across a room." (She doesn't know
what I know.) "We will see," I say, "We will see." And so I start
to print... err... write.

My name is Peter N. Jackson. What does the 'N' stand for? You
might ask as people have done before you. You will have to guess.
You might ask for a second letter. The second letter is "A". Some
cotton-on fairly quickly and others take a little longer. So, dear
reader, I will insert the letters in their correct order as we progress
through this book. Let us see how well you do.

I was born on the loth of November, l927. (To save you working
it out I am 76 years old.) I was born to Sally and Walter Jackson.
We lived at 60, The Crossways, in a two-up and two- down, in
the little town of Otley, in the Wharfe Valley, in West Yorkshire.
Otley is a thriving market-town. There's an Auction Mart, the
'Butter Cross'- a low-roofed building open all round, supported
on metal columns. It used to be called the "Barter Cross." Where
people would come to sell and barter their goods. The Jubilee
Clock stands in the middle of the Market Square, a four-faced
clock that celebrates Queen Victoria's Diamond Jubilee, and it cost
under £200 about 186 quid I think. Inlaid in the south-face is a
stone plaque, presented by Belgian refugees in gratitude for how
they had been welcomed and looked-after by the townsfolk during the l9l4-l9l8 War.

I am 76 years old, nothing extraordinary has occurred in my
life: no fame, wealth or glory. Well, maybe wealth, a wealth of
memories: some happy; a few sad. As I write, other memories are
vague. If I do not recall all the facts accurately I beg the reader's
indulgence. My very first memory is that I am laying in my pram,
and this thing, (I do not know that it is a head.) looks over and

nuzzles my arm. This thing, apparently, was a beautiful "Airedale" dog. It was my father's pride and joy. It would stand or lay for hours by my pram.

Unfortunately, one day one of the neighbours bent over my pram, as neighbours do, to tickle and coo, and Nance, short for Nancy, went for her. There was no serious damage or injury but it was decided Nance would have to be put-down.

When I was old enough to understand, my father told me that he could command the dog to obedience at all times. At meal times, he would put food in a bowl for Nance. She would sit or lay with her nose to the bowl until our meal was finished. He would say "O.K. Nance," and then she would tuck-in.

When the sad day came, Dad tethered the dog with a piece of rope, we did not have a lead- he didn't need one. Dogs were put-down at the Tan Yard. As Dad progressed along the main street- Kirkgate, Nance broke-loose and ran back towards the Jubilee Clock. Dad called and she crouched-down. She ignored his shouts. He gave a piercing whistle, as he did when training Nance, and she crawled slowly back towards him, quietly whimpering. Dad always said that she knew that something was going to happen, as they walked up to the Tan Yard, Nance looked-up at him. Dad said, that after a short distance, he could not bear to return the look. In fact, he almost turned round to come home, but he knew that he could not. So the deed was done. The following day Dad finished his meal and said, "O.K. Nance." and then he cried. I did not know that some years later, I would have a similar experience.

I am five years old and the proud owner of a Rolls Royce. It is about five feet long. It has a silver Rolls-Royce bonnet, (No Spirit of Ecstasy though!) a dickey seat at the rear. (This is an open seat situated where a car boot is today.) and wheels with silver hubcaps. There are three gears, the same as a bicycle system and a reverse gear. It has number plates to the front and rear: "PETER 5." The car is coloured a bright yellow with silver trim. It is powered using stirrup like pedals. Additional power is provided by willing-hands. The dickey seat can accommodate a small boy. (No girls.).

We lived in a cul-de-sac with a circle at the top, for horse and carts to turn. It was shaped like a giant keyhole. Anyone who pushed the car four-lengths of the cul-de-sac was entitled to sit in the dickey seat and ride for two-lengths. We frequently over-loaded the car, breaking the back-axle. Dad would go to the Blacksmith for a replacement. How my parents managed to buy the car I will never know: it may be because I was the first surviv-ing child- my Mother lost three babies before I was born. That car was my pride and joy.

Tommy came into my life when we were five years old. We started school together; we drank our milk together; laughed, and, cried together. I suppose one could say we did most things to-gether. We started school after the Christmas holidays.

It is January, 1932 and we are at school. One morning, we were drinking our milk, (It had just been delivered.) "This milk is ice-cold," I said, "I can hardly drink it." "Me neither," echoes Tommy. "I think I will stop having it during the cold weather." Next morning Tommy said to me, "I've got an idea." "What idea?" I ask. Tommy put his index finger to the side of his nose and winked. I think his father used to do that mannerism. "Please Miss!" (Always "Please Miss!") "Yes, Thomas," answers Miss Stead. "Please Miss, our milk is very cold." "Is it Thomas?" "Yes it is Miss. Please Miss, could we have the milk crates put on the heating pipes to warm it up a little?" "That's a good idea!" says Miss Stead. "Yes, I know it is," replies Tommy. "Thank you Miss Stead." We never had ice-cold milk after that. This was the first of many ideas that Tommy was to have.

One morning, I was sat on the front-gate, swinging to and fro, as you do, and the lad from next door came out to play, his name was Charles. "Morning, Charlie Chuck!" I cried. He never answered. "When are you going to get your hair cut?" No reply. "They don't use a basin at the Barbers you know." (It was alleged that some youngsters had a basin placed on the cranium, and any-thing showing was cut and shorn off, so depending on the size of the basin relative to the nut this would determine the hair-style, if you see what I mean.) Silence. "Cat got your tongue then Chucky!" He said nothing and went back into his house, leaving me to swing on the gate as you do. A few moments later he reap-peared. "Charlie Chuck married a duck…" I did not get any fur-ther. Wham!

When I came round, I was lying on the sofa. Mum was strok-ing my head. "Wha… What happened, Mum?" "Charlie from next door hit you on the head with a sweeping brush." "Why?" I said. "I don't know," she replied. "Well, I can't remember." "No, neither can Charlie," said Mum.

Tommy told me that he came just as I was regaining consciousness. "We were all worried. The Doctor said you must have a ruddy thick skull, and you should lie quiet for today and to keep away from brush wielding Charlie Chucks." According to Tommy, somebody said, "Put a poultice on his head." Other suggestions were: "He will get meningitis; tap him on the other side of his head to help him to regain his balance." I think he was nedding (kidding) me. However, I seemed to recover O.K.

The Doctor called to see me today, yes, I had got it, most of my mates had got it, anyone who had not had it would get it. I had contracted Scarlet Fever. The Doctor said he would telephone for the ambulance, ('Fever Van' to us.) which duly arrived. It was more like a box on wheels rather than an Ambulance. The driver was a small thin man with wire spectacles; a wire-like grey moustache; a peaked-cap, and, brown knee- length boots. His colleague was a small thin man also with wire spectacles and a dark wire-like moustache. He wore black knee-boots. If they had swapped one boot each, that would have made them much more interesting, I think.

They lifted me on to a stretcher. We went down the garden path, Tommy muttered, "Be careful they don't always come back from there! They do experiments or something." "I hope you never come back!" whispers Charlie Chuck. It can speak after all. I begin to feel unwell, my lips are quivering, I want to cough, I seem to be short of breath. I am leaving home for the very first time and going miles and miles away, (Well three miles actually.) but I won't cry. So I was going to the Fever Hospital for six weeks and my home will have to be 'stoved', (fumigated).

> Mother, mother, take me home,
> From this Isolation Home,
> I've been here a week or two,
> Now I want to be with you.
>
> Here I lay like a log,
> Can't get up to use the bog.

Mother, Mother, take me home.

Here comes Dandy Doctor Dick,
Swanking with his walking stick,
Here comes the Nurse with a red hot poultice,
Slaps it on and takes no notice.

Mother, mother, take me home,
From this Isolation Home.
I've been here a week or two,
Now I want to be with you.

Mother, mother hear my plea,
It's not so bad here.
So let me be.

I was the youngest patient in the male ward, but even in those days, there was always one rotten-apple in the barrel of good fruit- he was a Bully-Boy called Luther. Every day he would promise to "Twilt!" me. Every night I used to lay with a bedfellow, uncontrollably shuddering, wondering what a "Twilt." was.

Normally a Scarlet Fever patient would spend about four weeks in bed and two weeks convalescing. Apart from Luther time passes quite pleasantly, being the youngest in the ward, I am spoiled rotten by the Nurses. I have jelly or ice-cream everyday, (Once a flood at home if we are lucky.). I will be in Hospital over Christmas, I am looking forward to the big - big- party when I get home.

One week into the New Year then, I haven't been "Twilted." yet, but I have been promised one before I go home. I can't bear it any longer, I will bribe Luther with an apple to tell me what a "Twilt." is. "Would you like this apple Luther?" "Yep." "If I give you this apple, will you tell me what a 'Twilt.' is?" "Certainly Sonny! A 'Twilt.' is…"- he thumps me in the stomach; clips me round the ear-hole, and, he attempts to kick my ars-, err my backside. "That's a 'Twilt.' my son! But a good 'Twilt' is a lot harder, and it lasts much longer." I wish that I had never asked.

Today is " Showing-up Day." whatever that means. My feet are soaked in Vaseline; (Don't know why.) a urine sample is taken (Don't know why.); 'Dandy Dick' will come in the morning to pass or fail me for going home. " Showing-up Day," then! (I still don't know what it means.) Hello! Luther's bed is empty, nobody seems to know where he has gone, maybe he has been transferred, or gone home, maybe he has snuffed it, and gone to Heaven. I can't see that, if he <u>has</u> copped it he has probably gone the other way. So I didn't get a full blown "Twilt" after all. Hooray! I pass and arrive home in mid-January.

A belated Christmas party then. All my friends (No girls!), all my wonderful presents bought for Christmas. How my Mum and Dad managed it, I will never know. It takes about a month taking it easy before I am ready for School.

Tommy calls for me each morning to go to school. It is a journey of about a mile and a half. We usually call for 'Tiger'- so called because his flowing gold locks look just like a Lion's mane. We called him 'Tiger', because he doesn't want to be called 'Lion'. This particular morning, we called for Tiger, who was always slower than the clock. He was attacking two doorsteps (Thick slices of bread.) spread with jam, and drinking a mug of cocoa. His black and white sheep dog lay at his feet. Tommy was idly doodling with two knives. Suddenly Tiger jumped up and scattered the cutlery. "What's the matter mate?" says Tommy. Tiger said, "The night my mother died, we noticed crossed knives on the table." "That's rhubarb!" said Tommy. "Well that's what happened! It's an omen or something." Tiger replied. "You don't mean 'Amen' do you?" said Tommy. A few moments later, Tiger's dog lifts his head, gives a tired bark and puts its head on the floor. "There you are mate!" says Tommy. "He has only gone to sleep."

When we called at Tiger's house the following morning, he told us that when he came home from school the previous day, his dog was dead. As a practising Catholic boy, to believe in such things was a sin. I wonder, as God is my witness this is a weird memory.

"You're going to be an altar-boy," says Mum. "What me?" "Yes, you!" "Why me?" "Why not you?" "Because I don't want to be an altar boy." "You've got to be an alter boy," said Mum. "What me?" "Yes, you!" "Why me?" "Because – Oh, don't start that again! Now shut your cake-hole (Mouth.)! Open your lugs (ears) and listen. Father Dean says he wants you to be an altar boy." "Why just me?" "Not just you! Thomas has volunteered to go on the altar." "What's 'volun-', 'volunt-', what's 'volunteer' mean?" I spluttered. "It means, you do what you are told." "But I thought, 'vol-er – volonter – ', what you just said, meant you had a choice." "Not when Father Dean wants 'volunteers'," replied Mum. If the Parish Priest said black was white, It was white, but he could be 'wong'. (Chinese joke!)

Father Dean would decide who he wanted to serve on the altar- the parents were informed. It was like being ordered into battle: no question; no protest; over the top and at 'em'!" "I don't fancy going on to the altar," moans Tommy. "Join the Club!" I reply. "When we go to Confession, he will know who we are," says Tommy. I reply, "I think he knows already." "How's that?" "Well last Saturday, when I was in Confession, Father Dean asked me how my Mother was, and to tell her, he hoped she would soon be better." "That's not on!" says Tommy, "I thought it was unanimous when you went. I thought that you were unanimous, and he didn't know who you was." "Well, he does," says I.

"Mum! what does 'unanimous' mean?" "Well, it means everybody agrees." "Awe! Right!" "What does it mean when you go somewhere and they don't know who you are?" Mum said, "Let me think, err- , I think you mean 'anonymous'." "Awe! Right!"

Tommy and I are resigned to our fate. We start learning Latin. "Dominus vobiscum." (The Lord be with you.) "Et cum spirito tuo."(And with thy spirit.) After about four weeks, we are allowed to sit in our vestments on the altar, and watch. Two or three weeks later, we begin our altar-boy duties. Light the candles. Have you ever tried to light a candle about eight-foot high with a blazing taper, bent-down, stuck on the end of a long pole praying "Hail Mary! Help me please!" in front of a church full of people. (You want to have a go some time.)

"Bless me, Father, for I have sinned!" "How long is it since your last confession?" "A heck of a long time since." "Good! Good! You should go every week. Why has it been so long?" "Well, I thought if I saved my sins up, it would save us both a lot of time and trouble," I replied. "Good! Good! That is a good idea! I may start doing that." "Shall I spread the word, Father?" "Yes, I will announce this at the Sunday Masses, and will put a notice on the Church door." "Good! Good! Father." "I know it's good. Now how about your sins?" "Well, Father, we have been talking for so long, I have forgotten them." "Good! Good! Are you sorry for your sins that you have forgotten?" "No, Father, because I can't remember them." "Good! Good! Now for your sins that you cannot remember, recite "Ten Our Fathers" and if you remember them, say twelve 'Hail Marys'." "That's a heck of a lot of penance, Father!" "It's a heck of a lot of sin my son! Now if you can remember it, make a good Act of Contrition." ("Oh my God I am sorry!") "Thank you my Grandfather!" "You're welcome my Grandson, Bless you!" "And you Father!"

I leave the Confessional, closely followed by Tommy. We are face-to-face with Father Dean. "What have you two been up to?" "We've been praying quietly, and contemplating," says Tommy. "Oh have you? Well if you feel the urgency to pray: remove your vestments; go to the altar-rail; kneel and pray; say five 'Our Fathers' and five 'Hail Mary's', and may I suggest, that one prayer should be, 'I must not make a mockery of my Religion.' You can contemplate for another ten-minutes, and then hop it!" "That's a lot of penance! Father." "That's a lot of sin, my sons!" As we kneel at the altar, Tommy whispers, "I thought when you were at Confession, it was unanimous." "You mean 'anonymous'," I replied. "Yes, that's it! Well I am sure he was listening and he should confess it too!" says Tommy. "Too true mate! Too true!"

Altar-boys should attend Benediction each Sunday evening. We take it in turns to be in charge of the collection. Tonight, Tommy is on duty. As the collection-plate was passed to me, I put my penny in, I gasp, the penny on the plate is a bob I had put a shilling, (5p in today's money, but a heck of a lot of money in those days.) on the plate. Too late! Tommy has whisked it away. That leaves me with tuppence (Less than 1p today.) in my pocket that has to last me until the following Friday when I will receive my pocket-money- unless it is docked for any reason. Benediction ends and we sing a hymn 'Sweet Sacrament Divine.' and shuffle with the congregation out of Church.

As we emerge, I turn to Tommy and say, "You're not going to believe this!" "Try me!" said Tommy. "I put a bob on the plate by mistake." "You never did!" said Tommy. "I did! I am a twit!" "I know that!" replies Tommy." "Oh thank you!" "You're welcome, twit! Well twit! Here's your bob!" says Tommy. "You saw what happened then?" I said. "Yes, you owe me tuppence, (about 5p)"

"Why tuppence?" I ask. "We only put a penny on the plate." "I agree" "Well why tuppence?" "A shilling whipped-off the plate, a penny I put on, and, a penny salvage-fee," quipped Tommy. "Gerrout of it! But thanks anyway!"

Mrs. Murphy has won the Irish Sweepstake. I am waiting for the men in white-coats coming to take her to the looney-bin (Asylum.) because Mum says she has gone mad since she won all that money. One day I asked my Mum, how Mrs. Murphy was going on. Mum said she had recently been talking to her, and asked what she would do when all the money had gone. "Oh that will be no problem," she replied, "We will live on the interest!" "Ah well!"

"What's a 'Senry' dad?" "I don't know! Do you know what 'Senry' is Mum?" "I think it's where they train priests." "I think that that is called a 'Seminary' Mum." "Are you sure?" "Well, not sure, sure." "Well, are you one sure?" "Well, I am about half a sure." "Well, you are probably wrong, anyrode." "Yes, Mother." "Well do you know what a 'Prins' is, Dad?" "I don't know," he replies. "Do you know what a 'Prins' is Mum?" "Don't ask me!" "But I just did, Mum." "Don't get clever with your Mum," chides Dad, "I don't think that there are such words. Why don't you ask Miss Johnson?" "She doesn't know either," Mum says, "What's put these words into your head?" "Well Mum! As we were walking home from school, Tommy said, " 'Prins Senry' is a long road." "I think he meant; 'Prince Henry's Road'," replied Dad. "Awe right, Dad!"

Tommy and I live about one and a half miles from St. Joseph's Catholic School. We trot or run to arrive in good time to play cricket or football in the School Playground. School starts at 9 am, the dinner hour is from 12 noon to 1.30 pm. I never did figure out why it was called the 'Dinner Hour', when it was one and a half hours long. Comes twelve o'clock, Tommy and I dash home, gobble-down our meal and are down in the Park below the weir. We know exactly when Garnett's Paper Mill starts drawing water from the river. Sure enough, water ceases to flow <u>over</u> the weir, and we are able to cross on stepping- stones to the islands.

There are several rock-pools wherein trout can be trapped, occasionally a fish can be stranded on exposed rocks and the hardest part to catch them is having to bend-down. Tommy could never kill anything, so it fell to me to dispatch them with a quick blow to the head, usually with a short piece of round wooden rod (Known in the trade as a 'Priest.' because it administered the last rites.) We hide any fish we capture in an old drainpipe in the riverbank and collect them after we finish school at 4 pm.

One day, Tommy said to me, "When you take a trout home, do you get 'owt (anything) for it?" "No nowt, (nothing)," I reply, "not even a thank you." "I've got an idea," he says. "What sort of idea?" "Well!" Tommy said, "We could sell them." "That's a brilliant idea." "I know it is," replies Tommy.

"Would you like to buy a trout. Mister?" "How much?" Tommy says, "Thruppence, (three pennies) up to nine inches long; a half-penny for every inch over 9 inch, and, a tanner (six pennies) for a fish over a foot long." "I will give you four pence for any size fish," says the Mister. "Done," says Tommy. "And done you have been" is the reply. "Why?" says Tommy. "Because I am the new Water Bailiff."

Oh ye Gods! We are in deep ca-ca. (Use your imagination.) My mind races and becomes confused. I close my eyes and try to think. " Is it worth while praying?" thinks I. Well! I think that it will be a waste of time: I can't pray whilst I am more or less committing the sin at this moment, can I?

"You will both come to the Police Station with me, and go and collect any fish and bring them with you." "We can't do that Mister," says Tommy, "and you can't take us to the Police Station either." "And why not?" "Because we haven't copped any yet!" quipped Tommy. Well done! Thomas.

"Morning! Charlie. What are you doing?" "Nowt. (nothing)." "You must be doing summat, (something.)" "Well I am not!" "What are you looking at then?" "Nowt." "Everybody is looking at summat unless they are blind. Are you blind?" "No I am not." "I will give you my apple-core if you will tell me what this 'nowt' is that you're not looking at." "All right then!" "Mornin'!" "Mornin', Tommy!" "What's he looking at?" "He says he's looking at nowt." "He can't do that unless he is blind." "Everybody has got to be somewhere looking at summat (something)." "That's what I have just been telling him. He is going to tell me when I have finished this apple. I am giving him the core. Here you are, mate, now what are you looking at?" "Nowt!"

Charlie Chuck,
Married a duck.
The duck died,
Charlie cried.
Poor Charlie Chuck.

"Am still looking at nowt." "Right you're not looking at summat that isn't there?" "Yes, that's reet, (right.)" "Right, now we are getting somewhere, for this almost brand new, slightly rusty looking apple-core, what's this nowt that you are not looking at then?" "I'm waiting for the smoke to come outer (out of) Smith's chimney." "You'll have a long wait, mate." "Why?" " Because it is an electric fire ont' tuther (on the other) end o' <u>that</u> chimney."

"That gives me an idea," says Tommy. We are on our way home from school. We stop at the end of the bridge overlooking the River Wharfe above the first archway and gaze into the water. Tommy points downwards. "What are you looking at?" says a bloke. We put our fingers to our lips. "Shussh" Tommy points again. Soon we have about a dozen people, looking into the Wharfe. Most can't see anything, some say they can but are not sure what it is. As we walk away, Tommy says, "It's the biggest one I have ever seen." "Me too!" I reply. "Thank you Charlie Chuck for being somewhere busy looking at nowt".

About a couple of weeks later, Tommy says, "I've got an idea." "Is it a good one?" I ask. "They are all good ideas," Tommy replies. I am standing in the same spot once more, again looking down into the water. It is running about two-feet deep under the arch and beautifully clear. About half a dozen people gather around. Somebody says, "Look at that!" "What is it?" "Don't know!" "There was something here a couple of weeks ago," said this bloke. He turned to me and says, "You were here, did you see anything?" "Yes, I did, but this one is bigger." More people are talking and looking at the thing. Some say it is an eel and it must be at least twenty foot long, (about lo ft. actually).

I slip quietly across the road, give Tommy the nod, and sidle back. "Ooh it's moving!" squeals a girl. "You're right! Goodness what is it?" "It's a giant eel," says another. The thing moves and disappears under the arch. The crowd troop across the road. There's nothing to be seen. Eventually when they disperse, Tommy appears, and says, "I enjoyed that. It's surprising what can be done with a length of old fire hose, a bit of clothes line and some imagination." "Where's the giant twenty-foot eel then?" says I. "Safely tucked away under the archway," says he.

"How is Mrs. Murphy going on Mum? I hear that her daughter is not too well." "I was talking to her the other day, and when I asked her what was wrong, she said that Mary had Chicken- pox, but that she could not understand it, because she hadn't been any where near the Chickens." Hey ho!

It's Sunday lunchtime. Dinner's over. We have had a piece of roast pork, roast potatoes, and cabbage. Mum has made a rhubarb pie, and custard for afters. A meal fit for a King. A knock,- knock,- knockknockknock, at the front door, (That's our knocking code.). I go to greet Tommy. He says, "I am going sledging (tobogganing)." "A couple of secs. (Seconds) to finish my dinner and I'm with you," says I. "Come in and have a cuppa." "Cheers!"

I finish my meal, tog-up, and off we go along Parker's Lane, and climb up 'Giant's Arse',- err 'Giant's Bum'. The Protestants call it 'arse'- err that's what they do. We would have to confess so we settle for 'bum'. 'Giant's Arse' err- 'Bum' is so called because the two adjacent hills are shaped like a giant's bottom or bum. We race down the track. We are a racing car, a speedboat, an aeroplane, etc. We are anything we want to be. The favourite position is to lay face-down on the sledge and steer left or right, as required, by digging either boot toe into the snow.

About an hour on the slope, and I am whizzing down the track. What was that? I come to a stop. "Oh law! Oh heck! Oh law! Oh heck!" "What's up?" asks Tommy. "I have ripped the sole off my boot." That's bad luck." "Oh God!" I gasp, "They're my best boots." "That is bad luck," says Tommy. (We only wear our best boots on Sundays and Holy Days etc, or the odd Funeral.)

In my rush to go sledging, I had forgotten to change into my old boots. I have just managed to ruin my best pair. "What am I going to do, Tommy? What am I going to do?" I wail. "My dad will bray (hit) me." (Dad could lay a good hand on the arse – er bum, or on the back of the legs). "He will kill me and my pocket money will be docked." "I've got an idea," says Tommy. "My Father is away and my Mum never hits me." "But what can we do?" "This is what we can do." "What?" says I. "When we get home, we will swap, I will let you have my best boots." "But your Mother is sure to find out." "Don't worry about that," says Tommy. "That's a brilliant idea!" "I know it is," says Tommy. We swapped. Tommy's Mother did find out. He got a clip round the earhole, the rounds of the kitchen (a good telling-off) and sent up the dancers, (upstairs) missed his tea and had four week's pocket money docked. Greater love hath no lad, than to lay down his "sole" for his mate.

Monday morning. Knock! Knock! Knockknockknock! "That's Tommy at the door," says Mum (She's broken our knocking code; we will have to change it.). "Mornin' Tommy!" "Mornin' Plug!" "I've got an idea!" says I. "Let's hear it then!" "For the next four weeks we will share my pocket money fifty fifty."

"Mum, what's a 'damn sell'?" asks Mick. "I've told you before about using such words; you will have to confess it." "Which word is that?" "Why 'damn' of course," Mick says. "You will have to confess it also." "No I won't!" "Why not?" "Because I was only saying what you said," said Mum. "Well! 'damn' should be the same for everybody." "You do your confession and I will look after mine. Anyhow, what put this lot into your head?" "Miss Stead says we are going to do a play about a 'damn sell in distress'." Mum said, "She meant a 'damsel' idiot!" "Well! Why didn't she say so? I thought it was a crab in a shell trapped in a dam or something, or, maybe something stranded or caught in a net." "Really?" "Yes, really. Mum! What's a 'damsel'?" "Go out and play! You can ask Miss Stead tomorrow." "Right! I will Mum." From that day on, young Mick was called 'Thick Mick' affectionately.

"I have been chosen to go see the Pope." I announce loftily as we sit down to tea. "He's fibbing (lying)!" says young Mick. "He's blaspheming!" says Mum. "If you're going to be like that, I won't tell you." "You can't tell us 'cos (because) you're fibbing." "And blaspheming!" echoes Mum. "Let's give the lad a chance to speak," says Dad. "No, I am not going to tell you!" "I believe you!" said Dad. "So just tell me, and they can listen if they want." "Right then! I will."

"I have been chosen to go and see the Pope and receive a blessing." "I suppose it's got your name on?" says Mick. "Quiet you!" says Dad. "I suppose they will have to know which blessing goes to who, so it probably will have anyrode (anyway), so you could be right for once! Michael."

"I still think he is fibbing and he will have to confess it," says Mick. "And nearly blaspheming," echoes Mum. "So he will have to confess to a sin and a half for lying and almost blaspheming," says Mick. "The Pope lives in Rome," says Dad. "That's in Egypt," says Mick. "You're both wrong, he lives in Greece," argues Mum. "Egypt!" says Mick. "Why Egypt?" queries Mum. "Well! ' Out of the house of Egypt into a house on Bondgate.'" misquotes Mick. "That's not right!" says Mum. "It's 'Into the house of bondage'" "I don't think that's right either." One withering look from Mum and Dad says, "Aye, I think you're reet (right) lass!"

"Well! I can go to see him, and I have just to pay my fare." "But it's such a long way off and it will cost a fortune and we can't afford it, I still think you're fibbing," says Mum. "That's two sins for lying and half a sin for blaspheming," says Mick. "Oh, shut up young Mick!" says I. "Shut up, what?" "Shut up your cakehole (mouth) and anything else you can find! Why don't you go and play on the railway lines or something?"

"You will need new clothes and I don't know what, which we can't afford." "He's fibbing Mum!" "That's enough!" says Dad, who had quietly been eating his meal. Dad always ate his dinner with his eyes closed. I never knew if he was just tired because he worked very hard, or preferred to eat his grub whilst asleep. Maybe he just wanted to be on his tod (own).

"Write a letter, Mother, and let him take it to school tomorrow. I will make sure he gives it to Jenny," says my everloving Brother. "Miss Johnson to you, young man," gently chides Dad. "And don't you forget it!" "Sorry Dad!" says Mick.

"Miss Johnson has sent this letter for you Mum." "What did she say?" "Nothing really, she just smiled and said make sure your Mum gets this." "Read it out loud then:

Dear Mrs. Jackson.

I am writing to clarify any misunderstanding. Two pupils are chosen to take the Charity monies to Leeds Cathedral.

They will be presented to the Bishop and they will receive a blessing. I did tell them that the Pope would be very pleased. I do hope that Peter will be able to attend. He will be required to pay his fare and have a little money in his pocket. A meal will be provided.

Yours sincerely

Miss J. Johnson.

P.S. the other boy is Joseph Pickles.

"I bet that Leeds Cathedral is abroad," says young Mick. "It isn't, but if it was, it would be a heck of a lot more money than we could ever afford," says Mum. "I think that it could be about twenty miles away." "Well that's far enough away to be abroad," says young Mick. "If it makes you happy to say that it is abroad or what ever," says a steadily increasingly harassed Mum, "so be it."

"Mum! Mrs. Pickles is at the door." "Ask her in then," said Mum. "Good morning Mrs. Jackson! Isn't it a lovely day! I understand Peter will be going with Joseph to Leeds and to meet the Bishop." "Yes," Mother replies. "But it's going to cost a bit." Mrs. Pickles's husband is a 'Professional'. I don't know what that means, but they are "well off." We are poor but not poverty, as Mum would say. "I hope he can go," says Mrs. Pickles. "Joseph has some clothes I was going to send to charity, you could have them." "We're not poverty," answers Mum. "Well you could buy them," says Mrs. Pickles, "And I will give the money to charity." "Err I suppose so, I suppose I could do that. How much would you want." "How about two shillings?" "That's very fair. Thank you, Mrs. Pickles." "No bother, Mrs. Jackson, I will send Joseph with them tomorrow."

The great day has arrived. I am spick and span in my new/second-hand clothes. I even wear a tie, cardboard insoles in my new/second-hand shoes, (The first pair I had ever worn.) I feel wonderful. No cat-lick (A brief quick wash.) this morning. I have had a good wash. My hair is combed back using Council hair oil, (water). "Are you going abroad?" asks Mick. "Probably." "Well it's a long way off, so you must be, do you need an assistant?" "No." "Well I only asked!" "It's still a 'No' and it's not open to any haggling either."

To the Bus Station then to meet Miss Johnson. "O.K. good! It's a Double-decker." "Can we go upstairs, Miss?" "Yes, of course you can." "Thanks Miss." "One and two halves, Leeds return." And we're off! Two miles from home, and we are in a new land, maybe we are abroad, maybe we are not far off from the end of the world.

The rest of the day passes in a blur. I find myself kneeling in front of the Bishop. I manage to kiss his ring with my eyes shut. He smiles, and he blesses me. I have just met the man who has met the Pope, so now I must surely go to heaven. We have a nice meal and return home on another big red Double-decker bus.

"Have you had a good day then?" asks Mum. "Oh yes! Wonderful! Marvellous!" "Bless you Peter!" "Thanks Mum! I have already had a good blessing at the Cathedral." "Oh Peter! What about the thruppence (three pennies) I gave you to go with?" "The what?" "The thruppence." "Err the thruppence?" "Yes, the thruppence." "Err well! I err.." "Err, what?" I close my eyes, and ask Holy Mary to look after me and let me have a loving understanding kind gentle Mum just for today. I take a deep breath and say: "I've spent it." "You've spent it?" I just said I had, thinks I; she must be going deaf. "Well! What have you spent it on?" "On toffees." "On what?" I think she is getting forgetful, or going deaf, or both, maybe she is going doolally (stupid)as well. "On toffees!" "What all of it?" "Yes." "I give up!" says Mum. "Well, Joseph Pickles spent a tanner (six pennies)." "Oh aye! Just because young Pickles jumps into the river, doesn't mean that you have to do so, does it?" "I don't see why not!" "What?" "I've been a clot." "Well this clot can get up them dancers, (stairs) for a couple of hours." "Yes, Mother, thank you Mother."

After about half an hour Mum called me down. (She's remembered where I am then.) "I want you to go to the shop and get me two boxes of 'Top Mill Snuff'." ('Dope.' for short.) I now know why she is mad at me. When she is out of dope, she seems to get cross very quickly, I think it is like being without fags or something. "Yes, Mother, right away Mother." "And don't be long." "No, Mother."

The shop is only a mile and a half away. I trudge down Prince Henry's Road, (At least I've got that right.) and into the Park. Girls and boys are laughing; boys and girls are sailing; some are hailing; others are sailing and hailing. Everybody seems to wear a huge smile. There is happiness all over the whole world, for everyone but me. I am alone and miserable. I have just had the rounds of the kitchen, (a telling-off) and sent up the dancers (upstairs) for spending thruppence and my Mother is spending fourpence on dope. Life is just not fair, and the Bishop's blessing has been a waste of time, I probably got one with some other geezer's name on it who hasn't been to Confession, or Mass, for a heck of a long time and deserves bad luck!

I have been to the first house at the Pictures with Tommy, we say our goodbyes. As I approach our front door, I can hear music. I enter the sitting room, and there's Mum and Dad dancing to music coming from a box in the corner. "I didn't know you could dance?" "There's lot of things you don't know, lad!" says Father. Giving me a big wink, "What is it then?" "It's a waltz." "Why is it called a 'Waltz'?" "I don't really know but it's something you can dance to." "But there's other things on it aren't there?" "On what?" "On the waltz." "What waltz?" "The waltz you are danc-ing to." "Dancing to?" "Yes, that thing in the corner." "That's a wireless," says Dad. "You said it was a waltz." "No, I did not." "Yes, you did." "Well if you will listen, I will explain." "Yes, Dad." "That box in the corner is a wireless. The wire running round the picture mould is called the 'aerial'." "What does an 'aerial' do then?" "Well it sort of draws what's being broadcast in along, and into the wireless." "How can it be called a 'wire less' then?" "I don't know, son. I just don't know. Anyrode, the wireless is play-ing a waltz and we were dancing to the music. Got it son?" "It got Father." "Where's Michael?" "He's staying overnight at Gerry's house. Right?" "Right!"

"What's that box in the corner?" asks Mick next morning. "It's a wireless and that's the aerial." "How can it be called a 'wire less' with that wire stuck up all round the room?" "Ask Dad when he comes in." "Right, I will." (Nice one there Peter!) "Come here Mick! Let me lift you up to the aerial." "Why for?" "To see if you can hear any noise coming in to it." "Can you hear 'owt?" "No nowt." "Reet! Then let's go see if we can hear owt at the end." "All reet!" "Canter (Can you?) hear 'owt?" "No nowt."

Dad was working part time for a garage as a taxi-driver. They charged accumulators, (batteries for wirelesses)- anyhow, he brought this wireless home, He had bought it from the garage for half a dollar, (half a crown – two shillings and six pence). I reckon that was one of the best half dollars we ever spent. We listened to: Radio Luxemburg; 'The Ovalteenies.'; 'Fu Man Chu.'; 'ITMA'

('It's That Man Again.') with Tommy Handley; 'Dick Barton.' and many others.

I remember after the war, there was a radio show called: 'The Piddingtons.'. I believe they were Australians. They had perfected their act whilst being Prisoners of War in a Japanese Prison camp. It was a telepathic performance. One night, listeners were invited to take part in an experiment. Two people sit facing each other. The 'willer' held his or her hands out; the other (to be willed) holds the 'willer's' wrists and attempts to clear the mind. Mick says I should find that easy to do. "Shut up, Thick Mick!" We sit quietly, (even Mick), I am gently holding my Mother's wrists, I try to clear my mind and a short while later say, "You want me to move the box on the sideboard?" "Goodness that's right!" says Mum. "Are you sure, Mum?" "Yes, quite sure." "It's magic!" says Mick.

I have told this story many times. One day, as I finished speaking, somebody in the group I was addressing said: "How do you know it was genuine?" "How do you mean genuine?" "Well your Mother could have agreed with whatever you said; she could have been nedding (kidding/ lying to)you." "Mum, I think I have been conned!"

It's been cowboys and Indians for the past couple of days in the playground. We have all seen a cowboy film, Tom Mix (No, not Tom Mixing cement!) where they round-up horses. Two other lads and myself are horses, because we are wearing clogs, (Wooden soled boots, shod with iron.). They make a great deal of noise as we gallop around the yard. The cowboys make futile attempts to lassoo us, (No chance!). Suddenly, I am pulled sideways and fall to the ground. There's something gripping me around my neck! I can't breathe! I have been lassoed. I should not have said "No chance!" and this would never have happened.

I am floating. I want to go to sleep; my eyes are heavy. I can hear a gentle voice, "Sweet Jesus, save Peter!" It will be alright my Mum is here. The pressure on my throat has eased, air rushes in. Somebody says, "He is going, he is talking to his Mother." "I'm not going anywhere and my Mother's here anyrode." That's strange, I open my eyes, look up and see Miss White. "Where's Mum?" I ask. "She is not here," whispers Miss White. "I have sent for her."

Miss White had managed to loosen the noose. She had stroked my head and prayed for me. She wasn't an ogre after all, well not at this moment. "Where's Tommy?" "Here mate! The Doc's on his way." "Well done, Thomas!" says Miss White. "Well done!" "Thank you, Miss!"

The Doctor took me in his car, a rare treat this. We saw Mum walking down to school. We picked her up and the Doctor took us home with orders that I should rest for two or three days. For about a week, I was spoilt rotten. Then it was back to normal.

"Will you be joining the 'Diddleum' this year, Sally?" enquires Mrs. Bentley. "Yes," Mum replies, "Have you fixed how much yet?" "Most people are paying a tanner (six pence) a week for two shares, but you can have one share for a dodger, (three pence)." "No that's fine! I will have two shares for a tanner." "Right!" says Mrs. Bentley.

"What's a 'Diddleum' you may ask." A 'Diddleum' is a Savings Club usually commencing about the end of February each year. Monies are paid in weekly and held by Mrs. Bentley until the end of November. It is then paid out in time for Christmas. You received the exact amount that had been paid in. No interest because no one went to the Bank in those days. As Mum used to say, "We've nowt to put in anyrode." When the big day comes no problem everyone gets their savings.

Every thing settles-down; monies paid in; savings books marked. Then, out of the blue, just before the big payout, it leaks out that the 'Diddleum' money has gone missing a couple of weeks before. Apparently, Mrs. Bentley had put the money in an old vacuum-cleaner to save it in a safe place, (Well you do don't you?) Mrs. Bentley had to go into Hospital for a couple of weeks. Mr. Bentley decided to have a good tidy-up, and the vacuum, which must have been past its time and sell-by date-along with other unwanted items, had been taken away by the dustbin men to the tip.

Inevitably, it soon became known on the Estate. Everybody knew everybody else in those days. Neighbours would argue, fall-out, and fall-in, call each other names, and gossip; they would fall-in and then fall-out again. Oh! the gossip I have heard in our house, when I have been pretending to read , or be asleep. A lot of it was a waste of time though, because a lot of it I didn't understand anyrode.

Well, everybody knew everybody who was in the 'Diddleum'. A 'Mrs. Jones' and my Mother went round the Estate to break the sad news officially- to take the pressure off Mrs. Bentley. There was only one upset person, as Mum said, "They were probably more poverty rather than poor," but everybody mucked in, and contributed what they could. Mrs. Bentley was very reluctant to take the money, and it took a lot of persuading before she did so. It was decided that the monies gathered would be shared equally amongst all members.

People were very honest in those days. In a crisis everybody rallied round. There were no robberies. Household keys were hung behind the letter-box on a piece of string; other keys were left hanging <u>outside</u> the door. Some keys were lost; some were never replaced. One could go out for the day and leave the doors unlocked, probably go on your holidays except that no bug- err- body could afford one.

A couple of weeks after Christmas, the missing money was taken to the Police Station. The old vacuum had been found with the money inside. (More honesty here folks.) So we celebrated a fairly lean Christmas in December, and a heck of a nosh-up to- wards the end of January, the following year.

About this time, I asked my Father why Harry, (a lad about 16 years old,) had been sent away. He said, "Summat, (something), to do with a young lass." I never asked him anything about this and I never heard what had happened.

"Mornin' Tommy!" "Mornin' Plug!" "Have you ever thought about space?" "Not really," replies Tommy. "What's brought this on?" "Well last night, I saw a Shooting Star. Dad says they travel millions of miles through space, and young Mick says when you see one, it is a soul going to heaven." "Yes, I suppose it could be, but what's this about space?" "I asked my Dad what is space and young Mick said it was what I had between my ears." "He could be right, you know! Sorry, only joking!" "Dad says space goes on forever, there is no end to it."

"There must be." "Must be what?" " An end to space." "How?" "Well it's… it's… Well, there must be!" "How?" "Well somehow." "That's not an explanation." "Right clever-clogs! You explain!" "I can't!" "Can't what?" "Explain space." "Then why are we talking about it then?" "I can explain why we don't know about space."

"Go on then!" "Right, I will! Miss Johnson says our brains can only grasp so much, err like a goldfish swimming round a bowl, like your fish at your house." "How do you mean?" "A fish has a very short memory, right?" "Right!" replies Tommy. "So my fish is swimming around its bowl, it stops." "Right!" I reply. "Then it swims round and stops in the same place." "Yes, that's right," says I. "It looks out and says, 'Oh I have not been here before!'" "You have got it!" "I don't believe that," says Tommy. "I think there is a big hollow ball, thousands, err even millions, of miles away round the Earth." "You think so?" "Yes, I think so," says Tommy. "And what's on the other side of this great big ball?" "Err, another." "And on the other side of that?" "Another." "And on the other – side?" "Hang on!" says Tommy, "We could go on like this all day, or for ever." "Exactly!" says I "Ah, I see what you mean!" says he.

Tommy goes quiet as we walk to school, then after a few minute's silence, he says, "I have been thinking." "Has it given you a headache then?" "No, shut up and listen! I think that when people die, their souls go up into the first ball- which is the start of Purgatory. As we say prayers for them, they go to the next ball. They don't need doors because spirits can pass through walls and things, and as more prayers are said, they get to the last one, and, if they are O.K. they pass and go through into heaven." "And we both know what Miss Johnson says, don't we?" "Heaven will always remain a mystery, right?" "Right! But how do the unholy souls go on?" "They probably send them the opposite way, right?" "Right."

No T.V. in those days (Thank goodness!); we had to make our own amusement. Popular games in Summer were: 'Whip and Top.'; 'Piggy.', and, 'High Ball.', and of course, Football and Cricket.

We had two types of top. One shaped like a short stumpy carrot. We coloured the 'Top-top.' (I like that.), 'Top-top.' with crayons, and as they spun, the colours blended to a pleasing effect. The boys' favourite was a 'Window Breaker.' It was shaped like a mushroom on a good sound stalk. When whipped correctly, they would fly through the air. Tommy was the only lad I know who actually managed to break a greenhouse window. Result: whip and top burnt; the rounds of the kitchen; a clip round the earhole; up the dancers and four week's pocket money docked.

'Piggy.' was played with a piece of wood about 5" long and an inch square pointed at each end. The four faces were marked one to four in roman numerals. Each team member would spin the 'Piggy' into the air and the face showing the highest number denoted how many attempts that player could have. The pointed end of the 'Piggy' was struck with a piece of wood called a 'Striker.'. As it flew up into the air, the player gave it a good whack. The team covering the greatest distance won.

'The Crossways.' is a long fairly straight road with cul-de-sacs on each side at right angles- hence its name. We played a game called 'High Ball.' This takes two teams and a tennis-ball. The teams start about thirty yards apart and throw the ball at their opponents. The team who drive the other team to the end of 'The Crossways.' won. The ball would be thrown-over, straight at, or round the opponents. If it landed on the footpath, it incurred a five-pace penalty; into a garden a twenty pace penalty. A game could last a week or longer- except when 'The Crescenters.' played.

To the west end of 'The Crossways.' is 'The Crescent.'. It is at a right angle to 'The Crossways.' and is shaped like a running track. 'The Crescenters.' gang is feared by all other gangs. They always seemed to be bigger and older. Usually when we play High Ball, they come and ask politely: "Can we play?" "Of course you can," we say, even more politely, because if we say no, we are in for a good whacking. I don't know why it is called a 'good whacking', a 'bad whacking' is nearer the mark. If we say yes, we always fall out and get a good hiding anyrode. They win every time- the gert (great) big bullies.

On winter nights, we play: 'Stealth.'; 'Tin, Can Squat.', and, 'Dick, Bob or Tom.'. 'Stealth.' is a popular pastime. One has to pass from one end of the Estate using the back-gardens only. To be successful, one has to complete the course without disturbing people or pets and causing no damage. (How different now.)

'Tin, Can, Squat.' One person is 'It'. A can is placed on the ground; any player can kick it. The 'It" player retrieves the can and brings it back to its spot. The other players are hiding. As 'It' tries to find them; a player will emerge and kick the can behind 'Its' back, and shout, "Tin, Can, Squat!" If the 'It' player beats any other to the can, he kicks it and shouts: "Tin, Can, Squat!" We then have a new "It" player.

'Dick, Bob or Tom.' (Say four in a team.) The Anchorman from the other team stands with his back to a fence or wall, (A post-box or pillar box in our case, so we call him a 'Postman'.) The team members bend down in a line, each grasping the waste of the player in front facing the Anchorman. The other team jumps on to their backs. The first jumper shouts "Dick, Bob or Tom." A raised thumb is Dick, index finger is Bob and the middle finger is Tom. The first bender has to guess correctly. The Anchorman can see if we cheat but we never did. The jumpers jumped onto the backs of the benders until the first bender guessed correctly.

We were rarely interrupted during these activities by road traf-fic. There was a small bus: "The Newall Flier." Every half an hour, horse and carts delivering: coal; coke and firewood, and, there was one cart which delivered parcels. These horses knew when to stop and would turn the carts round the end of the cul-de-sacs without any command. We rarely saw any other vehicles apart from: the mobile grocer; the rag and bone man, three ice cream men, and, the dustbin-men.

The grocer was a Mr. Rainforth (We called him: "Reign Fifth."). He had a small round face with red cheeks. He looked like one of his apples. He had an open back vehicle with a canopy. He would normally call on a Friday evening. The produce was displaced down each side of the vehicle, in Winter, these were illuminated by paraffin lamps. After the customers were served, he would turn round in the cul-de-sac. We would follow and chase the vehicle, hoping something would fall off. I had heard my father say many times that 'It' must have fallen off the back of a lorry!

Mr. Garforth, ('Go Fifth.'), the rag and bone man, carried ev-erything but the kitchen sink (He could probably get you one on order.): pots; pans; sweeping-brushes; Peggy-sticks, wash boards, Possers, and, Paraffin etc. A 'Peggy-stick.' consisted of a circular piece of timber with six short legs or maybe that could be five legs attached, (Like a small stool.) This was attached to a shaft with a cross-piece at the top end. The Peggy-stick was stood in the wash tub and rotated too and fro, or fro and too-whichever you fancy. We have agitators today. A 'Posser.' was usually copper, a conical shape with holes around the bottom. It was attached to a shaft, the Posser was also vigorously worked up and down, and round and re-round (That's the opposite way, I thought everybody knew that!) The water flowed in and out through the holes- this action cleaned the clothes, (I hope!). A washboard was a frame with two legs. The rubbing area was a corrugated zinc sheet. Clothes were pulled out of the water and rubbed vigorously up and down. (I think that they were specially designed to cause as much damage as possible, I wonder if that's why we always seemed to have holes in our socks, and things).

The ice-cream men came round on motor bikes and sidecars. Mr.Granelli ('Groaning Granelli.'), he would call: "Iiiissreeem!" or something like that. He would say it as though he might be falling asleep. Mr. Buntin ('Billy Bunter.') was the second one, who also rode a motorbike and sidecar. Finally, the third was 'Walls Ice-cream.' ('Stop me and buy one! Knock him down and pinch two!' was our slogan for 'Wall's Ice-cream.'.) This man came on a pushbike, a box like contraption with a bicycle wheel either side. The driver sat over the rear wheel. A fixed steel bar ran the full width across the container in front of him. The contraption swivelled between the box at the front and the driver. Pulling on the bar with left or right hand would determine the direction of the vehicle. He wore a gray uniform, brown knee-length boots (Or they might have been black.)- I can't remember.

One day a man on a motorbike pulled up and asked the way to the Golf House. This was the best part of 3 miles away. I said I would show him. Off we went at loo mph, (Well maybe 25 mph.). My very first ride on a motorbike. I gripped his belt very tightly. The wind tore through my hair. The ride came to an end much too soon. "Thanks son!" he said, "You can walk back and I will give you a tanner, or I will run you back." "I'll walk," I replied. I would gladly have walked six miles for a tanner that would have worked out at a penny a mile.

As I walked along The Crossways, I could see my mother, feet apart, hands on hips with sleeves rolled up. Oh dear! These are ominous signs, I think I am in a spot of bother. I was in a spot of bother: I got the 'rounds of the kitchen': two clips round the earhole. To describe two clips round the earhole then: a solid right hand swings and makes contact with the left lug-hole (ear); this forces the nut (head) sideways- just in time to bring the right lug into an even more painful meeting with a well aimed left hand. I was sent up the dancers not because I have gone off with a stranger but because I had missed my dinner.

"Mum, if you heard someone say they had stolen from someone, what would you do?" "Well! That would depend." "Depend on what?" "Well if they were very poor, or if they stole a <u>lot</u> of money?" "What would you do if you heard someone say they had robbed the Church?" "I don't really know! There are a lot of very poor people about. Anyhow! Why do you want to know? What's brought this on?" "Well! I heard Mrs. Barker say to Mrs. Jennings, that she was going to have to rob Peter to pay Paul again this week." (Well done, Mick!)

"Mum, that girl at number eighty has had a baby." "Yes, I know." "Well, she seems very young to have saved all that money to buy one. I don't understand it, how did she manage it?" "Well err! Well err!" "Mother, should she have gone to St. James's Hospital?" "She could not go because she was poorly, she sent Mrs. Simpson to get a baby for her." "Awe right!"

> Ring a ring o'roses,
> A pocket full of posies.
> Atishoo! atishoo! all fall down.
> Ring a ring o'roses,
> Wipe your dirty noses.
> Atishoo! atishoo!
> Use your handkerchief.

It's a lovely day. It's a Holy day (A day celebrating a special day in the Catholic calendar.) and we have a holiday, as Tommy says, Holy days and holidays go together quite nicely. Mark and I call for Tommy. We are going on the islands at the bottom of the weir. Down Prince Henry's Road and into the park. The river is flowing at a normal level. Off with our boots and socks and we wade across to the biggest island. The sun glints on the water as it chuckles and gurgles round the larger stones. It scampers away between the islands, only to be captured by the main river after a few moments of freedom. As we approach, two swans glide lazily down to land on the river above the weir just like a couple of big flying boats; half a dozen land gulls rise squawking into the air and circle overhead protesting at our intrusion.

We have our provisions: a large pop-bottle of coloured water; thick slices of bread; a towel, and, an old tent for shelter. We are going to tickle trout and cook them on a wood fire. There are several rock-pools on the islands. We will approach ever so cautiously and quietly; lay down, and gently, oh so gently, move our hands either side of the fish. A first delicate contact; a gentle stroke forward and backwards; slowly oh ever so lightly, and, slowly gently increasing the grip- then whoosh, throw the fish on to the bank.

The tent is rigged, a fire spitting and crackling fills our shelter with thick smoke, but we stick it out, because it is Pissi err it is raining heavily outside. We place our catch on the fire, one small trout. "The kid in the Bible did better than us," says Tommy, "With the loaves and fishes." "Of course, he did," I reply. "Why of course?" "Well he had to be there to fulfill the prophesy." "He did very well," says Tommy. "Maybe he had a little bit of help," says I.

We have wined and dined on raw/cooked fish and begin to play "snap" and "I spy." "I spy" being rather limited in a smoked-filled tent. After about an hour, Tommy says he will have to have a slash. Out he goes as Mark calls, "Don't slash on the island or you will sink it! Slash in the river." "Oh heck and flipping heck!" shouts Tommy. "What's up Tommy?" I shout. "Have you slashed in the river and flooded it?" "No, mate! The river has managed to flood without my help. We're cut off!"

"Oh Hail Mary! We can't be! We are in deep ca-ca!" Out of the tent we dash. "We <u>are</u> cut off!" Like greased-lightening, Tommy, with his boots tied round his neck, is already wading across the river. Tommy is the only one of us who can swim. Fortunately, he doesn't have to; he wades to the river bank; turns and gives a thumbs up and dashes away.

The River Wharfe is one of the fastest-rising rivers in the country: heavy rains up the Dales and the wind a couple of days before have affected the river level. We know the river well enough to know we have at least one hour before the island is flooded, but, nevertheless, it is an anxious wait.

After about fifteen minutes, two men appear on pushbikes. I recognize them- they are policemen. One is carrying a rope. "Don't worry young 'uns!" shouts one. "We will soon have you out of this." "Thanks, thanks," we reply, "but hurry up." One man ties the rope to a tree; the other takes his shoes and socks off. He wades across the river and secures the rope to a fallen tree. No question who is to be first; he whisks me onto his back and away we go. In no time at all, we are safe, slightly sodden, and somewhat shaken on the riverbank.

Apparently our rescuers were just coming on duty at the Police Station as Tommy arrived there. They took us back to the 'Cop Hole.' (Police Station). Tommy was waiting there. We had hot drinks of cocoa and were rubbed down with towels, and warmed off in front of a blazing fire.

One policeman said to our rescuer, "You will get a citation for what you have done today." The Policeman says, "This young man is the hero." "What? Err I- err don't want anyone to know." "Why not?" "Well my Mum's not too well and she's saving up for a baby; my Dad's away, and I promised her I would never go on the islands unless Garnett's were drawing water and the weir had stopped running. I don't want to upset her." "Well," said our rescuer, "If you can keep mum so as not to upset Mum, we can." (I think he said that as a joke).

"Oh heck! Flipping heck!" moans Tommy. "What's up lad?" "I have left my socks on the islands." "Don't worry son, what colour were they?" "Dark gray wool with a hole in the left one just above my ankle." "We will get you a new pair." "Oh thank you! But can you get a pair with a hole in the left sock, near the ankle and then my Mum won't twig." "Surely she won't cotton-on (realise) will she?" "I bet you she will because she always seems to buy them with a hole in the left one near the heel." "No problem son, no problem." Tommy probably saved our lives that day. Mark and I certainly missed getting brayed (hit); the rounds of the kitchen, and, up the dancers. "Tommy?" "Yes." "Where did you get to slash then?" "You don't want to know, mate, you just don't want to know." Little did I know but Tommy would possibly save my life years later.

> "If a fella met a fella,
> In a fella's field,
> How many "f's" in that?"
> "None."

"Correct."

Sometimes, Michael and I would walk the longer route to school- on Kirkgate and along Bondgate. On the right hand side, Mr. Majerrison is making nets with a very big mesh- one end of the rope is anchored to the front wall of his house. He stands a few feet away, and with a template, he weaves and knots to produce the net. As Mick would say, "Its magic!" A small, dumpy man- he wears a permanent smile. I think he is a happy man who loves his work, (as I would love my work some years later). He makes the nets for farmers and fishermen I suppose.

"Mornin', Mr. Majerrison (Always 'Mr.'), "How are you today?" "I am fine and yourselves?" "Fare to midlin! Ok!" we chorus. "He is making those nets for fishermen," says Mick. "Clot! Any fish would swim straight through- the mesh is too big." "He is making them for abroad fish, 'cos (because) they are very, very big, Isn't that right? Mr. Majerrison?" "Aye lad! That's right! They catch whales and kangaroos: it's called 'Whale Meat' and 'Kangaroo Meat.'." "I've never seen any in the butcher's shop or the fishmongers," says I. Mr. M. looks at me, smiles and says, "Well you wouldn't would you?" "Why not?" "They only sell abroad fish to them that live there." "Awe! Right," I reply, " I think Mick could be right there." "I never knew that kangaroo was a fish?" I said, "I always thought they were animals what lived down-under something." "You can learn something new every day so you can."

As we said our goodbyes to Mr. Majerrison he said, "Be sure to stop and talk to me again." As we walked away he seemed to have a bigger smile than ever he seemed to be shaking all over and grasping his stomach, but then he always seemed to be laughing.

Still on the right hand side of Bondgate is the 'Model Lodging House.'. Destitutes, down and outs and tramps could stay for a night or longer for a copper or two (One or two pennies.), I imagine they could buy a meal (but I am not absolutely sure), making it a cheap bed and breakfast.

I remember these characters, in particular: 'Ginger Eddy'; 'Polly Nowt.' and 'Albert.'. Eddy was a tall thin man with beautiful flowing ginger hair. He would walk about six paces, stop, and nod his head up and down a dozen times. Another few steps and his right-arm would be lifted-up and down a few times and so

on, and so on, and so on, and still on and so on. I remember Polly
Nowt because of her name. She was a small slight lady who always
muttered as she trudged along. The best-known character was
called 'Albert.'- he was better known as 'Mothballs.'.

Albert was a smallish man. He had a full-face beard; wore an
old battered bowler hat and a long coat- just clear of the ground.
As he walked, we had a glimpse of his boots: usually several sizes
too big they were stuffed with paper, or straw, or whatever- depending on what size of boot that he was wearing. It's probably as
well that we never knew what packing he favoured. As he trudged
along, we used to follow to see if he ever walked out of his boots
but he never did.

"Hello, Albert, give us a mothball!" Sometimes we got one;
other times when we asked for one he would mutter, mutter,
"Something something off." It sounded like something to do with
sending a 'Duck going off somewhere'. It didn't sound very nice.
It was a long time before I discovered what he must have been saying, and as I have just said it wasn't very nice.

When Albert moved, there was a sound like pots and pans
knocking together. Heavens knows what he carried under that
coat. He always wore an old tie round his middle. Some said it
was his school tie and he had been to Eton or Harrow. I think
that it must <u>not</u> have <u>been</u> Harrow, because he always looked to
be moth-eaten! (Eton, eaten, Get it! Ah well!). Others said he belonged to a wealthy family, and they had lost all their money, or he
had been jilted on his wedding-day; some said he was a murderer
on the run. One story was that he owned a Mothball Factory and
gave mothballs away to advertise it.

The Wharfedale General Hospital, currently being replaced by
a new one, (cheers,) once was a Workhouse. One day, as I was
passing a man walked out of the Workhouse. I said, "Good morning!" "Hello!" he replied. "It's a fine day! It's good to be alive!"
As I started to walk away, a gruff voice said, " Herrllow." That's
Albert's voice I thought. I turned, and the man said in a pleasant
voice, "You don't know who I am, do you?" "Well you sound
like somebody I know." "Well, would you like a mothball?" "It <u>is</u>
Albert!" I cried. What a transformation!

Albert would go to the Workhouse where he would be bathed;
shaved and shampooed, and, given new/second-hand clothes and

boots. This morning, the long tied up coat was missing. I think that before he went into the Workhouse, each time he hid the coat and contents so that they did not confiscate them, but he always seemed to stick to that same long coat or maybe, just maybe, it was stuck to him. He must have had a heck of a job extracting himself from this garment.

He would disappear for about three months after each visit to the Workhouse. He had a round face and wore a lovely smile, he reminded me of Peppi one of the 'Marx Brothers.' the one with the curls. "But what a different person!" I cried. "Yes! Aren't I just?"

That morning, Albert told me how he had become a tramp. He made me promise not to tell anyone his story. I promised, "Cross my heart and hope to die." Spit on my right-hand and wiped it on my left sleeve. We said goodbye, and off he strode looking fifty years younger. Probably because he had lived more like a human being for a short time, something must have triggered normality for a few brief hours. Then he would slip back into some weird, vague world of mothballs and things.

I did not see Albert for about six months after our encounter. When I did I said, "Give us a mothball, Albert?" I did not get one, as he turned away, he was still muttering about that duck being sent off. When my wife read this she said. "What happened to Albert then?" I put my finger to the side of my nose and whispered, "Ssshh!" "Your secret's safe with me Albert, wherever you are."

Up to the age of nine years, I lived on the "Crossways." and belonged to the "Crossways." gang. The gang on the Crescent was called the "Crescenters.". We were terrified of them. They all seemed to be bigger and older than us. If I was sent on an errand to the 'Ivy Cottage Store.' about three quarters of a mile away, in order to avoid the 'Crescenters'.' territory, I would detour down Prince Henry's Road, along Farnley Lane and up Billams Hill. This was a round-trip of about two and a half miles. My mother would always ask me why I had taken so long. I never told her because she would not understand and she would not want a Son who was a coward. I'm sorry folks but I must confess that I was a dedicated, devout coward when it came to dealing with the 'Crescenters.'.

One day, Mum said that she had nearly saved enough money to buy a baby, and we would shortly be moving to a new house because we would need more room. "Where are we going then?" I asked. "On to "The Crescent." "What!" I cried. "On to 'The Crescent.'," said Mum. "Where?" "On to the Crescent. Are you going daft or deaf?" "No Mum." "Do you feel alright?" "Yes Mum." "Well you don't look alright to me. You have gone very pale." "So we are going to live on 'The Crescent.' then?" "Well done son! I think you've finally got it," says Mum. "You have not got cloth ears after all!" "No Mother!"

I certainly had got it, it was like being thumped between the eyes. They felt blurred- and I had got a headache. What will I do? What will I do? They will kill me! What will I do? There's nothing else for it- I will run away. I have got four doorsteps of bread; some milk in a pop bottle- topped up with water; some jam in the bottom of a jar, and, two apples. I am ready to run away. I will go after dinner, might as well start on a full stomach. One thirty and I am off. Up into the fields to bypass the Crescenters' territory, along Parker's Lane, and up on to the top of the Giant's Arr, err Bum.

It's a lovely afternoon. I have a slice of bread. I've forgot to bring a knife so I break the bread, push it into the jam and hook it out with my finger. A good swig of milk. My that was good! I lay back. A couple of lapwings are wheeling diving and turning. (Gosh, I wish I could fly like that!) They give their plaintive cry 'Peeewit, Peeewit!' (We call them 'Pewits.' or 'Chewits.'.) I know they are agitated: I am too near their nest. One bird drops to the ground; looks at me, and, starts to walk with its right wing hanging down as though it is broken. It stops, starts, stops. It's trying to lure me away from the nest. Don't worry little one! Your home is safe. I follow the bird for a few yards. Suddenly, its wing is miraculously cured! It flies away with its cry 'Peewit, peeewit.'

I can hear a Skylark singing. It takes a while to spot it. There it is hovering high in the sky on trembling wings, and singing its heart out. It looks like a puppet on a string: controlled by somebody or something high up in the heavens. A Curlew calls as it descends in a long slow glide, 'Coor-wee, coor-wee!'. As it nears the ground the call increases in pace then one long last 'Cooor-weee!' as the bird lands, and disappears among the long grass.

Two young rabbits are playing close by. I wonder if they will
have to run away from home to avoid bigger rabbits or giant
hares, I hope not. I lay back, close my eyes, and let the sun gently
warm my face. It's not bad at all- this running away lark. I will
have to decide where I will run away to. I could run away to sea
but I don't know which way the sea is. Let's have another drink
and then lay back and take it easy. I must have dozed-off. I am
awakened by loud shouts, hoorays and halloos. Oh, Hail Mary!
It's the Crescenters! "What <u>will</u> I do? What <u>will</u> I do?" I hope I
die quickly. Too late to do anything, they have spotted me. I am
surrounded.

"What have we here?" says Bill. (Bill is the gang leader.) "What
have we here?" "What are you doing up Giant's Arse all alone?"
He seems to be seven foot tall: everybody is bigger than me. "I err
I'm…" "Speak up lad!" says this seven foot giant. "Spit it out, but
not at me!" (Laughter alround.) "Come on! Let's have it!" "I'm
err, I'm running away." "Running away! Where from?" "From
"The Crossways." "I'm not surprised at that," says Bill. "If I lived
on The Crossways, I'd run away." (More laughter.) "Well young
'un, why are you running away?" "Because we are going to move
on to "The Crescent." "Well, that's not so bad, is it?" "No, I
err- err… I suppose not." "I bet I can tell you which house you
are moving into." "Can you?" "Yes, you're going to live in number twenty one." "That's right! How did you know?" "Magic!"
said Bill. "When you move house, you will have to join 'The
Crescenters.' gang (Cheers.). Do you understand?" "Yes! Oh yes!
I do, I do, I do!" "I now pronounce you and 'The Crescent.' man
and wife. Ahem Gentlemen! Order please! I propose that –what's
your name?" "Peter, Sir." Call me Bill." " Err, right, Sir Bill,"
"No young 'un, Bill will do." "Peter, have you got a nickname?"
"Yes, err, it's 'Plug.'." "Plug. That will do nicely!" "Do you smoke
a pipe?" "Err no, why do you ask?" "Well you must have heard
of 'plug tobacco' haven't you?" "Err no, Sir, err Bill err Sir Bill!"
"Whoa slow down nipper! Forget it! Listen up all you lot! I propose that young Plug is under our protection until he becomes a
full member of 'The Crescenters- Second class'. (More cheers.)
Everybody agree? Raise your right hands. That's unanimous."
(More cheers.) "Right lads! Are we ready to move off? Right
then." As Bill turns to go, he whispers to me, "I live at number

twenty three." He smiles and gives me a wink. I blink bank.

I arrive home about four thirty- just in time for tea, My mother wants to know what I have been up to. "I've been for a walk, just for a walk," I reply happily. Now I can go directly to the Shop by the Crescenters' territory without fear.

I have just got some sweets and a box of snuff for Mum from the Cottage. I come face to face with four members of "The Oval "gang (Known as the 'Ovalers.'.). This gang is second only to The Crescenters. "What are you doing here?" the leader of the gang demands. "I've been for some sweets and snuff for my Mother." "You can keep the dope. You're one of 'The Crossways' gang." "No, I'm not." "Oh yes you are." "I am a member of 'The Crescenters' gang, Second class!" "Pull the other one!" says the Leader. "Oh, dear! We are all shaking with fright!" says another. I could be in deep ca-ca here. What can I do?"

"Hi, young Plug! How are you?" I turn and it's Bill on his bike. "Hi, Bill," I answer. "Your mum sent me to take you home. Hop on the seat and I will pedal you home." So I sit on the saddle; Bill stands on the pedals, and off we go. "That was a close shave, laddie, but they won't bother you again." "Thanks Bill." At the time this happened, it was a great pity that I hadn't a clue what two raised fingers meant.

A few weeks later and we moved to twenty-one, The Crescent. Our furniture was loaded on to a horse and cart. My mother put her special things on a hand-cart, Mick and I moved the coal and coke on my bogey. As we set off on a journey of about a good half-mile, neighbours on either side of the road held sweeping brushes aloft and clapped us to our new home.

There's a knock at the door, Mum answers. "It's for you, Peter." "Thanks Mum." I open the door and Fred is standing with a piece of paper in his hand. Fred is the smallest and probably the youngest member of The Crescenters' gang. He is a 'Gopher First Class.'. What's a 'Gopher'? You may, or may not ask. If you are one of the askers, a 'Gopher.' is told or ordered to 'go fer this.' and ' go fer that'. Don't tell the others though. "A note for you, young Plug." "Thanks," I reply. "See you this afternoon." "Cheers!" "Cheers!" I open the note and read. "To young Plug, you will attend a full meeting in the Newall Park at 1.30 pm. Prompt. If you do not turn up, you will have to pay a forfit. (Forfeit.). Your Boss, Bill. P.S.

Don't be late or you will have to pay two forfits."

Saturday afternoon in The Newall Play Park, everybody is there. Bill stands on the wall. He raises his right arm and says, "Gentle folk! Come to order, the Crescenters! (Cheers.). The Crescenters (More cheers.) are now in session." Bill clears his throat and says, "I propose that young Jackson, now known as young Plug, is to be a member of The Crescenters (Cheers.). Everybody agree?" A pause. "I can't hear everybody saying 'agree'," says Bill, menacingly. "Good! Then that's agreed all round." He turns to me and says, "Young Plug, from today you are Gang Member Second Class- officially. Congratulations!" (Cheers). As a new second-class member of The Crescenters, I cheer with the gang this time. "You are entitled to one wish. If we can grant the said wish, we will do so. So wish away young Plug."

A wish, what can I wish. "Take your time, young 'un," says Bill, "But you must say your wish by the time I count to twenty." I close my eyes; my mind races; what can I wish? I can have anything, well something. "Time's up, young Plug." "What?" "Time's up, have you got a wish then?" "Yes." "Well, spit it out, but not at me." (Laughter.) "Well err- hmm, I wish Tommy could be a Second Class Member of The Crescenters." (Cheers.) "O.K," says Bill, "I will put it to the vote. Any objections you lot.?" "I object," says a lone voice. "I see, Master Jack has an objection, may I ask why?" "Why, because young Jackson, err young Plug is a Roman Catholic." "So what? So what?" "Well Tommy is a Catholic also." "Yes, go on," says Bill. "Well if we allow Catholics to join we could be over-run," says Jack. "You've lost me at this moment in time, would you care to explain?" "Certainly Bill, my father says Roman Catholics breed like rabbits, and, before long they will outnumber the rest of us." "But I haven't any rabbits, and neither has Tommy." "Well," says Bill, "I think it will be a long time before that happens, let's put it to the vote. Everybody who votes 'yes' will receive half a napple (apple) over the next two weeks, and any objector up to this moment, will receive one whole apple if the vote is unanimous. What do I hear then? Right, I hear all agree, and one 'suppose so'. Is that a: 'Suppose-so.'; a 'Yes.', or, a 'No.'?" "It's a 'Yes.'." "Are you sure?" "I suppose so" "Are we all right Jack- not half left then?" "Yes all right, Jack," says Jack.

The vote is unanimous, I am a full second-class member of The

Crescenters (Cheers) and Tommy soon will be.

"I propose we have a stew-up next Saturday," says Bill. "All in favour? All agree? Good, no 'Suppose-sos.' then? No? Right, we will depart from this spot next Saturday morning at ten o'clock. Anybody coming late will pay a forfeit."

"What's a 'stew-up' Bill?" "What's a 'stew-up', what's a 'stew-up'? Don't they teach you anything but religion at your school?" "Yes!" "What then?" "They teach us Latin." "What good is that then?" "Well, if you want to be a priest..." "I don't want to be a priest. Any of you lot want to be a priest? All agreed that we don't want to be a priest? Unanimous is it? O.K. carried!" "You could be a Doctor," I suggested. "I could manage that," says Bill. "And it would come in handy if you travelled abroad." says I. "True! Anyhow, young Plug a 'stew-up' is we bring tins of soup; Oxo or Bovril, and, anything else we can scrounge; sling it in a bucket or pan, and, cook it on a wood fire."

"Now, young Plug, to be a full First-class Member of The Crescenters (Cheers.), you have to do something for the gang." "What?" "Well, you can supply the bread, two large loaves and a bread-knife. You must buy the bread with your pocket money. That makes it a sacrifice for the gang, for your fellow-man. Dost thou understand?" "I dost," I reply.

Come Friday, and I am going to the Co-op for two large loaves of bread. "Could I have two large loaves of bread please?" "Certainly, there you are." I give the lady the money. "That's just right!" "I know it's just right because I have been for lots of bread for Mum and our neighbours. "What's your Divi (Dividend.) Number then?" Oh gosh! I can't remember! What can I do? What can I do? Mum always writes it down. "What's the number then?" "The number?" "Yes, the number." "The number is... err- the number is one two three four five!" "Are you sure?" "Err, yes, that's it! One two three four five."

"What's your name then?" "Jackson- Peter Jackson. My Mother is called Sally Jackson." "Where do you live?" "Twenty one The Crescent," I reply proudly. She looks in her book, "Right name; wrong address." "Oh sorry! We have just moved." "Where from?" "From sixty the Crossways." "That's more like it! Your number is six three double five one." "Six three double five one," I repeat. "Yes, here's your Divi Cheque and your bread. Don't eat it all at one go." "We probably will," I reply. All the way home, I kept looking at the Divi Slip and memorising the number and I never forgot it after that day. It's a six and a three a five and a four. No! That four is another five I think, and, a one- 1 think.

I supplied the bread and the knife. We had our stew-up, cooked on a blazing fire in Weston Wood, burning Weston Wood wood- if you see what I mean. On that day, I became a full member of the Crescenter's gang (Cheers.); a full First- class Member.

Shortly after this great day, Tommy was accepted after 'Doing his forfeit.' He had to clean the boots of all the Crescenters' gang (Cheers.); the only time the gang had clean footwear was when a new member was admitted.

One day I told Tommy about Roman Catholics and rabbits. The following morning, Tommy called to go to school. "I've got an idea," he says. "What idea?" I ask. "It's a good one," says Tommy. "They always are," I reply. "Yes, I know," says he, (big head). "Come on then, what's this brilliant idea?" "They were on about us Catholics breeding like rabbits." "Yes." "Well, let's get a rabbit each and when they have young ones, we could sell them as pets, and we could sell the !to eat." "That's a brilliant idea." "Yes! I know it is," says Tommy.

First, we had to get permission to keep rabbits. No problem here, so we start to build a couple of hutches. Dad gives us a hand. They are all duly completed and he says he will buy us a couple of bunnies from the Auction Mart.

"We're in business!" says Tommy. "We certainly are!" I reply. Time passes, we bed, feed and clean them out. After a couple of weeks, no young ones, nothing happened. "We'll give it another two weeks then." "Agreed," says I. A month has passed, noth- ing. Tommy says, "If Roman Catholics breed like these rabbits, it won't be long before we are all wiped-out and extinct." "I agree." "I will ask my Dad what's gone wrong." "That's a good idea." "Yes, I know it is," I reply.

"Dad," "Yes son," "Err Dad," "Yes." "About these rabbits?" "What about them?" "Well, we have had them for about a month now and nowt's happened." "How do you mean: 'Nothing's hap- pened'?" "They haven't had any young ones." "Arrh well! I don't think they will have any." "Why not?" "Why not? Because you need two rabbits to have babies." "But we have two: I have got mine here and Tommy's got his at home." "You ask Tommy to bring his rabbit down here." "And his rabbit hutch?" "No, he doesn't need that," says Dad, "We will put them in one hutch and I will help you to look after them." "Why have they to be in one hutch?" "Why? Well, err, it needs two of them to look after young ones: it can be too much for one to look after them- just like people. The husband goes to work to buy food and clothes and the wife stays at home. So you ask Tommy to bring his rabbit down here and then leave them alone so that they can get to know each other." "Thanks Dad!" "You're welcome Son! You're welcome!"

"But how can they have young ones if they don't go to St. James (St. James Hospital, Leeds.), or, a place like it?" "I think St. Francis sends young animals and birds with an Angel." "That's alright then," says I. Sure enough not long afterwards, the Angel delivers six babies. They must have arrived during the night. As they grow, Dad says we can put them into Tommy's hutch.

We sell them all for a dodger (three pence) each for pets. One day, Tommy says, "Let's sell the big rabbits for eating." "That's a good idea," says I. "I know it is," says Tommy. "You kill them when we have got someone to buy them." "Why me?" "Why not you?" "Not me because I don't want to. Why not you?" "I can't kill anything," says Tommy. "What are we going to do then?" "I don't know but I will think of something."

"Morning Tommy!" "Morning Plug! How's tricks?" "Fair to midlin', have you come up with anything?" "Yes, I have." "What?" "We will sell them to the Butcher." "That's brilliant!" "Yes, I know it is." We sold the rabbits for four pence each and as Tommy said, "It has been a privilege to be able to look after God's creatures."

Young Michael caused a bit of a panic the other day. He came home and went straight upstairs to the bedroom. Mum called him down for his dinner, "In a minute Mum." "Dinner's out." "Sharn't be long." "There's something wrong with that lad," says Mum. "Nip upstairs and see what he is up to- he's always sat down before his meal is ready." "Right-o Mum!" I go to investigate. "What's up Mick?" "Nowt." "Well your dinner is out on the table. Come on laddie! Let's have you!" As Mick turns towards me, "Oh heck! Oh flipping heck! What have you done?" Michael's right eye is closed and swollen and he has a few flecks of dried blood on his cheek. "What have…" I am interrupted. "Oh Holy Mary! What have you done? What's happened?" screams Mum. "You've lost your eye! You've lost your eye do you hear? And you say that's nowt? That's nowt?" "No," says Mick. "I have had an accident up Giant's ar-err –bum." "Peter," "Yes Mother," "Go phone for an ambulance." "Yes Mum." "Right away."

On my return, Mum told me what had happened. Apparently, Michael and two other lads had tried to carry someone sitting on a bicycle inner-tube. Why would anybody want to do a thing like that I wonder. Somebody let go and the valve clobbered Mick in the eye. Mick was lying quiet, Mother had put a cold compress on it. He did not seem too bad. "The ambulance is here," "Good!" says Mum. The two ambulance men have a look at the injury; they ponder and have a quiet discussion. One of the men tells Mum that they will have to take him to The L.G.I. "What sort of an 'eye' is that then?" asks Mick. "Nay, it's not an eye lad; it's the Leeds General Infirmary." "I'm going abroad; I'm going abroad," shouts Mick "I think he must be concussed," says one of the men.

"Peter, will you go to Leeds with him?" "Yes, Mother." Before we even get mobile my almost dying younger brother shouts, "Can I sit in the front? Can I have a go at the gears?" "If you don't behave yourself, you won't go." "Awe Mum!" "Well just settle-down and behave." "How will we get back home, Mum?" "Well err.. I err…" "Don't worry Missus, we will get them back to you." "Thank you very much." "It's a pleasure, Missus."

Three miles out of Otley, "Are we abroad yet? Can I sit in front? Can I have a drive?" "All right, all right, if you promise to be quiet, you can come into the cab, but you can't have a drive?" "Awe! O.K. then."

We arrive at the L.G.I, the driver reports in at Casualty Reception. A wheelchair is provided. "We could do with a cou-ple of these chairs at home," says Mick. "What for?" "Then we could race down Giant's arse in—." "You know you haven't to say that." "What?" "'Arse', look now I've said it." "Well, it doesn't matter." "What doesn't?" "'Arse' doesn't." "Why?" "Because it doesn't count when we are abroad." "What I was going to say was that we could race down Giant's Arse in Summer and sledge down in Winter."

"Any chance of a couple of old wheelchairs, Mister?" "No

chance," says the wheelchair man. "No chance at all, they have to go back to be recycled." "And who gets the cycles when they are done?" "No, they are not made into cycles, they – Ah, here we are young man." "Thank you, mister." "You're welcome son."

The Doctor arrives in Casualty to examine Michael. He seems to be very good but I can't understand a word he says- perhaps we are abroad. I catch the Ambulance Driver's eyes; spread my hands towards him and give him a perplexed look. The driver comes over and whispers, "The Doctor's Welsh." "Welsh, is that abroad?" "No." "Well, he could have fooled me." "He comes from Wales." "Well that's abroad, isn't it?" "Well, not really," he replied, "It's sort of another country over the border." "What's the border?" "Well, it's a sort of... a sort of a line between two countries to separate them." "Well if they are separate, they must be abroad from each other." "I guess so, I suppose so," he wearily sighs, "You can learn something new every day, so you can."

The Doctor said, according to the Ambulance Man, that Michael would be alright and he could go home and rest quietly for a couple of days. I couldn't understand a word he said and I said to the driver that it sounded like Greek to me. (Mum used to say this when she could not understand something.). "Now <u>that is</u> abroad," he replied.

We leave the L.G.I. Mick up-front, me in the back peering through the cat-flap or maybe head flap into the driver's cab. The driver does a quick turn of his head; looks at me; winks, and, says to Michael, "Would you like to see some more of abroad?" "Ho! Yes please!" "Right then! We will go the Canal way home." We divert a little off our normal route home and travel along the Canal. Huge pairs of horses are pulling carts laden with timber, huge boxes, and bales. (The driver says they are bales of wool and cotton). The horses clatter and snort as they move off; others wait-stamping impatiently and whinnying. Giant cranes swing to and fro like fairground rides. Barges are sailing, smoking, and hooting; men are shouting, smoking and hooting- well hollering; some are swearing and a couple of dogs are barking. I look at Michael; his hands are up either side of his face; his eyes are wide and bright in awe and wonder, and, for once, he cannot speak (Hooray!).

Michael notices my gaze and he says, "Peter." (He never calls me Peter, it's usually 'Hey you!' I will say, "I am not a Chinaman."

But never 'Peter'. "Peter," he says, "Truly, today, I am abroad." "Of course you are." We echo," Home at last! "How is he? Will he be alright?" "He will be fine missus." "Oh good! Thank goodness!"

"You will have to say a prayer of thanksgiving," says Mum. "Why, is Tea ready?" "It will be in ten minutes." "Well, in that case I will say one thanksgiving to cover tea, and my eye." "He's alright, missus, he's alright." "Go upstairs and wash your hands and face for tea, and don't have a cat-lick (A cat-lick is the line which marks the end of a briefly washed face, and the start of an unwashed neck.). "O.K. Mum." As he walks upstairs, he calls, "I have had a wonderful day abroad." "No, you haven't." "Nay, Missus," says the Ambulance Man, "Don't say owt; don't shatter the poor little bu... err- boy's dream." Mother didn't take offence at this remark because as she says, "We're poor but not poverty."

Tonight is Mischievous Night, the Tiger has paid us a rare visit. I have to obtain a unanimous vote from The Crescenters (Cheers.) for him to do so. "What are we going to do then?" he asks. "Well, we can tie two door knobs together and knock on both doors at the same time. Or, we can go window tapping. To window-tap, a button is hung down from the window frame attached to a drawing pin on a short length of cotton; a long length of cotton is attached from the button to the operator. As the line is pulled back and forth the button taps the window.

"That sounds very exciting, I don't think," says Tiger. "Surely, you can come up with something better than that." "We annoy Mr. Neal for ten minutes." Nothing happens, he must be out or asleep, or Kaylide (drunk), so we gather under the lamp to play flics-on. Each player throws a cigarette card using the index and middle fingers. The player who lands his card on any one of the cards wins the lot.

Some burn 'Wheeli' and swap tales of nights passed. 'Wheeli' is a slow-burning fuse for lighting fireworks. When cupped in the hands, it scorches the skin brown, and hard, I don't know why we did this, but we did.

Suddenly the night is shattered by a voice, "Nobody move! Stay where you are! I have got you all in a corner!" "Flipping heck! It's Nealie!" All except Tiger are veterans of the game of 'Stealth.' We leap over the fence into the gardens and melt away into the darkness. Tiger makes the fatal mistake of legging it closely followed by Mr. Neal.

We look over the fence wondering what has happened. Suddenly clattering feet and Tiger gallops past, head thrown back, mane flowing- closely followed by Nealie. The Tiger has become the hunted. The Crescent is shaped like a running track. In the darkness, Tiger has missed the turning off into town. Half a minute later, "Here they come again." As they pass us the second time, a voice calls out of the darkness, "Take the second left Tiger!" About ten yards behind, Nealie seems to be keeping a steady gap. Tiger disappears; Nealie reappears; passes our hiding places, and, disappears into his house. Tiger avoided capture. Two months later he moved to London. I will probably never see him again. He could be dead by now- or something.

As I grew up, I became friendly with Mr. Neal. He told me that he could have caught us any time but did not as he enjoyed the chase, and, that he got a buzz from almost frightening the ca-ca out of us.

Bonfire night is approaching (Well it's towards the end of September.); all able gang members are ordered to be in Newall Park to go 'Chumping.' (Gathering anything that could be burnt.) at ten o'clock sharp. Members must bring at least two doorsteps of jam and bread, and, any old tools that may be useful.

We set off armed with long and short shaft axes and a miscellany of knives. (They would be regarded as offensive weapons today.) One member turned up with a 'Diana' air rifle. When Bill spots the weapon, he inquires sarcastically, "Why! Oh why if it's not too much trouble, have you brought that? "No trouble at all Bill. We might shoot a rabbit and cock it." "Good idea Scotty! But I think you mean 'cook it', don't you?" "I suppose so." "Is that: 'Suppose-so'; a 'Yes' or a 'No'?" "It's a 'Yes'" "Are you sure?" "I suppose so." "That gives me an idea," says Bill. "When we have collected enough "chump" for the biggest bonfire in Otle, (Cheers.), we will go 'snickling' (snaring) (Cheers.) and these two new members can be bloodied." "I don't like the sound of that," whispers Tommy. "Nor do I. It sounds too much like a 'Twilting' to me." "Do you know what 'sninkle' and 'bloody' means, Plug?" "No, I don't, but I think you mean 'snickle', not 'stinkle'." "It looks as though we are going to find out what bloody is," whispers Tommy. "And 'snickling'," says I.

Off we go, past "The Workhouse," (Good old Albert!); along Parker's Lane and up Giant's err, err, what the Protestants call it. Here we have our first stop, a doorstep and a swig of water. Bill gives the order to move off. We cross the long field and into Weston Wood. We know the Keeper and he knows us. He can trust us to take only the wood we have permission to collect.

We spend a pleasant morning cutting and trimming the branches- we are actually clearing the dead wood, which is a great help to the Keeper. We should be getting paid for this I think. We drag our 'chump' home. We didn't see a rabbit. Tommy and I are looking forward to bonfire night but not to being 'bloodied' or 'snickled'.

The bonfire grows week by week. Different gangs raid each other's 'chump'. We raid theirs; they raid ours. One night we send a raiding party to The Ovalers' bonfire. They return empty handed. "Why haven't you got owt?" demands Bill. "Because they've nowt left to take." "That's a shame, a great shame! I enjoyed the raids, things are a bit flat now." "Well their bonfire site is ruddy flat also at this moment", says one of the raiders.

"I've got an idea," says Tommy. "O.K." says Bill. "Carry on, your ideas are usually very good." "Yes, I know." "Well young Tommy, let's have it?" "Have what?" "What you've got." "What have I got?" "I don't know what you have got." "Then why do you want, what you don't know that I haven't got?" "I didn't say that I want summat that you have not got?" "I asked you to let me have summat that you have got." "But I haven't got owt" "I think someone is pulling your leg mate," says Scotty. "No he isn't!" says Bill, "Yes he is!" says Scotty. "How do you know that big head?" "Because you're walking with a limp mate." "Very funny Dotty Scotty! Now can we get on." "Have you something to tell me Thomas?" "Well William! Let The Ovalers raid some back." "And how will we do that may I ask? You know they don't have the guts to tackle The Crescenters (Cheers.). "Well let's make it easy for them, we just won't guard it." "I think you've got summat there, but what can we do?

"Any ideas you lot?" asks Bill. (Silence.) "No brainwaves then?" "No brains," says a lone voice. (Laughter all round.) "We could let it be known that we have all got the plague." "No good! They wouldn't believe that." "Tell them we are all going abroad, that's what young Mick would do," says Tommy. "That's no good either," says Bill.

"Half a mo'," says Tommy, "Just tell them that as we are approaching the Season of Goodwill, they can take back what their consciences will allow." "That's brilliant!" chortles Bill. "I know it is," giggles Tommy. We all chortle or giggle, and pass the idea unani... err unanimously. "That's good, young Tommy! If I ever wanted to rob a bank, you would be the best planner I could have." "Yes, I know, Bill, I know."

'The Ovalers.' are happy; we are happy. Two nights later their greed has been satisfied. They took a heck of a lot of chump- a lot more than we had taken off them. Justice must be seen to be done." William err- hmm- Bill calls the meeting to order. "All able bodied members will meet at seven o'clock tomorrow night." "What for?" "What for?" echoes Bill, "We're going to raid The Ovalers. (Cheers.) and pinch everything (Cheers.) and more beside. By the time we have finished there will be a ruddy great hole standing where their bonfire should be." (Cheers.)

Two weeks before Bonfire Night, Bill has called a meeting for six o'clock, Friday, all members must attend or pay a forfeit. "Order good people! Order! I propose that tomorrow morning, we go snickling." Tommy looks at me and says, "This is it then! Did you find out what 'bloody' means?" "Well not this one, but I know what the other means." "Well every bug... err every body knows that." "Do you think they cut your wrists like the Indians do to be blood brothers, so that we are full members, and a bit extra?" "When you two have stopped gabbing like two old washerwomen, would you kindly let us know, and then we might just be able to get on with the business in hand."

"Sorry, Bill, sorry, err please carry on." "Yes please carry on." "Thank you ladies. Quiet everybody." Bill gives a little cough to clear his throat. "Ahem! Err good gentle folk, each member must bring at least one snickle, two each would be better, but bringing one will avoid a forfeit. Agreed?" "Agreed – err Yes. I suppose so." "Is 'suppose so', a 'Yes' or a 'No' then?" "It's a yes." "Thank you, are you sure it's a 'Yes'?" "I suppose so." "Thank you." "We will need a hammer," says Bill. "Two would be better." "I will bring two," says Mark. (His father is a joiner.) "Thank you, Mark, fullmarks to Mark."

"Everybody meet at the end of Parker's Lane at nine o'clock in the morning, any late comers will pay a forfeit, to be decided. Bring the usual provisions: coloured-water- the best coloured water will receive a prize. This will be a 'napple' which I will contribute. I will test each bottle to see which one tastes the best and the winner will get a 'napple'." (Cheers.) Crafty old Bill! "Bring at least two slices of bread; at least one inch thick to qualify for a doorstep with enough butter, jam, or treacle, if possible, to cover both sides of said bread- and bring a knife each. We will proceed along Parker's Lane and up Giant's Arse, (Bill is a Protestant so he doesn't have owt to confess or nobody to confess it to.). Here we will have a short break, then we will cross the Long Field (So called because it is a long field.) and into the woods." "Can we have a fire?" asks Mark. "I've got the matches," says Bill (Cheers). "After refreshments, we will proceed to snickle up," Bill drones on.

"Go on then! You ask!" "No! You ask!" "I'm not asking!" "Right then! We will toss for it." "I haven't got owt to toss with," says Tommy. "Well! I have a penny," "Go on then!" "Right! You call!" "Heads!" "Hard luck mate! It's tails! You lose!" "Err, best out of three," says Tommy. "You never said that!" "No, but I meant it, and thought it." "Go on then, I will toss again right?" "Right, I call tails," "Its heads! You lose! Tails! I win! Hard luck mate!" says I.

"Err, Bill," calls out Tommy. "Yes, young Thomas," (Cringe.). "Please William, don't call me Thomas." "O.K. point taken, Tommy, point taken." "Thank you, Bill." "OK! Spit it out! But be careful where you spit it. (Laughter all round.) Come on let's have it!" "Well, Bill, what's a 'snickle'?" "What's a 'snickle'?" "What's a 'snickle'[? What is a 'snickle'? Don't they teach you anything at the Catholic School?" "They teach us Latin." "Don't start that again young Plug." "Sorry, Bill," "I should Coco (Think so.) So you don't know what a 'snickle' is then?" "I wouldn't be asking if I knew." "Watch it young Tommy! Watch it!" "Sorry Bill!"

"Is it something to do with cutting grass?" I venture (Laughter.). "That's a 'sickle', you ignoramus." "Sorry!" "Young Tommy, and young Plug are excused supplying 'snickles', because they know naff all about them, We will show them how to make one tomorrow, but I propose they bring double bread ration. (Cheers.).

The meeting is now closed. Remember nine-o-clock sharp in the morning, or pay a forfeit."

Saturday morning 8.30, knock – knockknock- knock – at the front door. "Thomas, (Cringe.) is here," says Mum. She has broken our knocking code- we will have to change it. "Hi Tommy!" "Hi yourself! Come in, it's a lovely morning." "A bit nippy," Tommy replies, "and it's a lazy wind." "How do you mean that it's a 'lazy wind'?" "Because it goes straight through you: it's too ruddy lazy to go round." "That's very funny Tommy." "Yes I know it is." I lead the way into the kitchen. "Morning Mrs. Jackson." (Always full title with respect in those days). "Morning Thomas!" (Cringe: we will have to do something about this, calling Tommy - Thomas, lark.). "Come and sit down. Peter has nearly finished his brekka. What's it like outside, Thomas?" (I give up.) "It's bright and sunny; I think it may snow, but by gum, it's a lazy wind." "What's a lazy wind then, Thomas?" (Goodness, it does sound soppy.) "It's a wind that too lazy to go round, instead it goes straight through you." "Ah yes! I see, very good Thom…." "Tommy Mum," says I.

"Would you like some bread and jam or treacle?" "Treacle, please, Mrs. Jackson?" "And a mug of cocoa?" "Yes please." "What's it to be then, two slices or a doorstep?" "Ooh! A door-step please Mrs. Jackson." We finish our meal. "Thanks Mum!" "Thanks Mrs. Jackson!" "You're welcome Thomas!" (Ouch!).

As we troop out, Mum calls after us, "Dinner for twelve o-clock and don't be late home." Nobody ever had a watch but we were always back home in time for meals. "Right Mum! What are we having then?" Mum answers, "Fish and chips, parsley or fish cakes and chips, or scallops." (Scallops are slices of battered potato.) "If you have scallops, you can't have chips." "Why not?" "Because five scallops make a good meal without chips." "Aw Mum!" "Come on lad! What's it to be then?" "Right, I will have parsley cake and chips." "Well, I am glad we have got that settled, off you go." "Bye Mum!" "Bye, Thomas!" (We really will have to do something about what Mum calls Tommy.) "Will you get me a ha'poth (halfpenny) of scraps, (Small pieces of batter that fall off the fish being fried.) Mum?" "We will see, remember if you are late home there may be nowt left." "Aw Mum!" "Only joking," she laughs. "Off you go then and have a good time." She does not ask us where we are going, or not to speak to strangers, she doesn't need to.

"Have you got any idea what's going to happen then?" "Not a clue," I reply, "we will just have to face it, but I will tell you what..." "What? "We are going to have to sort something out about my Mum calling you Thomas." "I couldn't agree more," says Tommy.

Ten minutes to nine, some of the gang are assembled. Greetings are exchanged as we wait . Five to nine then, as we approach Parker's Lane, most of the gang have turned up. Greetings are exchanged as we wait for Bill. "You can learn to make a snickle, while we wait," says Alan, who is Second Leader. First class. "Right!" "O.K. then!" "Well you get a piece of Old Granger's fire-wood- point it at one end; you then make a lassoo with the wire that he uses to bind his firewood into bundles; you fasten the other end to the pointed wood. Are you with me, so far?" "Yes." "Yes, with you," we echo. "You knock the peg into the ground with the wire loop sticking out." "But, Alan, what is it for?" "What is it for? What is it for?" (I wonder if he is going deaf). "Yes, what is it for?" "Well for the benefit of Catholics which don't seem to be too bright, except for breeding, and doing Latin, it is for catching rabbits." "How?" asked Tommy. "You. knock the peg into the ground on a rabbit-run." "What's a 'rabbit-run'?" I ask. "About thirty miles an hour with a tail wind! A 'tail wind'- do you get it? "Err yes" "I should think so." (Laughter.) "Aw come on Alan! Fill us in." "O.K. then! A 'run' is a narrow track what Mr. and Mrs. Bunny use regularly. You knock the peg into the ground with the wire loop across the run. When our furry little friend hops along, it sticks its bunny nut into the loop; pulls it tight as it tries to run, and it's curtains. "Do they take a long time to die?" "Of course they do," says Alan. "Course they do.

The Parish Church clock is striking 9 o'clock. Bill appears round the corner. "Mornin, gentle folk!" and to Tommy and me he says, "It's a fine morning, young sirs. Do you now know how to make a 'snickle'?" "Yes, Bill," I reply. "And you also, Thomas, err young Tommy?" "I suppose so, William err Bill," replies Tommy. "Point taken! Point taken once again, but is that suppose so, a 'Yes' or a 'No'?" "It's a 'Yes' Bill," "Are you sure it's a 'Yes'?" "I suppose so," says Tommy. "Good! Good!" says Bill, "At least you are learning something useful at last to help you to travel on the rocky road of life. Right then! Is everybody here?"

"Everybody except Freddy," says Alan. "Oh! I am not surprised at that! He will be too late for his own funeral! We will give him till quarter past nine by the Church clock when it strikes a quarter past." A couple of minutes later, Freddy appears round the corner. I wonder if he comes just a bit late and waits round the corner, out of sight, and then appears at least 5 or 6 minutes late so he can keep his reputation of never turning up on time. I know that Bill waits, and appears as the Church clock is striking, I think that they must have had many a natter (Chat.) just out of sight of us lot.

"Come on Steady Freddy! What's your excuse today?" "Sorry Bill! I couldn't find my boots." "You would forget your head if it wasn't screwed on tightly!" "That's what my Mother says." "Well, glad you could make it; you will be fined two forfeits." "Nay Bill!" "Three forfeits." "O.K. Bill! I accept." "Good, now can we move off?"

We walk along Parker's Lane and up to the top of Giants. "Oh Bill!" "Yes, young Plug," "What's, what's…?" "If you have got summat to say, say it!" "Right I will!" "Go on then!" I take a deep breath. "What's 'bloodied'?" "What's 'bloodied'?" "I just said that!" "Well you still have a lot to learn! You should change schools young Plug, so that you are not a total ignoramus." "What's 'ignoramus' Bill?" "I give up! Let's stick to your first question, right?" "Right!" "Thank goodness for that! Now listen and do not interrupt!" "Will not do," I reply.

"To be 'bloodied', you will cut and gut the first rabbit we snare. Each member of The Crescenters, (Cheers.), will smear you with blood of the said, sad victim. O.K?" "Yes," I reply. "I suppose so," says Tommy. "Is that: 'Suppose so'; a 'Yes' or a 'No'?" "It's err, a 'Yes'," says Tommy. "Now, are you absolutely sure it's a 'Yes'?" "I suppose so," says Tommy. "That's unanimous then." "I feel sick," whispers Tommy. "That makes two of us," I whisper back. "What can we do? What can we do?" "Don't worry, I will think of something." (The third letter is "U").

About half way across the long field, we stop for refreshments, coloured water, and doorsteps. Bill tastes all the bottles of coloured water, and declares himself the winner. When Bill declares, nobody has the bottle to object, even if he swigs and swigs (drinks) and empties most of them. Having dined and supped, especially Bill, we troll off and arrive at Weston Woods. Bill and Alan show us where to lay our snares. We build a fire and have toasted/charred bread spread with jam or treacle, and other nameless substances. We play a good un-bloodied game of Indians and Cowboys until about eleven o'clock. Even without a watch, we knew we would be home by about twelve thirty.

"Right, lads! We will scoff the food and swig the water at the top of Giant's Arse, agreed?" "Agreed." As Tommy and I part company, I say to him that I could not bear to be bloodied. "I am more concerned about killing a rabbit." Tommy could not kill anything; not even a fly; not even a wasp. He would try to catch them in a tin or a jar and then release them.

I remember the day when just outside Weston Wood in the long field we discovered a wasp's nest in an old fallen decaying tree. We decided to raid it for the wasp cake and sell it to a fisherman for bait. It was highly prized: the grubs would be gently baked in the oven to toughen them up a little. It was regarded as a killer bait.

We attack the nest- all except Tommy, and. we <u>all</u> got stung- except Tommy. He stood quite close watching our efforts, suddenly he called out, "Look! Two wasps have settled on my hand." I thought he was going to caress them as though they were friends and believe it or not, he never did get stung. (Ye shall reap as ye shall sew.)

Saturday, just after tea, Tommy calls, "Hi Plug!" "Hi yourself!" "I have a message from Bill, we are going to Weston Woods at two o'clock on Sunday to check the snares." "Oh heck! What <u>are</u> we going to do?" "I've got an idea," says Tommy, "this is what we can do."

Sunday afternoon about 1-45 pm. "Everybody here, everybody?" "Yes!" "Here!" "Present!" "The Crescenters (Cheers.) will now move to the killing-grounds." "Ugh! I wish they were all Catholics." "Me too," says Tommy, "and that they would behave in a civilised manner." "And learn Latin," says I.

"We will have our usual stop for refreshments and proceed into Weston Woods," announced Bill. Having supped and dined, we set off and troll across the long field to Weston Woods. As we approach the gate to the wood, Bill stops and shouts, "Halt!" and

bellows "Hoody blell! Hoody blell!" Bill can get things mixed
up a bit when he is really annoyed or whatever. "What's up Bill?"
"I'll tell you what's up! Look at that sign. Everybody read it, including the Catholics, if they can read English. In fact, young
Plug! You can read it out loud." "Right Bill! I will, Bill!"

TO WHOM IT MAY CONSERN,
WESTON WOOD HAVE BEEN
OVER RUN WITH SNIKLES
ENUFF TO START A FIRE WOOD FACTORI
ANY WUN CORT WILL BE SNICKLED
AND SHOT THIS MEANS YOU

"Hoody blell,! breathes Bill, "Hoody blell! Let's go home." As
we set off on our return journey, I whisper to Tommy, "You made
a flipping good job of that Notice but why did you get the spelling
wrong?" "I know," smiles Tommy, "I know that I made a good
job of things. But why did I get the spelling wrong?" "Everybody
will think that it was that uneducated Game Keeper because, although Bill asked if I could manage to read the sign, he knows that
us Catholics are pretty hot when it comes to reading and writing."
"Crafty Tommy!" says I "Yes crafty me!" says he. Tommy had
made the Notice on Saturday night: we got up very early Sunday
morning to fix it and pull all the snares up. We were both very
happy because no rabbit had been caught we hadn't been bloodied,
and we could go to eleven o clock Mass with a clear conscience.
"One to the Catholics I think.
   For several weeks now, we have all been in various Firework
Clubs. I am in Bryant's Club: this is a Toy Shop by the Maypole
in Otley. This is the shop that sells dope(snuff) remember? We
pay our half pennies and pennies into the club and Mr. Bryant
marks our cards to keep a record of payments. The average savings would be about two shillings (About ten pence- an absolute
fortune.). Into the Toy Shop then, brightly lit, always nice and
warm. Set out the full length of the shop, under a glass counter for
safety are millions, err- thousands, well alot of, fireworks: rock-
ets, some even cost thruppence and a tanner; Roman Candles;
Little Demons; Pom-pom cannons; Jumping Crackers; Pin-wheels
(Catherine-wheels); sparklers, and, many more. I will get all half-

penny fireworks. It is a time of big, big decisions. I might even get a tuppenny rocket. I could take an hour or more to make my choices and spend my two bob so don't wait for me.

Bonfire Night at last. It has rained most of the day, every thing is pis-err- very wet. The damp wood, newspapers, and whatever else are eventually coaxed into life (Cheers.), spluttering, protesting, spitting and smoking. Soon flames are reaching up through the bonfire and high into the sky (More cheers.). Mothers and sisters come round with treacle toffee, Parkin Pigs etc- sisters have limited uses after all. I have perfected a toffee taking technique. When offered the tray, I will go for a piece of toffee whilst covering the biggest piece under my palm. I then withdraw my hand, sliding the toffee off the tray into my left hand (Yum yum.). "Thank you very much Missus!" "You're welcome young man! You're welcome!"

The flames are reaching heavens high, no smoke now, the heat of the fire is glowing fiercely red. Right coat pocket-Bangers; left coat pocket- non-Bangers. Off we go with a bang then. "Drinks anybody?" (Cheers.) We light our wheeli and begin to set our fireworks off. "What's that you're holding?" says Tommy. "It's a Union Jack," I reply. "I don't reckon much to it," says Tommy, "I thought that one was a bang…" Flash! Boom! "God! Tommy is right!" Someone had blundered (Me): the firework had thundered. "God! Tommy, I have blown my hand off! I must have put a right pocket Banger into my left non-Banger pocket by mistake."

My cheeks puff up; my eyes start watering. I can't feel a thing. Tommy says, "Sit down for a few minutes," Now I <u>can</u> feel something; my hand is throbbing with pain; my fingers are swollen, and, they feel as though they are glued together. My hand feels as though it is going to burst.

Eventually, Tommy says, "Do you think you can walk home?" "I think so." "Steady does it mate!" We arrive home, Mum asks me what happened and applies a cold compress. After a while, Mum gently dries my hand and suggests I lay down for half an hour. "Aw Mum! Aw, Mum!" "Go on then! Off with you as long as you feel alright." "Thanks Mum." "Bye! Mrs. Jackson." "Bye! Thomas." With today's fireworks I could have blown my hand off, or my head (Which would be the greater loss I wonder.).

Half an hour later, we are back at the bonfire; cheating with the toffee; eating Parkin Pig, and, drinking pop. Eventually, the fire begins to die down. People drift away: some to bed and some to beer: leaving about a dozen of us lads seated around the glowing embers. They glow fiercely, gently spit and splutter, an occasional burning branch cracks and scatters a shower of sparks, some of us have to hurriedly draw back. Into this Devil's Cooking Pyre, we place our spuds. After a short while, we attempt to retrieve them; they are charred black- sometimes the skin is so burnt and black you cannot hack a way into them but, believe it or not, if you do manage it, most of them are still raw inside anyrode.

Have you ever noticed when you sit, or stand around a bonfire, your ars…, err bum is always cold. If you turn to warm your bum your front is always frozen (I know how the brass monkey must have felt.). "Ah, well! Roll on Christmas! Roll on!"

Young Mick is in a spot of bother, someone has snitched (grassed) on him. As he comes in my Mother says, "Have you been smoking Woodbines?" "No." "Yes you have!" "No I have not." "I know you have been smoking." "How?" "Someone told me." "Who?" "Never mind who! You have been smoking, haven't you?" "Yes." "Why have you lied to me? You will have to confess." "I haven't lied." "Of course you have; you've been smoking Woodbines." "No, I haven't!" "That's another lie!" "No, it isn't!" "Just a minute," says Mum, "let's start again." "Right!" "Now Michael! Have you been smoking?" "Yes." "Now we are getting somewhere." "Ask him what sort of cigs he has been smoking," I suggest. "Alright then!" says Mum. "What sort of cigarettes have you been smoking?" "Not Woodbines, Mum, I have been smoking Craven A." "Well, I reckon you have three sins to confess; one for smoking and two for lying."

Mick approaches me and says, "Have you many sins lined up for Saturday's confession?" "Not many," I answer. "Will you confess you did my smoking; I will give you a couple of fags." "But I don't smoke." "Well, you could <u>start</u> smoking or sell 'em." says he.

It's Christmas Eve: Tommy and I are going to Midnight Mass for the first time. We are being allowed to go by ourselves. Tommy is going to call for me about 11.15 pm. Meanwhile Dad, Mum, Mick and I are sat round a cheery coal fire. It throws out a warm comforting glow. We look for smoke gently escaping from the coal. "Just like a steam locomotive," Mick says. His engine is going faster than mine; we argue gently; I let him win seeing it's Christmas.

Mick and I lay on our rug and watch soldiers climb up the fireback. The soldiers are small pieces of soot; they glow red with the heat from the fire and creep upwards and outwards only to be shot- well they disappear. It's the same thing innit anyrode ('Isn't it.'; 'Anyhow.').

Most people make their own rugs. A rug-frame consists of two pieces of three inches by two inches of planed timber with a mortise hole (slot) through towards each end. Two pieces of three inches by two inch timbers slide into these slots. They have a series of holes. The heavier timbers are spaced apart by inserting pegs into the holes as required thus forming an adjustable frame.

'Harding' a sack like material is fastened to one three inch timber and rolled round it. The other end is fastened to the second three by two inch timber, stretched and pegged. If anyone started to 'brod a rug.'. Neighbours would bring suitable material and give it to the 'brodders,'- who, in turn, would then supply them with materials when they were 'brodding'. A 'brodder' was a steel spike with a small knob like handle, usually varnished. Strips of material about four inches long and about one inch wide were used; usually old coats; trousers; skirts, or, any cloth like material.

The brod was pushed down into the harding. To make a hole: the tab was inserted into this hole using the brod and pulled through to about two inches; another hole was made adjacent to the first hole; the other end of the tab was inserted and pulled through. The trick was to get both ends matching but the tabs could be trimmed with scissors. The tabs were very close together. This stopped them from working loose. Some people made random patterns; others with a border. The more ambitious brodders marked out the harding and selected their pattern colours.

During the war, I remember our Family made a 'hooky' stair carpet. We joined the harding long enough to cover the staircase. Any material used was cut into long thin strips and rolled into a ball: stockings; dyed vests- in fact most materials - some unmentionable, I think. Silk-like materials were not used. The harding was stretched on the frame; the strips were held in the hand underneath the harding and were drawn up with a tool similar to a brod but filed or machined to leave a flat area at right angles to the point- like a crochet hook. This allowed the strips to be hooked through from underneath and looped on the face, in and out (Snake like as you might say.). Our stair-carpet had black or navy borders with a dark strip across at intervals. This was in filled with random colours. To get the length of the carpet: we carefully laid a clothes-line across the landing; down the stairs, and, across the hall to the front door.

Any member of the family would have a hook, or a brod, at the rugs. Neighbours would drop in for a cuppa, a chat, and do some of the rug-making. One day I came home from school to find two neighbours working away. They had called; nobody was at home; they let themselves into the house (The key being hung down behind the letterbox on a piece of string. It could even have been left hanging outside.). They had made themselves a cuppa and got cracking. (I nearly forgot, most rugs had backing- usually sacking).

Back to our cosy fire and tab rug then. The radio is quietly broadcasting some dance music. I suppose it would be quite lively but we have the wireless turned low, "So we can hear ourselves think and speak," as Mum would say.

Our presents lay round the tree. It's not artificial (I think it wandered to our house from Farnley Woods looking for a good home,). Usually we receive presents that are useful, as Mum says: a new vest; nearly-new boots or even a new pair (If Dad is in a job.)- only to be worn on Sundays or Holy Days. If I had grown out of any of my things, they would make up some of Michael's presents. Mum would say that they were gifts from baby 'Jesus' and we should treasure them.

We play 'I Spy.' and listen to Dad's yarns. Mum has made some sausage rolls: two each tonight and four each tomorrow. She brings out the pies and home-made Ginger Wine. "We are living like Royalty," says Mum. "I've got a riddle for you," says Dad. "What?" "A riddle," says Dad "Go on then." "Right! I will. Think of a number." "Have we to think of the same number? We could whisper it." "No! No!" says Dad. "Just think of any number." "Up to ten?" says Mick. "No! No! Any number." "Right!" "Think of a number (Pause.). Thought of one?" "Yes," we chorus. I have thought of number four and Mick has whispered to me that his is number eight. "Double it." "Err yes! Hang on!" "Add six." "All

of us to add six?" "Yes." "Divide your total by two." "Right!
O.K. yes!" "Take away the number you first thought of." "Hang
on! Right!" "And your answer is three," says Dad triumphantly.
"That's clever!" says Mum. "How can we all have three if we all
thought of different numbers?" asks Mum. "Magic! Just magic!"
says Dad.

The evening passes pleasantly. Mum says, "I wonder how many
will be going to Midnight Mass who don't go to Church the rest
of the year?" (That's not like Mum.). "What I mean is something
seems to draw them at Christmas." "Probably the beer and the
spirits Love!" (Now that's like Dad.) "Do you know what I think?"
says Mick. "I think, because all the year round, Jesus is a man,
when he changes back to a baby for Christmas and it's the middle
of the night, lots of people come to make sure he is alright." He's
no mug is our Mick.

Tommy and I are walking to Church (About a mile from
home.). I mention about what my mother had said about people
only attending Midnight Mass, and not the rest of the year. As
we enter Church, there is a whiff of incense, candles are flicker-
ing, an occasional cough, the odd sneeze, a youngster cries. I don't
think that it should be out at this time of night: it sounds to be
too young to be at Midnight Mass. The organ is quietly playing
'Away in a Manger.'. Some people are praying. I can smell: incense;
tobacco smoke, and, a faint whiff of beer and spirits.

"Let's go have a look at the crib," whispers Tommy. It looks so
beautiful and peaceful. Baby Jesus seems to look straight at me. I
wink at him. I think he might have winked back. "Let's go sit at
the back of the Church! I've got an idea." As we sit down, Tommy
whispers, "Which side do you want, Epistle or Gospel?" "What
for?" "We will toss for it." Tommy has a coin cupped in his hand.
"Call!" he whispers. "Heads!" "Heads it is. Which do you want?"
" I will have the Gospel side. Now what's this about?" "Ssssh!"
whispers Tommy, "And listen."

"As people enter the Church, we will check the: one point for
one that comes late; two for a staggerer; three points for a drunk-
ard, and, four points for a repenter." "How will we know a repenter?" I ask. "They will be crying." "Awe right!" "Whoever sits on
the Epistle side are my points; Gospellers are yours." "Right!" We
kept track: some come late; others arrive about halfway through

Mass; some just managed to get there before the end of Mass-
coming in as we were going out almost. Tommy won of course.
Thirty points to twenty four and as Tommy said, "It passed an
hour on."

Christmas morn, it's nearly half past eleven when I wake up.
A quick cat lick; a hurried comb through my hair. I rush downstairs: "Can I have a mince pie, Mum?" "I think Michael has eaten
them all." "Awe Mum!" "Only joking," she laughs. "Anyhow,
Merry Christmas! Come here you're not too big to have a kiss or
a cuddle!" "Neither are you Mum!" (She is about four foot nowt.)
"Cheeky!" says Mum.

"Where's Mick?" "He's gone for a walk to Weston Woods with
Father." "I could tell you a tale about Weston Woods." "Not now,
I am too busy." "What's that smell?" "What smell?" "That smell."
"You will have to wait and see." "Well it smells good," says I.
"What does?" asks Mum. "That smell does." "What smell?" "That
sme... Awe Mum! You're kidding me!" "One point to Mum
then?" "Yes! A point to you Mum!"

Now you're not going to believe this: I have been to Midnight
Mass- so I won't tell a lie. For our Christmas dinner we had:
Yorkshire puddings for starters; sprouts boiled; roast potatoes; and
carrots, and for afters, we had Christmas pudding and white sauce.
"What's so special about that?" you may ask. Oh sorry! I nearly
forgot. We had a goose! Yes a goose for our Christmas dinner!
(Cry your eyes out Tiny Tim!). "Not many people in Otley will
have had a goose for dinner today," said Mum.

Father had won the bird in a raffle at the Catholic Club in
Crow Lane, close to the School. Mum and Dad had decided to
keep it secret until Christmas Day.

The holiday passed quite pleasantly. Tommy and I went for
walks in the countryside and woodland. We pulled up snickles and
made one or two bundles of firewood with the pegs and bound
them together with the wire. We sold the bundles for tuppence
each. We managed to get two days sledging in up Giant's. All in
all a very good Christmas.

I come in from school. Father is sitting in his easy chair. He
is crying; his trousers and long johns are crumpled round on the
floor -round his feet, A steaming bowl of water by his side. Mother
is bathing his right leg on the inside about ten inches above his

knee. His shirt hangs discretely down his front. I don't need to ask. "Dad's leg has made up." Every night we would end our Prayers, "Please Jesus make Daddy's leg better."

Mum is bathing the wound with water, as hot as my Father can stand- in the hope that it will start to discharge again. His leg is full of scars from previous operations that our Doctor describes as: "A surgeon's battlefield."

When he was a very young boy, he had an accident with a rusty nail and it penetrated his leg. He could not remember much about how this happened but for him to "get by" as he put it, the wound had to discharge permanently. I have known my father to be off work for up to a year at a time: this created havoc with our finances. God knows how they managed! Mick and I never went hungry; we did not appreciate the hardships, worries and sacrifices, my parents made. "Please, Jesus, make my father's leg better when you have got some time to spare."

"I chased a bug around a tree, I chased a bug around a tree." chants Mick.

"What's that you're singing?" asks Mum. "I chased a bug around a tree," sings Mick obligingly. "You've been told many times about swearing." "But I'm not swearing," protested Mick. "Of course you are." "No, I'm not." "You just sang 'bugger' twice." "No, I haven't." "But you've just said it, so you will have to confess it." "No! I will not!" argues Mick. "Why not?" "Why not? Because I was only repeating what you said." "Well! 'Bugger' is 'Bugger'- no matter how or when you say it." says Mick. "You have said it twice more." "Yes! I know but I was only repeating what you were repeating, Mum! But I wasn't singing 'bugger' before." "Well it sounded very much like what we have been saying." "What have we been saying Mum?" "We have been saying, err, we have been saying what we should not have been saying." "Well! Now you have got me all mixed up Mum!"

"All right clever Dick!" "The name's 'Mick' Mum!" "All right, clever Dick/Mick! What were you singing?" "Do I have to?" asks Mick. "Of course you have to! Come on let's have it!" "O.K. here goes! I chased a bug... Pause Mum! ... Around a tree." Score Mum 0; Mick 1.

Tommy and I knew each other from the age of four. When we were five years old we started School together; we drank our milk together; laughed and cried together. I suppose you could say, we did most things together. St. Joseph's Roman Catholic School was situated in Crow Lane. ("You could be dead in Crow Lane and nobody would know." as Tommy would say.)

The school consisted of three main rooms and two cloak rooms. A narrow yard with girls' and infants' toilets at the back. Diagonally across the front playground from the main doors were the boys' toilets tucked between a high wall and the end wall of the school. In the main playground was the Coke Store. The School had Gasometers (Gas Holders.) and Gasworks on three sides and Crow Lane on the fourth side. There was a permanent smell of gas and sulphur, or whatever, but it was said that St. Joseph's was the healthiest school in Otley! (Pull the other one!)

Tommy and I have just moved into the middle classroom. From being "Cocks-O-the-Midden," we are the lowest of the low. This is when the bullying starts, there's always one. Intimidation: a bit of arm twisting; taking our milk and sweets off us- even the promise of a good twilting. "I am getting a bit pissed off with this carry on!" said Tommy one day. "I've just about had enough of this lark!" "What can we do?" I ask. "I don't know but I will think of something."

Nine o'clock Monday morning, Miss Johnson calls out the Register: "Attwood?" "Here Miss!" "Bolton?" "Present Miss!" and so on. "Robinson? Robinson? Is Robinson here?" "No Miss, but I saw him before school this morning," says Mark. "Where did you see him?" "In Crow Lane Miss." (Where you could be dead and nobody would know.) "Quiet! Err quiet every body! Thomas would you please go and see if he is out there?" "At once Miss!" "Thank you Thomas!" How is it that when a teacher calls Tommy 'Thomas', it doesn't sound too bad. I suppose that you can get used to anything with practice,

Thomas (Now I am saying it!) returns, "I have looked in the toilets and everywhere." "Have you looked in the Girl's toilets?" asks Mark (Giggles all round.). "Yes I have, clever clogs!" resounds Tommy, "He just isn't out there!"

"Thomas!" "Yes Miss!" "Will you please go and see if he has gone back home?" "Yes Miss! At once Miss!" Tommy duly returns to announce that James Robinson is not at home and neither is anyone else.

"Peter!" "Yes Miss!" "Will you go to the Police Station? I will write a note." "Yes Miss!" When I return, Tommy whispers, "I bet he has gone missing because of the bullying." "You could be right," I whisper. Tommy whispers, "I know I'm right, I just know it."

Two policemen arrive, ask us a lot of questions and write a lot of answers down in their notebooks. They have a good look round and leave. I wonder if they ever read what they write.

Playtime at last! We dash out; talk about James; play games; talk about James. He just seems to have disappeared. Miss White comes out and rings the bell. We form up: girls in one line; boys in the other. As we sort ourselves out, Tommy comes from the toilet and whispers, "I know where young "Robbie" is." "Where is he?" Tommy spreads the palms of his hands towards me and raises his eyes towards heaven. "You don't mean he's dead," I gasp. "No you idiot!" Tommy nods his head a couple of times; lifts his eyes gently and whispers, "He's on the top of the Gasometer. I have just seen him peeping over the edge when I was at the toilet."

"Good God Tommy! What are we going to do?" We troop into School. Tommy says, "Say and do nowt." "Nowt!" says I "That's reet! Nowt"

"Please may I leave the Room, Miss?" "What for Thomas?" "To go to the toilet, Miss." "But you have just been! I saw you come out." "I have a chill Miss and I need to go to the toilet often." Well he did say that he was 'pissed off' thinks I. "Very well Thomas! Don't be long." I won't Miss! Thank you Miss!" (Well done Tommy!)

About ten minutes later, Miss Johnson says, "Where's Thomas?" "I don't know Miss!" "Haven't seen him Miss!" "He went to the toilet Miss!" "I know he did! Peter go see if he is alright!" "Very good Miss! At once Miss!"

I know where I should look but Tommy is terrified of heights. He jokes that he wished he lived in a bungalow because he can get dizzy just going up the dancers and, if he walks near the edge of the foot path, he has to step down into the gutter- so he says but I think that he is nedding me.

I look up and see Tommy clinging to the vertical iron ladder about ten feet from the top of the Gasometer. A Gasometer rises and falls according to the pressures inside. I guess at the moment it is about forty foot high. I dare not shout, or call, or anything but I can pray. "Oh, Lord! Look after Tommy and James! He's moving! He's moving!" breaths I. Very slowly Tommy is inching his way upwards. He's stopped again, a short pause and he climbs a little quicker this time as though it could be one final effort. I stand there hands on hips; gazing towards Heaven- mouth wide open. I cannot think; I dare not think, and, I cannot breath properly now I have got neck ache. One last effort and he disappears over the top.

I run back into class. Miss Johnson says, "Where's Thomas?" "Err… where's Thomas?" "Yes! Where's Thomas?" "He's err…on; he's err…" "Well!" "He's on top of the Gasometer Miss!" "That's enough of that! Where is he?" "Err… where is he? He is with James Robinson Miss!" "Oh good! Where is James?" "Err James?" "Yes James! Are you going deaf Peter?" "No Miss!" "Well! Where is James?" "On top of the Gasometer Miss!" "Good gracious! What's he doing up there?" she gasps. "He's with Tommy Miss!" "Quick Peter! Come with me! The rest of you stay here in class and read your history books."

Miss Johnson and I dash into the yard- and look up. Tommy appears and then disappears. "Are you alright Thomas?" calls Miss Johnson. "Not too bad Miss!" responds Tommy. "And James, is he alright?" "He is fine Miss!" says this voice from above. "But we can't get down." "Don't worry, Thomas, Peter is going to the Fire Station." (no phones in those days). "Oh good, Miss. Thank you Miss." "Off you go, Peter." "Yes Miss, I will be quick." "I know you will."

The Fire Engine arrives. The firemen raise a very long extension ladder, and soon James and Tommy are on terra firma. They are both shaking. "What on earth were you thinking of James?" "Don't know Miss." "Are you alright to stay at School?" "There's nobody at home Miss." "Are you alright Thomas?" "I am now, Miss. I am now." "Well done, Thomas. Well done." "Thank you, Miss."

"Was it because of bullying, Tommy?" "Yes," says Tommy, "Well, James hasn't blabbed has he?" "No," says Tommy, "I told him to keep stum.(quiet) I promised him that the bullying will stop." "Were you scared up there?" I asked. "Too true mate, too true. I'll tell you what" "What? Saint Peter and Paul got more that their fair share of prayers today." "Well, it's all over now mate." "That's all over, but we have to sort this bullying out." "There's only one real bully and that's George Black, agreed?" "Agreed."" Well when I was up there near to heaven, I had time to think. I've got an idea." "I bet it's a good one." "It is" says Tommy, "It is."

"Black, come out here," commands an annoyed Miss Johnson. "There's a page missing from your sum book, explain." "Can't explain Miss, there can't be." "Well there is a page missing, stay in half an hour after school." "Yes Miss, but Miss half an hour?" "I could make it an hour, "Do you understand?" "Yes Miss."

"What's this, Black?" "What's what Miss?" This black ink blotch on your writing book." ("Black on Black," whispers Tommy.) "What black blotch Miss?" "This black blotch," says Miss Johnson as she holds the book aloft for all to see. "Explain?" "Can't Miss "Half an hour after school." "Yes Miss, thank you Miss."

"Black!" "Yes Miss!" "Why have you turned all the corners of your exercise book?" "I don't know Miss!" "You don't know why you have turned the corners down?" "No Miss!" "No what?" "I did not know that they were turned down." "Well! Stay behind after school and unturn them!" "Err…" "Err… what?" "Nothing Miss!" "He doesn't seem to be a happy camper," whispers Tommy.

A week passes; we have got to Wednesday. "George Black!" "George Black!" says Miss Johnson almost in a whisper. This is a Miss Johnson I have never seen before. She is always sweet and kind but today she has got her dander (temper) up. There's a sort of gasping and gulping from Master George Black, esq., "Are you listening to me, Black?" Gulp! Cough! Gasp! "Err! Yes Miss!" "Come here and read what is written in your essay book!" "In my essay book, Miss?" "Yes, in your essay book Black!" "He's in the 'black books' is Master Black," chortles Tommy- without making a sound. "Err yes Miss!" another gulp, cough and gasp- not necessarily in that order. George half- staggers to Miss Johnson. "Now Black! Read this!" "What this Miss?" "Yes this? George glances down at the book; shuts it and gives another gulp etc. "Please Miss! Do I have to read this Miss?" "Yes this!" "She's punishing him," whispers Tommy. "Please Miss! Can I give this a miss! Miss?" pleads Inky. "If you do not read what is written in the book, out loud, I will send it to your parents and inform Father Dean."

George's face is a picture of torment. He gasps for air; wipes his nose with his shirt sleeve; wipes his brow with the same sleeve and puts his right index finger in his ear. "Remove that finger at once and read this out loud!" "Read this, Miss?" "Yes this!" There's no escape for Master Black. He gives a gulp, gasp, gulp in that order and in a quavering voice I hardly recognise, he starts to read. "When I, Master George Black, stop bullying smaller, younger people, I am sure I will have a more pleasant easier journey along the road of life." George slams the book shut, and throws it on to Miss Johnson's desk, as though it is red hot.

"Please Miss! May I leave the Room?" "Well! You can't take it with you!" giggles Tommy. "Behave yourself Thomas!" says Miss Johnson as G. B dashes out. "Sorry Miss!" "And so you should be!" retorts Miss Johnson, "So you should be!" I think her lips are quivering and she seems to be holding back like we do, to avoid a fit of giggles.

Tommy's idea had been so simple. We had recruited some lads from our class, and, a couple from Blackie's who we could trust. He didn't have many friends and those he had were afraid of him. The operation commenced. We knew where our bully boy was at all times. One of us would be on guard at the classroom door and Tommy would do the business. The bullying ceased and any would-be bullies got the message.

After Prayers the following morning, Miss Johnson makes an announcement. "George Black is not feeling too well and will be off school for about a week." Her lips are quivering again. Tommy says to me, "Have you heard that saying: 'Brain beats brawn every time.'?" "No, I haven't," I reply, "but I tend to agree."

"I have bought this electric fire," announces Mum, "But it needs this flex joining to it then we could plug it into the light fitting on the landing (One socket upstairs in our house and one downstairs.). "We could use it in the bedrooms." "I will do it for you, Mum," says I. "O.K." says Mum, "but be very careful." "I will Mum!" "O.K young Mick! Switch on!"

"Right!" Flash! Bang! "Quick! Turn it off!" "Reet! What happened?" asks Mick. "Don't know!" says I. "Better leave it for now." "I think you had better leave it altogether for ever," agrees Mick.

Tea time: "Switch on the light, Michael," "O.K. Mum!" "What's the matter?" "It's not working Mum!" "Try the other lights." "O.K. Mum! (A pause.) Nowt's working Mum!" "I will have to report it, I will go to phone the Electric Company." "Oh Mother!" "Yes." "I err I err… I did have a go at the electric fire; there was a flash and a bang." "But no Whallop!" says brother Michael. "That's enough of that!" chides Mum. "I bet that's what has caused it. Hide the fire in the coal hole." "Right Mum!" Mum nips out to the telephone-box to call the Electric Company.

About three hours later, the Electric man arrives: a big, fat, red-faced man- full of rush and bluster. "Wer… err… What's up Missus?" "I don't know but nothing's working." The man puffs and pants and pants and puffs as he wriggles under the keeping-slab in the pantry. Have you ever noticed how Gas and Electric Meters are always fitted in the most awkward places? "You have blown the Company's fuses. Have you been using an electric fire or something?" I close my eyes and cross my fingers: "Me! An electric fire! How could I afford an electric fire?" "Well it beats me!" says the fat red-faced man. Mother has beaten him also- thinks I. Hey Presto! All the lights are on. "Thank you very much!" says Mum. The man retreats muttering that it beats him. I hope all this beating doesn't hurt him.

Will Mum have to confess to a lie. The man asked her is she had an electric-fire and she said: "How could we afford one?" I never worked-out whether she was a sinner or not. I took the fire to my Uncle. He had a look at the fire and said, "It was not a good idea to join all the bare wires together." Here endeth my electrical career- and even today, I confine myself to a bulb and a fuse.

Tiger's back, I never thought that I would ever see him again in this life. I spot him in Church. As we shuffle out, from behind, he taps my right ankle sideways with his right instep hoping that my right toe would hook round my left heel and therefore tripping me up. (I hope you have worked that out.). He failed: he will have to get up very early in a morning to catch me. We meet up on the footpath opposite the Church. Tommy and I greet Tiger: "Hello! Hiya! Err, are you back for good then?" "Ugh!" "For bad then!" inquires Tommy. "He must have been abroad" says Tommy, "and only knows abroad language." Tiger nods his head. "You come us?" says I. Another nod. "We go Milk Bar." Nod. We walk up Bridge Street and into the Milk Bar. in Manor Square. "What you drink?" Tiger points to a lemon milk shake. "You have one."

Tiger grunts, or maybe it could be a growl.

We spend about half an hour in the Milk Bar, not getting very far on the communication front. As we walk across Manor Square, I realise we have a common language, the Tiger suddenly understands English, and more to the point, he understands Yorkshire English. Tiger's back! He told us that his family had left London and returned home because there was going to be a war. "A War! Who with and where?" "I haven't a clue!" says Tiger. "I can't think there will be any War," says Tommy. "Me neither!" says I.

Mr. Granger was an old retired man. He had been a bound Apprentice Joiner they must have tied him to a tree or something. He left School and served a seven-year's apprenticeship. To make a bob or two, he chopped and sold firewood. He was a small man and very bow legged; always ready with a yarn to tell; he always wore a big smile. All his customers would be offered a drink by Mrs. Granger: hot soup in winter and cold drinks in summer.

He would sit on an upturned log with a cushion nailed to it for comfort. I think that it was all this sitting that had made him bow-legged. He would be surrounded by all types of cut joinery timber and split logs. When the weather was bad, he worked in the kitchen. He chopped the wood and bound it into bundles with thin wire. I think he got the off cuts from where he used to work. He had been with the same firm from leaving school to retirement (Yes, it did happen!). You could buy a bundle of firewood for a penny or tuppence depending on its size.

"I've got an idea!" says Tommy one day as we collected two bundles each. "What idea?" I ask. "Well! The firewood is chopped about one-inch square or more. Right?" "Right!" "And the log and branch pieces can be quite bent, a lot more bent than the Joiner's timber. Agreed?" "Agreed!" I respond. "Why are they chopped so thick?" I ask. "Because the lazy old bug err... so and so is too idle to chop them thinner." "Aw right!"

"Here's what I propose." says Tommy. "We buy half a dozen lengths of branch firewood." "Why branch firewood?" "Because branch firewood is all bent, right? I thought that I had just explained it to you right?" "Right!" "There will be a lot of air space in the bundles, they will look bigger. Are you with me?" "With you!" I reply. "So what I propose is that we saw the branches into shorter lengths to get more bundle lengths out of them and chop the wood thinner. Get some wire to bundle it and deliver it to our customers." "When we get some," says I. "We will!" says Tommy. "We will!" "And you know," says Tommy, "it will light more fires more easily because it is thinner and has more pieces per bundle." "That's brilliant Tommy!" "I know it is," he replies.

So we go into business, all bundles are two pence each, delivered each week. We buy lots of timber from Mr. Granger. He is happy; we are happy; our customers are happy and as Tommy says, "Smart thinking is what makes the world go round."

It was about this time that I became interested in aeroplanes. I made them from wood, bought or scrounged from Mr. Granger. I borrowed my father's cobbling knife and rasp. (I could sole and heel my boots when I was ten years old.) With these tools I could turn out a fair model, usually bi-planes, (For the dedicated ignoramuses: a 'bi-plane' has two wings. Yes two!) Using matches for struts; cotton for wires, and, buttons, when I could scrounge them, for wheels. A propeller was made from a cigarette-card cut to shape and held with a pin; tapped into the nose. If I could manage some paint, especially red, they looked fair to midlin.

I sold these models for tuppence and threepence each. When I became proficient, I made a model Gyro-copter (Auto gyro.). The real one we called it 'The Motorbike Engine Auto-gyro.', because it made a noise just like a motor bike. It had a small propeller on the nose and a huge rotor above the pilot. As the plane moved along the runway or grass, the rotor was powered by the engine to about 400 rpm. When the rotor lifted the coptor, it was disengaged and spun freely. The Autogyro could almost hover. I remember the first copter we saw flying from Yeadon Aero Club (Now Leeds/Bradford Airport.) was painted vivid red with a broad silver band along the fuselage. They had no wings- just short control stabilisers. I thought they were wonderful and that the pilots were very brave. They were used during the war as guinea pigs to perfect Radar (Radar Detection and Ranging- incoming enemy aircraft. Not everybody knows that!).

Otley Swimming Baths were open air. The exit was partially obscured from the main pool area. A turnstile rotating clockwise only, allowed bathers out but not in but if you were thin- you were in. Horizontal crossbars prevented people from entering the Baths but we could squeeze between them, as one of us rotated the turnstile. We all seemed to be thin in those days. I only knew one fat lad and people said there was something wrong with him.

"I'm pissed off!" said Tommy. "What are you moaning about now?" "I will tell you what I am moaning about." "What about, what about?" "I'll tell you what about. Oh chuck it Plug! Just chuck it and listen!" "Chuck what? Where? Sorry only kidding! I'm listening." "Have I got to listen also?" asks Mick. "You can if you want to," says Tommy. "Want to?" says Mick. "Hooray! At last I can get-on." "On what?" "Oh, shut up Mick! You're worse than Plug!" moans Tommy. "That makes me better than you young Mick!" "Can I get on? Err get started?" asks a steadily losing temper Tommy. "The stage is yours!" says I. "And all the world's a stage!" echoes young Mick. "I'm going home!" "Don't do that!" says I. "No, don't!" echoes Mick, "We're all ears!" "And theres," says I.

"I am pissed-off because I have to confess every Saturday to stealing into the Swimming Baths." "So what! We all do it!" "I know! But Father Dean says that if I persist in breaking in, he cannot forgive my sin because he says I can't be sorry for them, and for once, I don't know what to do!" "Hang on!" says young Mick. "I've got an idea." "Has it given you a headache then?" queries Tommy. "No! But my feet are throbbing." "Oh! Your brains are in your feet then? That's what Father Dean says when he watches us in the school-yard playing football." Anyhow young Mick! What's this great idea?" "Well! If you save all your stealing in sins till the end of the Swimming Season, you can then confess to them all at one go, and you can say that you are very, very, very sorry or as many sorries as it takes to make Father Dean happy." "That's a brilliant idea young Mick! But what will I say on Saturday at Confession if Father Dean asks me if I have been swimming with a clear sin free mind." "Have a swim in the river and tell him 'Yes'." "That's a brilliant idea!" "Yes, I know it is!" says Mick. "Here have a napple." "Thanks Tommy!"

It's a lovely afternoon. It is playtime. I have stayed in the classroom to finish painting a picture. A tennis-ball comes whizzing in the window. I pick it up and forcefully throw it back out. My timing is perfect: Miss White is passing and is looking into the room to call people out to form up and walk back in again. (I always thought this a bit daft.) Wham! The ball hits Miss White just above the right eye; her head goes back accompanied by a cry of shock and pain.

Oh my goodness! <u>What</u> can I do? I panic and run out of the classroom through the middle room into the girls' porch and out of the back entrance into the girls' toilets; slam the door and sit; wondering, and, quaking- knowing I am being hunted by the now fearsome Miss White.

Footsteps sound. Oh! Hail Mary! A steady purposeful tread of feet (Someone has snitched.); the footsteps stop outside the toilet door and a gentle voice calls: "Peter!" I am in deep ca-ca- but at least I am sat in the right place. Another gentle: "Peter!" "Err... yes! Err... yes Miss!" She never calls me 'Peter': it is either 'Jackson', or 'Peter Jackson' or 'Nosey Parker' "Can you open the door?" ""Err... yes Miss!" I stand; close my eyes; my legs feel weak; my hands are clammy, ah well here goes: "Are you alright?" "Yes Miss! Sorry Miss!" "It <u>was</u> a silly thing to do but it <u>was</u> an accident." "Yes Miss! Thank you Miss!" I complete my 'Hail Mary' as I walk to line-up to go back into school. She isn't the ogre I thought she could be. The next encounter in the boys' toilets would turn out a little bit different.

"I've heard that they are going to have a baby at Mark's house," says Mick. "Mark told me they have been saving up for a long time. They have to save currants you know," says Mick. "Are you sure?" "Of course I'm sure." "How sure?" I ask. "Sure, sure," responds Mick. "Sure?" says I. "Sure," says Mick. I thought it had something to do with love," says I. "Well, you could be right because last Christmas, I heard Mum say that she couldn't get any currants for love or money." "Are you sure about the currants?" "Of course I'm sure," "How sure?" says I. "Oh! Don't start that again! I am sure because it was on the wireless that all goods would be paid for in currants." "Now I will make you unsure," says I. "Why?" queries Mick. "Well I heard that as well." "Well?" "It said that goods would be paid for in English currency." "Ah! Is that what it said?" asks Mick. "Yes, that is what it said, idiot!"

Summer holidays: a whole four weeks off school. We always seemed to have glorious summers with beautiful sunny days; with rain and thunderstorms at night. Summer games are in progress: Indians and Cowboys; Bows and Arrows. Today, I became a member of the 'Black Arrows.'. To become a member of the

'Black Arrows.'; one had to make a throwing arrow. The shaft was a straight, small branch off a tree- about two, and a half feet long, pointed at one end, and card flights at the other. A groove or notch was cut round the shaft adjacent to the flights. The string was a length of thin string (We called it 'Sugar Band.' because it was wrapped vertically round blue sugar bags to keep them closed.). A length of Sugar Band with a knot at one end. This was wrapped once round the groove and over the knot and held taut from the pointed end.

The missile was launched with an over arm throw. To qualify, one had to throw it the full width of Jennings Field, which is to the east of the Crossways, a distance about one hundred yards- well a heck of a long way anyrode! Members of any gang would compete. They and their supporters would be immune from attack or whatever at these events, which usually resulted in fall-outs, etc. and punch-ups, anyrode.

Pea-shooters were very popular. These were a tin tube about a foot long and about three eighths diameter. They had a circular tin mouthpiece; we bent this over to accommodate the lips comfortably. The ammunition was pigeon peas. They were about a quarter of an inch in diameter and very hard. One could fire a single shot, or rapid fire with a mouthful of peas, but this was uneconomical and rarely practised.

If we were broke, which we were more often than not, hollow stems of 'Black Man's Porridge' (A wayside weed called 'Cow Parsley'.) and Elderberries were used. The stems were rarely straight and, of course, they were very inaccurate but a few ripe berries could cause a bit of a mess.

Conkers was played when they fell or could be knocked off the Horse Chestnut trees. If a conker floated in water, it was a good un; if it had a fault, or decay etc- it would sink. Or was it the other way round? I must confess I cannot remember. Some cheats would bake their conkers in the oven. (I did mine for about ten minutes.)

The conkers were drilled or pierced. Fine string was knotted at one end (I wonder if the saying: 'Get knotted.' stemmed from this.) and the conker was held in one hand. The opponent could steady the hung conker that might be swinging in a lazy wind by a devious movement of the hand. Victory was claimed when the opponent's conker was broken and none remained on the string.

For each success, the winning conker was awarded one year old (Eg Ten victories ten years old. Some cheats claimed a conker to be a ten, fifty, or a hundred years. (I usually started mine at fifty.) Nobody disputed these claims because a winning conker could claim the loser's years and add it to his own score. (I hope you got that.)

"Mornin Tommy!" "Mornin Plug!" Tommy has called for me to go to school with him. "It's a nice morning." "Fair to midlin," I reply. "I've got a riddle for you," says Tommy. "Not a jimmy riddle." "No listen! This is a real good un and you won't solve it." "You want to bet?" "Yes! As much as you like," offers Tommy, "As much as you like! Ooh big head!" says I, "Right then! What's this super riddle?"

"Here we go!" says Tommy. "Go where?" I ask. "Do you want to hear it or not?" "Not not!" I reply. "Right! We'll start again," says Tommy. "Right! Start then!" says I. "Three men go to a newly opened Restaurant for a meal. Right!" "Right!" says I. They each pay with a ten shilling note." "Go on!" "The manager says to the waiter: 'As a sign of goodwill, give them five shillings back.'. Are you with me?" "With you!" I reply. "The waiter thinks: I will give them one shilling each and I will pocket the other two shillings. Do you follow?" "Follow!" says I. "Right then!" says Tommy, "They each pay ten shillings and get a shilling back. Right? So they have each paid nine shillings." "Correct!" I say. "So three times nine shillings is?" "Err twenty four err... six, twenty seven shillings." "And two shillings the waiter pocketed," "Twenty nine shillings," I reply. "Well where has the other shilling gone?" "I don't know! Where has it gone?" "Magic!" says Tommy, "Pure magic!"

"Where have you been, young Mick?" "I've been playing with Mark. He says his Mum has gone to St. James's Hospital." "So what?" "Well! Mark says that she has saved enough for a baby and St. James looks-after all babies and sells them when they are ready," says Mick, "and St. James lives abroad and teaches them abroad language. When you get them home, you can't understand a word they say, and they don't have a clue as to what we are on about, so we have to teach them British words." I think Mick could be right for once.

Today some of us are sitting for a Scholarship to decide our future education: Grammar School or not. "He should do well," says Miss White. "Peter…" (She never calls me 'Peter' only in the toilets.) " Peter is usually towards the top of the class generally, and in the mock Exams, he does very well. Mum did not seem too enthusiastic. She didn't talk about the Scholarship; she didn't wave her arms about like when it was something good or exciting- such as Dad getting a job after being on the dole and returning to work, or, when his gammy leg started to discharge again, and he could hold down a job.

"Knock! Knock…! Knock knock!" "Thomas is at the door," says Mum. (That's another Knocking Code broken. We will have to get a doorbell.) "Right Mother! I will be off then." No 'Good Luck!' or 'I hope you do well!' Just a 'Take care!' "Mornin!" "Mornin Tommy!" I reply. "All ready to do battle then?" "Yes!" says Tommy. As we walk to Prince Henry's Grammar School, Tommy says, "If we do pass, it will cost a heck of a lot of money," "How?" "Well! My Mum was talking to your Mum and she said that there would be books, uniforms, and loads of other things, and we would not be leaving school at fourteen." "That's it! That's it!" I cry. "That's what?" asks Tommy. "That's why my mother has been very quiet about this Scholarship: they can't afford it!" "Well they can't can they?" "No! They can't! That's it! I am not going to pass the exam!" "Don't be a clot! You know you can pass!" says Tommy. "I don't have a problem because I <u>know</u> I won't pass!"

We pass Prince Henry's every time we walk into town and to us, it is just a building set amidst playing-fields and sports- fields. We walk through the huge entrance gate- just like going to prison. As we progress up the wide drive, the building seems to grow bigger than ever. My heart sinks, I have a sickly feeling in my stomach, if Tommy is feeling the same as I, he is certainly not showing any emotion. We walk to the entrance of the school in silence. The building has grown taller and taller and I seem to be shrinking smaller, and, smaller.

Tommy and I are directed to the Exam Room. It's huge: the desks seem to be spaced yards apart; the teacher in charge seems twice as large as our teachers. (The next letter is 'G'.) Each candidate is allocated a desk.

"Any candidate who wishes to go to the toilet may do so now."

"When us toileters return and everybody is settled, this big chap directs and advises us how to go about answering the exam papers. "The bell will ring for you to begin and when the time is up.""

. I glance to Tommy. He gives a quick thumbs-up and a voice drones: "One minute to the bell and then you may start the first exam paper." Dingggg! I nearly jump out of my seat; give a sub-dued cough and attempt to settle-down. I think to myself that I should try to pass the exam even if I don't go to the Grammar School. Right then! Here goes!

I pick the paper up; glance down; glance down again; look from top to bottom; from bottom to top; turn it over and repeat the process. My eyes are unable to focus. I gulp for air. I'm get-ting a stomachache; my hands are clammy, and now I am starting with a headache. Apart from this lot, I don't feel so bad. I know I am kidding myself or anybody. I haven't a hope in Hellifield of passing this lot.

I turn to page two, three and four. I might as well be looking at an 'abroad language' as Mick would say, or as Mum says when confused, "It's Greek to me." A quick glance at Tommy. He is sat with glazed eyes; he spreads his hands, palms upwards across his chest; leans his head towards his left shoulder; raises his eyes and shoulders then he draws his index finger across his throat. "Candidates must not communicate in anyway," drones this mo-notonous voice.

I cannot believe it! Tommy said he would have no problem because he knew he would fail. I have just joined Tommy's Club. "How have you gone on then?" asks Mum, as I walk through the front gate "Oh! I have failed." "Are you sure?" "Yes, Mum! I have definitely failed." "Err... good! Err... good heavens! I thought you would pass. How do you know you have failed?" "I know I failed because I wrote nowt down." "Ah well!" says Mum, "Here's a tanner for trying your best." "Thanks Mum!" "How did Thomas (Cringe.) go on?" "He will probably get a tanner as well." A good many tanners changed hands after the exams from grateful par-ents to grateful ex-examinees- one kid even got a bob. It was a case of good rewards for abject failure. It puts me in mind of big business today: profits down the pan; job losses; top-people sacked and walking-out with a sack of gold, and, walking straight into another bullion sharing set up. So I did not become a Banker or a

Solicitor. I went into a job I grew to love and still do- but where every body earns every penny. I have no regrets.

"I can't understand it!" says Miss White to my Mother. "I was sure Peter..." (I am doing well, two 'Peters' in a week.), "I was sure Peter... (Three 'Peters'!) "... would pass! Nobody from St. Joseph's has passed this year!" (Tommy's Club is well and truly full- and rich!)

I could understand why we had failed after the exam experience. We have three classrooms and a small annex for the infants. Miss Stead taught infant and lower classes, Miss Johnson took the middle classes and Miss White taught the top forms. Our teachers would be teaching three different age groups in one room.

Miss Stead taught us to speak correctly and to communicate in good English. I hope that this little book bears that out. "That... That is... Is that... That is not... Is not... Is not that so? That... That is... Is not... That... That is not. Is not that so?" We recited our times tables every day: 'Seven eights are fifty six, etc., etc.' We were taught to use figures and numbers etc. 'Nine times nineteen.' We would multiply twenty by nine equals one hundred and eighty and subtract nine, equals one hundred and seventy one. Even today, if I had to answer: 'What's eight times fourteen?'- for example, I could comply without thinking about it. It's err... err... you work it out.

Miss Johnson was younger than the other two teachers and had had a more up to-date education. She taught us: English; full stops; capital letters; nouns; verbs, and, punctuation etc. A great help in writing this book. Miss White taught the top age groups and this is where it all went wrong: we were supposed to be taught decimals but were never shown how to do them. The same with long-division. We seemed to spend a lot of time on stocks and shares and percentages (All right if you're going to work in the City!) I had been working for quite a while before I realized that there wasn't a 'Left-angled Triangle.' to complement a 'Right-angled Triangle.'!

.Miss White kept the answer books in her desk. We had a rota to look up the answers from these books. We were clever enough not to get all correct answers. We took our turn to get some wrong. What a shambles! I am sure Miss White favoured the girls. Three of us were neck and neck in the annual exam- I was one mark in the lead. For the final part, we had to stand in front of the class and speak for five minutes on any subject. One of the girls went out, scored five marks and was awarded five extra marks for being the first to volunteer! I went second, gained five marks. The second girl got five marks and was awarded an extra five for choosing an interesting subject! (Something smells here methinks.) So from being top of the class, I finished in the third place. Disaster! I had been promised a Season Ticket for the Swimming Baths if I came top. I think this bribe to come out tops was that my Mum could have a little boast about her very clever offspring.

I was bitterly disappointed. It would have been smashing to be able to go swimming whenever I wanted. I could have cut down on stealing into the Baths saving time and trouble for Father Dean and myself in Confession.

Mum accepted my School Report in a sealed envelope. (Why do some people say 'Onvelope?' I always thought that to 'enve-lope' was to cover or contain something or anything- whereas an 'Onvelope' would only cover the top of whatever. Ah well!) "You have come third! I thought you said you were top of the Class?" "I was." "You can't be!" says Mum. "Well I am telling you I came top!" I protested. "How can you be top when your Report says third?"

I proceeded to explain what had happened. One of the girls corroborated (Gosh that's a big word!) my story and I got my Season Ticket. Cry your heart out Father Dean! When I look back there were many subtle favours given to the girls

I heard a bloke on the wireless talking about someone called 'Hitler' (That sounds foreign.), and, a place called 'Munich' (Now that must be foreign.). He said we would have peace in our time. I think it might have been a play being broadcast.

> Mary had a little lamb,
> It was a little glutton,
> She used to feed it on ice cream,
> And now it's frozen mutton.

Another Christmas is approaching. I think it will be a bleak one. Dad is off work: his leg has 'made up' (Stopped discharging.). Tommy says to my Mother that he will see if Michael and I can go to his house for Christmas dinner but Mum will have none of this. She keeps reminding us that we are "Poor not poverty." I think the thing I will miss most is the Christmas joint. Dad was going to buy a hen from Farmer Longfield and I have never eaten hen before. "Neither have I!" commiserates Tommy, "But I think that we might manage one at home."

Two days before Christmas I find a parcel at the back door. "Look what I have found!" "What have you found?" asks Mum. "Don't know!" "Well, how do you know if you have found some-thing, if you don't know what you may not have found?" "Awe shut up Mick!" "Yes be quiet Michael!" echoes Mum. The box is crudely wrapped in Christmas paper. As Mum lifts the lid, I rec-ognize it as a Gallon's provision store delivery box.

"Let's open it," says Mick "and see what it is you haven't found." "Right!" says Mum, "Here goes!" "Oh! Oh! Oh!" says Mum. "Oh what?" asks Mick. "It's a...Oh! Oh!" "What's a 'Oh! Oh!' Mum?" "It's a... Oh! Oh! Duck." cries Mum. "What's a 'Oh! Oh! Duck' then?" "It's not a 'Oh! Oh! Duck!'" says Mum, "but you said it was a 'Oh! Oh! Duck!'" "No! It's a... du...du... duck," stam-mers Mum. "What's a du... du... duck, Mum?" asks Mick. "It sounds like a speaking duck from China." "I think you mean a Pekin Duck," says I. "That's right Plug!" agrees Mick, "A speaking Duck." "No listen!" says Mum, she seems to have got her breath back: "It's not a 'Oh! Oh!' or a 'du... du...duck', and it can't speak, because it's a dead duck." "Well I am glad we have settled that our Mum," says Mick

Mum holds it up by its neck and says, "I wonder who has sent it?" "Maybe it was Scrooge," offers Mick ."I don't think so, and anyway he sent geese didn't he Peter?" "I am not sure Mother." "Well he managed to send one to Tiny Tim our Mum." says young Mick.

It remained a mystery over Christmas; Mother told us not to tell anyone because we were poor not poverty. Tommy called Boxing Day to play-out. As we played, Tommy said, "Did you enjoy your du...?" "What did you say?" I asked. "I said, did you enjoy your dinner without a hen or a joint?" "Err yes! We did." I said. I never asked Tommy; he never said anything but I had a feeling that Farmer Longfield was one duck short. How Tommy managed to bring himself to kill the bird, I will never know. Greater love hath no man than to lay down the life of a duck for his friends.

Christmas has come and gone. My father is going back to work. When he is off work it seems to drain him and affect the whole household.

I come in from school. It is about four thirty. Dad is back home (Oh lor! Let's hope his leg is alright.) "What's up Dad?" "I have had the Doctor to see me. I have to have an operation." "Oh heck Dad!" I gasp. "It's alright son, I could be cured at long last." "How?" "Well, as I walked to work, I felt something pricking just above my knee. I worked until dinner-time and decided to come home. As you know, Dr. Paine will come to see me any time at short notice." "Yes Dad! Dr. Paine has always said it could be a deceased bone." "I think you mean a 'diseased bone'." "Probably Dad." "He thinks a piece of the bone has been loosened, and for many years, has been working its way down my leg." The Doctor was proved right.

My Father was in Hospital for three days and he came home cured. It was the best Christmas present our family ever had. "Thank you Lord for curing Dad's deceased err diseased leg."

I am 11years old and working for a living. I am old enough to work after School and Saturday mornings. I proudly display my official badge on my right arm.

One day Mum came home from shopping and says, "How would you like a job?" "A job? What job?" "Working as an errand boy at Moss's Store on Weston Lane." "Well he can't be an errand girl, can he?" "Shut up Mick!" says I. "Yes shut up!" says Mum. "Sorry and very sorry!" says Mick, "That's a 'very sorry' to you Mum, and a 'sorry' to you Plug." "Thank you Michael!" "Thank you Mick!" "You're both very welcome." "What will I have to do?" I ask. "Well you will have a bicycle," "Ooh great!" says I. "You will deliver orders in boxes." "But how can I carry boxes and ride a bike, Mum?" "It's a carrier bike: you can put boxes in the carrier on the front." "Awe that's alright then!" "When you have no orders to deliver, you will make up orders from a list and put them into boxes. Then if you still have nothing to do, you will sweep out the Store and make drinks for the Staff." "That's smashing Mum! When do I start?" "You can start next Monday teatime, but you must let Miss Pepper know." "I will go and see her straight away." "Haven't you forgotten something?" "Sorry

Mum! I forgot to put some coal on the fire." "Not that!" "I forgot to wash up and make my bed." "Is there anything else you have forgotten to do?" " Oh aye! I will go upstairs and have a good wash, not a cat-lick."

"What I am trying to ask you is have you forgotten something to do with the job?" "Awe right! Err what?" "How much you are going to be paid?" "Awe right! How much then?" "You will be paid a shilling a week." "Eck! How much?" "A shilling a week." "A shilling! That's a fortune," gasps I. "And you will get tips." "That's no good, I don't smoke." I know young Mick has some-times smoked. "Tips err filter tips, that is." "No, not cigs," says Mum. "These tips are what people give you as a thank you for delivering their orders."

"How much do you want, Mum?" "I could keep the shilling, and you could keep all the tips, because you get more in tips than wages." "No, we can't have that," says I" "How about if I have the bob (shilling) each week and you keep <u>all</u> the tips?" "Smashing!" says Mum. "That's alright then," says I.

People are taking about a war with this bloke called Hitler and some Nazis. Someone on the wireless was talking about the 'Fifth Column'. Mum says the Fifth Columnists are spies in our midst. "What Mincepies?" asks Mick, sometimes I wonder about that boy.   .

All members of The Crescenters (Cheers.) are called to a Special Meeting at two-o-clock, Saturday afternoon in the Newall Park. Tommy calls for me: "What's it about, Plug?" "I haven't a clue!" "It must be something important." "Yes, it must be," says I.

Two-o-clock, Bill arrives, bang on time. "Everybody here?" he calls. "Everybody but steady Freddy." "Right then! We will give him a couple of minutes. I think they will have to postpone his funeral because he will turn up late. Ha! Here he is. Ready steady Freddy?" "Yes Boss!" "Now listen everybody, and listen good! It is my sad duty to inform you that as from two weeks today, I will no longer be your leader." " Hooray! Cheers!" "Well thank you very much!" "Sorry Bill!" "Only joking Bill! Sorry!" "I should co-co (Think so.). Well the sad fact is, our Family are moving to Sheffield." "Why?" "Because my Dad has got a better job and my Mother used to live there, dost thou see?" "We dost see."

"We must decide on a new leader." "How about Allen?" says

a lone voice. "I agree with that," says Bill, "but I have had talks with him, and he does not want to carry this heavy burden. He is quite happy to be Second leader, still First class of course, so any ideas anybody?" "What do you think Bill?" asks Mark. "What do I think? I will tell you what I think." "Go on then! Tell us!" "Right! I will! I propose that Tommy be the new leader." "What?" shouts a very whatish voice. "How do you mean 'what'?" asks Bill. "Well! I object!" "And so do I!" "O.K. We have two objections, let's hear them." "Well, I object because I think he is too young." "Too young for what?" "Well, he is too young for... err..., for... err... owt!" "And what owt is that then, that he is too young for then?" "Well! Too young for <u>any</u> old owt!" "Right and what's the other objection?" "He is a Roman Catholic!" "So, he is; so, he is," agrees Bill.

"Now everybody listen, and listen good! If any of you were in deep ca-ca, or a spot of bother, and someone got you out of it, would it matter if that someone were: Christian; Catholic; Protestant; Atheist, Jew or Black or White; Khaki, or. any other mix of the aforesaid? I ask you would it matter?" "No! I suppose no!" "Is that 'suppose not' a Yes or a No." "It's a No." "Is it a No for 'not', or a No for 'it doesn't matter'?" "For 'doesn't matter', Bill." "Thank you! And who is the brains of this gang?" "Well! After you!" says Mark, "It's Tommy."

"Now I think we have talked long enough. I propose, that if Tommy is willing, he be made the Number One Leader of The Crescenters (Cheers.). All in favour?" "That's unanimous then." (Cheers.). And so Tommy became the youngest ever leader of The Crescenters (Cheers) and also the First Roman Catholic.

Tommy has got a job delivering orders at Gallon's Store in the Market Place. His carrier bicycle has a small wheel at the front about twelve inches diameter (Just like my bike!) to accommodate a deep frame or carrier for the boxes. Two legs drop down as a stand to hold the bikes upright for loading and unloading. After a month's probation, we can take our bikes home, so, of course, Tommy and I use them for school.

One day, Tommy says, "I've got an idea! Let's give the younger kids rides round the playground, and those that like it, we can charge a napple, or sweets, or something." This turned out to be a nice little earner.

"Have you ever thought of going into the taxi business Plug?" "No not really! How do you mean?" "Well! If we see our young customers and offer them a service to take them home at teatime, we could probably make a tanner a week each or more." "But their Mothers won't like them riding on the bikes, will they?" "They won't know!" says Tommy, "We can pick them up and drop them out of sight of school- and their houses." "That's a brilliant idea! But we will have to swear the kids to secrecy." "We can do that! And we can tell them that if they snitch, we will get Father Dean to put them in sackcloth and ashes." "Brilliant as usual Tommy." "As usual," says Tommy.

Tommy canvasses for business and we get a couple of deep boxes from work. The business takes off. We ferry kids from school, on condition that they keep their heads down so that any inquisitive bu... err inquisitive nosey parker can't see them, then go to our jobs delivering orders.

All went well for a couple of weeks until some Mothers realized that their youngsters were getting home from school, which could be up to a mile away, in about four or five minutes or less. (We slipped-up there.)

I have been delivering orders for a couple of months. One teatime, as I get on to my bike, two men approach: a tall, dark, thin man and a small, thin man. They are both wearing dark suits. They both wear tall trilby hats and carry raincoats over their arms. "What time does it get dark around here?" says the small man. "Are they building Army Camps at Weston?" asks the other. What can I do? I don't like the look of them. "I don't know," I said. "I live abroad." (Thanks Mick!) and I shoot away on my bike.

"Mum?" "Yes son." "Err Mum!" "I am listening, son!" "Well! As I finished work tonight, two men asked me what time did it get dark and about the Army Camps at Weston- but I didn't tell them." "He's fibbing!" says Mick. "Be quiet Michael!" says Mum. "Yes be quiet! And go play on the railway lines!" "Sorry Mum!" says Mick. "Are you fibbing?" "No Mum!" "I bet he is!" "Do you want to go up the dancers?" asks Mum. "No Mum! But I still bet he's fibbing!" says Mick. "Cross my heart and hope to die!" "We should be that lucky!" says my ever-loving brother. "I think that could be blasphemy, " says Mum. "I wouldn't have thought so," says Mick. "Well! I think that you had better confess it next

Saturday. Better safe than sorry you know." "Awe Mum!" I think that I have convinced her. "If you are lying about something like this, you could go to jail" " And to Hell!" echoes Mick. (I wish someone would adopt him and send him abroad.) "And you can confess to that!" says Mum. "To what?" "You know what to what!" double talks Mum. "Do you mean Hell?" asks Mick. "Of course I do!" "So Mum, I have not to say 'Hell' then, and never say 'Hell' again then?" "That's right! Absolutely right!" Score Mum nil and Mick 4 <u>and</u> he says he won't confess because it's in the Bible.

"Right then! I believe you! I will go and see Bobby Hill and tell him what you have told me." Off she goes and returns ten minutes later. "Bobby Hill and Bobby Dale are coming to see you shortly. Are you sure what you will tell them?" "Yes Mum! I will tell them what I have told you." "Good! Now we will wait Bobby Hill and Bobby Dale arrive with another policemen. I think he was called Bobby Moore. I reckon they should have been selling camping equipment and outdoor clothes calling themselves: Hill; Dale and Moore. They are dressed in plain clothes. Why are they called plain clothes when amongst them we have: bright-coloured shirts; flashy ties; gray flannels and brown suede shoes?

They ask me questions and off they go on their bicycles - probably to Weston.

We never heard anything about what had happened to me. I have wondered many times if they were spies or 'Mincespies' as Mick would say. Maybe they <u>were</u> Fifth Columnists. If they were shot or hanged and I was responsible for their capture and execution... Well hard luck Krauts!

Tommy has called for me to go to school this morning. We walk out of the Crescent towards Billams Hill. I am chatting away merrily. "You're very quiet this morning Tommy!" I venture. "Err yes! I suppose I am." "What's up mate? Have you lost a bob and found a tanner?" "No! Nothing like that!" "Well as Bill would say: 'Spit it out but look out where you spit it!'" Tommy gives a wry smile. "Has something happened mate?" "No not yet! But I think it might." "Well that's as clear as mud to me! Can you be a bit more spe... spec... spec..." "Do you mean 'specific'?" "Yes that's what I mean! Err, yes what you just said." "Then why didn't you just say so?" "Awe pack it in Tommy! Pack it in!"

"Right then! I will tell you what I have been thinking about.

The Great War of nineteen fourteen to nineteen eighteen and the next war." "What 'next war'? I thought the Great War was the 'War to end Wars'." "That's what we all thought, mate! But my father says that there is going to be another War." "But Adolf Hitler has promised there won't be a War." "Oh there will be! There will be mate!" "How?" I ask. "Well! For a start, let's take the name 'A Hitler'." "Take it where?" "No stop messing about Plug and listen!" "Will not mess about and will listen," I reply. "Good!" says Tommy, "Take the letter 'T'." "O.K." "And then 'H' and 'E' and what have you got?" "THE." "Now the other letters in the following order." "O.K. I will. L- I-A-R." " Now what have you got?" "THE LIAR," I reply. "Well that's a bad start isn't it?" "Yes, it is Tommy." "And the word German sounds like a man with germs or the plague, or something nasty." "And what does 'nasty' sound like?" asks Tommy. "Err well Tommy! I don't see what you mean," says I. "Well, what does Nazi sound like?" "Ah! I see what you mean now! We are going to be fighting, Nasty Germ-ridden men who tell lies." "Spot on son! Spot on! And I will tell you something else. The cross on their flag is crooked! So we will be fighting Nasty Germ-ridden Liars, who are crooks." "You're right Tommy! You're right!"

One day an old lady, a neighbour, came to our house and asked my Mother if she could buy a bag of coke because she had run short. "Certainly not!" said my Mum, "I will lend you a couple of bags to loosen you out until you get some." I know my Mother would never ask for it back, but our neighbour would probably return two bags anyway.

"Sit down and have a cuppa and a couple of doorsteps." So Mrs. Borrows sat down to a mug of tea and two doorsteps of butter and jam. "When you have finished I will send Peter with the two bags of coke," says Mum.

Mrs. Borrows leaves and Mum says, "Can you manage two bags on your bike?" "No problem Mum!" I load up and off I go and return with a threepenny dodger. "You should not have taken anything!" chides Mum. "You know she's poverty rather than poor." "But she insisted Mum! Honest!"

"Hi Tommy! How's things?" "Fair to midlin! How is it with you?" "O.K. moggin (Carrying.) on! Just moggin on!" says I. "Err Tommy! I've got an idea." "You've got an idea! And not got a headache! That's very good!" "No! But my feet are beginning to ache," I joke. "Right then, what's this foot bending aching idea?" "Well the other day, Mrs. Borrows came to our house to buy some coke, and Mum lent her two bags, because as you know since her hubby died, she hasn't had much to stir on." "So what! What's your idea?" "How about us going into the coke delivery business?" "How?" "Well! We could carry two bags of coke in the deep, strong, cardboard boxes that we used for our short-lived taxi venture: two bags each trip to a customer. We could deliver on a Saturday morning. We usually finish delivering orders by ten-o-clock and if we work an extra hour Friday teatime, we would have most of the morning clear." "That's a brilliant idea!" says Tommy. "No wonder you've got footache if that's where your brain is! But I tell you what!" "What?" "Well when it gets to about half past eleven, we can deliver fish and chips." "I bet your feet are aching now!" "Just starting," says Tommy, "and so is my head."

We canvass about a dozen customers each. I ask Tommy if we can cope with so many. He thinks we can but suggests if it gets towards dinner, one of us can handle the coke and the other can collect and deliver the fish and chips.

Saturday morning then, our first visit to the Gas Works in Charles Street. (Not named after Charlie Chuck). Two huge Gasometers which rise and fall according to the gas pressure. A very tall processing plant. dominates the area, it seems to go as high as the clouds. On a foggy day it does disappear! Chimneys spewing smoke; steam hissing from faulty pipes- all happy to be free from their prison. The freedom is short lived, however, they soon disappear into nothingness. Gas and Sulphur fumes tingle the nostrils and irritate our throats- causing us to cough and splut-ter. I wonder if Mum suffers as we are doing when she sniffs her dope (Snuff.)...probably. My eyes gently start to water and they are beginning to be a little sore.

Tommy whispers, "My dad said it would be like this for the first few times." "Awe! Right!" I whisper back. "Tommy!" I whisper. "Yes!" he whispers. "Why are we whispering?" "I don't know!" he says. "Neither do I." "Perhaps it's because we are over-awed." "Perhaps." "That's it! We are in awe then?" "Awe right!"

We pay for two bags each and queue with our tokens in our hand- waiting to be loaded from the pile of bagged coke. As we wait, women, and men, with small or big prams; newish or oldish prams; prams with babes and bags; lads and lassies with carts and bogies coming and going home with their bags of comfort and solace- and fuel for cooking. A whip cracks! A huge horse whinnies, snorts, and with a great clatter of hooves, slips and slides as it attempts to move the loaded cart; a few words of encouragement; a couple of whip cracks and they are away.

Another cart pulled by two big horses clatter onto the weighbridge. "Whoa!" shouts the driver and applies the brakes. The cart load is weighed and amid much snorting, whinnying, slipping, sliding, sparking hooves, hoarse (Not horse!) voices shouting and whip cracking; they give a great heave and move away followed by the great lumbering cart. Well it would have to follow the horses wouldn't it- seeing that it was attached to them! Now it's our turn! "How many bags son?" "Two mister!" "Got your token?" "Yes Mister!" Here we go then.

As we move towards Charles Street, another whip cracks, a "Gee-up there!" Two horses whinnie and clatter; the driver shouts: "Make a clear way! Loaded cart leaving!" The cry is taken-up by the people. Tommy and I look at each other, shrug our shoulders and join in. We draw back close to the high wall as the 'Loaded cart leaving.' clatters by; delivering all that comfort and warmth and heat for cooking from whatever is trapped inside the coke. I think it's wonderful and mysterious.

The business is going well, we cope and complete the coke deliveries- tuppence a bag. We take and fulfill orders for: Fish and Chips; Fish or Parsley-cakes and Chips, and, Scallops (One slice of potato nicely battered.). Most people order bags of scraps for halfpenny or penny a bag. (Scraps are small pieces of batter that have fallen away from the fish etc., as they fry. I think I may have mentioned this before: about the scallops and the scraps. Old-age mate! Old-age.). Fish costs one and a half pennies; chips a halfpenny or a penny; Fish cakes are one penny and Scallops are five for a penny. All in all, with the delivery charges of two pence; a bag of coke and two pence for each order for fish and chips- or whatever, and, an occasional bottle of pop from the grateful fish-shop owner, life is pretty good, and profitable.

Mum comes in from shopping on Saturday afternoon and says, "Bless you! Bless you! You are my little Angel!" "What me?" I

ask. "Yes you! My little Angel! I know what you have been up
to! I have been talking to Mrs Borrows." I have refused a couple of young Mick's fags- they taste lousy anyway. I have even
avoided saying or thinking any swear words, lately, not even mild
swear words. I can't see any connection. I wouldn't qualify for an
'Angel' twice over and a 'little treasure' if she thought that I had
been smoking or sinning or owt else. "You are my little treasure!"
"What have I..." Mother comes and gives me a cuddle and kisses
me on my right ear and says, "Let it be our secret."

"Tommy!" "Yes!" "I don't know why but I have suddenly become an Angel twice over and a little treasure." "Oh you will
soon get over the shock! But mind you! Don't get your wings
clipped! How have you become an Angel twice over- and a treasure then?" "Search me! My Mother seems to think I have being
doing good works or something for Mrs. Borrows." "For Mrs.
Borrows?" "Yes Tommy for Mrs. Borrows!" "For Mrs. Borrows!
You mean our Mrs. Borrows?" "There's only one Mrs. Borrows,
Tommy! Not two or three as you seem to think, in fact, I am not
sure at this moment how many Mrs. Borrows you think that there
are!" "Sorry Plug! Of course there is only one Mrs Borrows! Well!
Only one Mrs. Borrows living around here at this moment in
time!" "Well! I am glad that we have sorted that out at long last! I
will have to go and see her and sort things out."

"Err... don't do that Plug!" says Tommy. "Why not?" "Why
not? Well I have been delivering coke free to Mrs. Borrows for
the past couple of weeks." "You haven't been charging delivery?"
"Err no!" "And what else have I supposed to have done?" "You
err... You have been letting Mrs. Borrows have the coke free as
well." "What free?" "Yes." "You mean free, free?" "Yes! Yes!" says
my very good friend, "But on your honour! Don't tell anybody!
Cross your heart and hope to die!" "I probably will when my
Mother finds out." "Then say nowt," says Tommy. "But why did
you do it?" "Well! I heard my Mother say that Mrs. Borrows was
very poor since her husband died, almost poverty, so I thought I
could help her a bit." "Well done Thomas!" says I, "Well done!
And thank you very muchly!" "You're welcome!" "Well your not!"
"Sorry mate!" "I should co-co! Well you have put me in a right
fix! Right in the deep ca-ca!" "Why?" "Why? Because my mother
thinks I am an Angel twice over and a little treasure. If she ever

finds out, she will bray (Hit.) me! I will get the rounds of the kitchen and sent up the dancers." "Well! Keep your gob (Mouth.) shut then!" "Yes! I will!"

A couple of weeks pass- business is booming. I still feel a bit guilty that I did not think of it: free, free coke- for Mrs Borrows that is. Guilty, because I think it could be a sin of omission- or something.

"Peeeterrr!" hollers Mum. "Yes Mother!" "Come here! Just you come here!" Oh dear! She doesn't sound very Angelic. I don't think that that is a nice way to treat an Angel twice over- and her sweet little treasure. "Peeterr!" "Coming Mother!" I will have to face the music. I get off the swinging gate; a crack on the head from the brush wielding Charlie Chuck would be better than the wrath of my non-angelic Mother. I shuffle up the path as slowly as I can to the front door to be greeted by a piercing shriek that sounds something like my name.

"Come here you nasty little sod! Err... so-and-so!" "Yes Mother!" "I think one Angel twice over has crashed, and a little treasure has been lost forever." "Yes Mother!" says I as innocently as I can manage. "Don't you sweet talk me, you sneaking little bug... err... bug... err blighter." I wonder why she isn't swearing properly. As I go into the kitchen, I find out why.

"Oh! Hail Mary! It's Mrs. Borrows. It seems she has come across the back garden to thank Mum for what I have done- but not done. Mrs. Borrows is sat in our best armchair, a steaming mug in one hand; a half eaten doorstep in the other. She hurriedly consumes her doorstep, splutters her drink down and says that she must go because she has some bread rising. 'Bread rising?' some of you younger readers or ignoramuses may say.

Well! To make bread: flour, yeast, and maybe salt, are mixed with water into a thick paste called 'dough'. The dough is placed into a glazed bow and covered with a cloth. It is then stood near the fire that causes it to rise. When it has risen, the dough is divided into suitable pieces to fit the loaf tins, further rising, and then into the oven to bake. You see, you can learn something new every day, so you can, and have new fresh baked bread every day as well.

"Yes, Mother, what's wrong? Can I help you?" "You are a liar, a sneak and a lot of other things I shouldn't wonder!" "I am <u>not</u>

an Angel twi —err- an Angel then?" "No you are blood… blooming well not! You have deceived me and others because I have told them what I thought you had done and now I have just found out it was Thomas all along." "Thomas?" (Now I'm saying it!) "How… err… what Mother?" "I will tell you what, what! I will tell you what! Mrs. Borrows called this morning and said what a good boy Thomas (Cringe.) is, and I should be proud to be his Mother. She thought that Thomas was my son! Well! I would be proud of him if he was <u>my</u> son! That boy is an Angel, an Angel, I tell you." "And a treasure Mother?" "Yes a blood… err… a beautiful treasure. He should go in for a Priest. God Bless him!"

"It will be St. Thomas next!" I mutter. "What did you say?" "I said, Thomas will be vexed because his secret is out, because someone has blabbed." "Don't you come it with me, young man!" says a once ever-loving Mother getting madder and madder, and quickly losing her love for her little Angel twice over, and the little treasure. "Right! That's it!" says this very irate lady. I don't know about Tommy becoming a Priest, but I would make a darned good <u>Prophet</u> because <u>I did</u> get a clip round the earhole; the rounds of the kitchen, and, sent up the dancers.

"Mornin Plug!" "Mornin Tommy!" "I think there's going to be a war," says Tommy. "You think so?" "Yes." "Why?" "The wireless is full of war talk about Poland; a place called Danzig; invasion and ultimatums." "What's 'ulti… ultimate'?" "You mean 'ultimatums'?" "Yes!" "Then why didn't you say so?" (I think Tommy is a bit upset. He can be awkward if something goes wrong, or whatever.). "Right then! What's this ult… err ul… err…what you said." "I don't know but there's one going about. And I will tell you another thing." "What?" "All the Russian Air Force has gone up." "Up where?" "I don't know where but it said on the wireless that they had." "But they must have gone up somewhere?" I insist. "Well of course they have!" "Why 'of course'?" I said still insisting. "Because they are designed to go up." "What are?" "The aeroplanes! Idiot!" "But wherever they go up, they <u>must</u> come down some time!" "They probably have come down the length of time we have been arguing!" says Tommy. He quickens his pace and leaves me behind. (Tommy <u>is</u> upset.)

Everybody is talking about a War. The wireless is telling us what might happen and what we should do in the event of hostilities. Whatever that means.

Will there be a War. I am eleven years and ten months old. I am serving Mass. I pray that there will be. Mass is interrupted: a slightly trembling Father Dean makes an announcement, and my prayers have been answered. We <u>are</u> at War! Father Dean motions for us altar boys to sit in the side pews. The congregation have got over their first gasp. Now a coughing steadily spreads throughout the Church: handkerchiefs are being waved and then put to a wet eye or a damp nose, or, a wet nose or a damp eye. (Take your pick but don't pick the nose!). A lot of people seem to have caught a cold all at once. Somebody starts to sob quietly; others take up the sobbing; some are crying silently.

Father Dean, his hands shaking more than normal for him, his voice quivers. I suppose it is filled with emotion or something. He is telling us to pray. Well I <u>have</u> prayed and we are at War. Who says that our prayers are never answered? Mass has ended; more people stay behind than is usual- they are knelt and praying quietly. People are lighting candles. Tommy and I take off our vestments and walk up the aisle; genuflect; bless ourselves with Holy Water, and, leave Church.

"Well!" says Tommy, "That's it! The ultimatum has run out." "Out where? Sorry Tommy I should not have said that! I am not being funny Tommy- but <u>what</u> is an ultimatum?" "A <u>very</u> serious thing." Tommy says, "Well! It was in the newspaper. An 'ultimatum' is like a promise or a warning depending?" "Depending on what?" "Well! Mr. Chamberlain told Hitler that if he did not get out of Poland, we would declare War. He told him that if we did not hear by eleven o'clock today, we would consider ourselves at War- and the bastard hasn't said owt, so War it is."

"Let's go to the Drill Hall, to see if there is owt doing." So up Bridge Street, through the Bay Horse passage along Boroughgate to the Drill Hall- the home of the Territorials (Part time volunteer soldiers.). There are quite a lot of people gathered. "Owt happening?" we ask. "There's going to be a parade at twelve thirty." "Ooh right! We will wait then." There are a few old soldiers who fought in the First World War: 'Old Sweats' we call them. One in particular we call him 'Battling Basher Bill'. He always carries a walking stick and he walks hunched forward. Today he is smart and upright with a load of Medals on his chest. He is following all the orders given to the parade. "Present Arms!" "Shoulder Arms!" He remains at attention, stick on his left shoulder and salutes the parade. "Right dress! Eyes front! Attention!" They look very smart. "Stand Easy!"

The Commanding Officer clears his throat twice, and tells the soldiers, and the rest of us, that we are at War and it is a just War. "God is on our side and we shall be victorious against the powers of evil!" I wonder if some Germans are hearing something similar. My Mother says she had heard that Hitler had said: "The Lord helps him who helps himself." Some of the soldiers are crying. I didn't know that soldiers cried. Our side won't get killed; only the Jerries will get shot.

Hello! Look who's there and he is crying also! It is Bully Luther from the Fever Hospital. Not so brave now! Serves him right! No I don't mean that! "Please look after him and all the other soldiers- and don't let any of them be killed."

The first night of the War. We recite the first of many Rosaries: one 'Our Father'; ten 'Hail Marys' and a 'Glory Be to the Father'. How is it that each time we pray, I always want to go to sleep, and Mum has to nudge me awake?

Off to bed then! Off to sleep! What's this dream? This nightmarish sound? Oh my God! It's the Air Raid Warning. Mum comes into our room and wakens Michael. "Quick!" she says, "Let's get up out of bed and get under the keeping slab in the pantry under the stairs!" Young Mick doesn't want to waken up. I half carry him downstairs. Mum says she will get our gas masks.

We are cowering in the pantry under the slab. I am terrified, even young Mick is quiet for once, but I think that all he wants to do is to go back to sleep. Mum seems very calm, she is in charge. Dad is away ferrying troops around the country, so we are alone. Half an hour passes, nothing has happened. Michael is hard and fast asleep; I must have dozed-off. Someone is shaking me! It's Mum! "Quick! I can hear some rattles. Oh my God! We are under gas attack! Quick!" says Mum, "On with your gas mask! I will sort Michael out."

Now I am terrified. I have heard stories about Mustard Gas in the First World War. I know men who have been gassed and they have told me that many soldiers died from gas poisoning.

The rattles are sounding again. Mum is very calm. (I think she is praying). Michael wakes up. I will say a prayer to Mary. Michael has gone back to sleep (Thank goodness for that.). We have had warnings on the wireless. If Church bells ring, we are being invaded. If a gas attack was imminent (Whatever that means.), rattles would sound. Well they <u>are</u> sounding now! I must have fallen asleep. I wake with a start. My mask is steamed up. I am cold and sweaty where the rubber is touching me. Mum says, "Take that thing off!" "Yes Mother!"

Michael is still asleep. Mum must have taken his gas mask off. "What happened? Mum, have we been gassed?" "No son," answers Mum. "I think it must have been a false alarm." "Thank God Mum!" "Amen to that son! Amen to that! Let's have some breakfast shall we and let young Michael sleep on?" "Yes Mum! But I bet he wakes up when the grub is up." He did.

Breakfast over, Mick and I are reading our comics; 'Film Fun' with 'Laurel and Hardy', and, 'Stainless Stephen'. Mum is spitting on the iron- which has been heated up on the fire prior to ironing. "Postman's here!" she cries. "I'll go Mum!" "Right Peter! I hope we have a letter from Dad. We didn't have one last week."

"Mornin, Postie!" "Morning son! How's tricks?" "Oh fair to midlin! What have you got?" "I have got two letters. I think they are from your Dad by the handwriting." "Good! Did you hear the gas rattles last night Postie?" "No I didn't! But I can tell you they were <u>not</u> gas rattles son." "But I heard them!" "No son! What you heard were horses!" "Horses! What horses?" "Well! You know about all those cart and dray horses that they have brought from Leeds and Bradford to escape any bombing." "Err yes". "Well, when the sirens sounded; they spooked the horses; they panicked and broke out of the field near the Workhouse; ran twice round The Crescent and up towards Clifton." "Well! That's good news. I was scared stiff!" "I bet you were son! I bet you were."

"Peter, do you think I will <u>get</u> my letter today?" "Sorry Mum-coming!" "Bye Postie!" "Bye son!" Two letters from Dad. He can't tell us very much: 'Careless talk costs lives.'. He is very busy. His leg is standing up to the rigours of life. Mum has finished reading most of them to Mick and I. "The rest is private," says she with a wry smile. I don't know what that sort of private 'private' really means but there we are.

"I want you and Michael to go for some blackout material from

Walkers on Kirkgate." Blackout material was a stiff black paper sold off the roll by the yard. Mr. Granger the Joiner has given me enough strips of wood to make blackout frames for the windows. The first night of war, we switched off all the lights and managed with an odd candle and the glow from a low fire. At least we had drawn curtains in the sitting room. We kept them closed that night. "How much do we want, Mum?" says I. Mr. Granger has written the measurements down and how much we need. "Right Mum!" "Off you go then!"

Across the Market Square: "Hi, Tommy!" "Hiya Plug!". Going for blackout paper then?" "Yep!" "Same here!" "You know Tommy! I would have thought we would be O.K. without blackout, as we did last night." "Don't you believe it mate! Do you know that they can see a lit fag- miles and miles away?" "No I didn't!" "Well they can!" "Ye Gods Tommy! Look at the queue!" "Now that is a queue!" says he.

Nothing for it, we wait and we get the blackout paper and some drawing pins. (For some inexplicable reason, I remember the film showing at Kirkgate Cinema. It was Barry K. Barnes the actor; the film, "This Man is news." Yes I know! That's what we call useless, time wasting, information.)

Home again. "Have you got everything?" "Yep! But who is going to make the blackouts?" "You are!" "Who me?" "How me?" "Well! Mr. Granger is coming round after dinner to show you how to make one and then you can do the others." "Cheers Mum!" "Cheers son!"

"Hello Mr. Granger!" "Hello Peter!" "I don't know how to make a frame. I haven't a Dolly Blue (Clue.)!" "Well! By the time I leave you will be able to make one." "Great!" says I.

Mr. Granger showed me how to measure the window and mark the wood. Four pieces were marked to size: each piece was cut about 4 inches longer. We made the frame on the kitchen floor. Two uprights were placed over the top and bottom rails on the marks. Mr. Granger put the heads of the nails on to Dad's cobbling last and tapped the points a bit flat. "Why have you done that?" I ask. "Well! If you left the point on it works like a wedge and can split the wood but the flat point compresses the fibres." "Awe right!" "You can learn something new every black out, can't you?" Mr. Granger knocks the nails in; turns the frame over lets the nail head rest on Dad's cobbling last and hammers the points over into the run of the grain of the wood. "That's called 'Clenching'," says he. "Now we cut off the surplus." "Why did you leave the ends on then?" "Less chance of splitting." "Good idea!" says I. "A very good idea!" says he.

We offer the frames up to the window. "That's a good fit," says I. "It's a joiner's fit," says he. "But how do we keep them up?" "Well! We cut slots in the edge of the frame: two in each upright and two across the top. We then offer the frames back up and knock in staples where the slots are. We then make pegs to drop into the staples. "That's brilliant!" says I. "Wait till I tell Tommy."

"Right then! Put the frame on the floor; cut the blackout over-size; glue and drawing pin it on to the frame and trim the over-hang." "Right! That's the first frame done then." "Not quite!" "Oh! Why not 'quite'?" "We have to glue and pin a strut about 9 inches long across each corner." "What's that for Mr. Granger?" "To keep the frame square." "Oh! Like a Kraut's head then!" "I suppose so." "Thanks Mr. Granger! I know how to make one now. "You're welcome son!" "Bye!" "Bye!"

Mum comes in from shopping. "How's it gone then?" "Brilliant! We have made a blackout!" "Let's see then!" Up goes the first pro-totype (Whatever that means. It sounds like a spinning type-writer or something.) "O.K! Switch on the room light!" "Right!" "All you do Mum is to lift the frame up into the window; it is marked 'Top', and, put these pegs into the staples to hold it in place." "That's blooming marvellous!" says Mum "Now pop out-side and see if you can see any light showing." So out I troll out to have a gander (Look.) "Can you see owt?" shouts Mum "Naff all!" I holler back, "Blooming marvellous!" says I. "Mum?" "Yes son!" "Can I be a Joiner when I grow up?" "We'll see! We'll see!"

Tommy and I are 12 years old. We have moved into the top classroom and will be taught by the dreaded Miss White- but I don't think she is too bad. Miss White makes an announcement: "Miss Johnson will be leaving us shortly." "Awe heck! (Shame.)" " She is moving to Birmingham to be near her parents." That's a shame! I like Miss Johnson. I think I could love somebody like Miss Johnson (Ah well!).

I am fed up, or as Tommy would say: 'A bit brassed-off.' I am confined to bed: I have a headache; a high temperature, and boy, am I sweating!   A hot brick wrapped in a towel at my feet. If the towel comes loose and I touch the brick "Ouch!" A jug of lemon and barley water and a mug stand neatly on my side table ready to administer (Whatever that means.) to my needs. Time for another 'Perry's' powder: Mum carefully opens the sleeve wrapper and forms it into a tube; I open my mouth and mum blows it down my throat.

Thank goodness! I have a mug of barley water but any poison would do. Someone has gone out of their way, and probably been paid a lot of money, to make them taste lousy and horrible, but Mum says that if they taste lousy and horrible they must be doing me a lot of good- I don't think!

I must have dozed off. "Peter!" "Err... Err." "Peter! Are you awake?" "I am now Mum." "Tommy's here! Shall I send him up?" "Yes please Mother!" Tommy thumps up the staircase: the noise seems to go right through my head. "For goodness sake Tommy! Quieten it down a bit!" "Sorry mate! How's tricks then?" "I feel lousy." "Pissed off then?" "Yes pissed off!"

"Right!" says Tommy as he sits on my bed. "Ask me what time it is?" "Why, have you got a watch?" "No, I haven't got a watch!" "Well why should I ask you the time if you haven't got a watch?" "Why? Because I can tell you what the time is without a watch. Well roughly what the time is anyrode?" "Oh! I suppose you can tell the time by the Sun then." "Well! If I could do that; I couldn't!" "Sounds like Greek to me." "I couldn't do it because the Sun isn't shining. I tell you what!" says Tommy, "What?" says I. "Let's start all over again. Here have a mug of barley water." "Thanks!"

"Mornin Plug! How's tricks?" "Worse than a couple of minutes ago!" "Sorry mate!" "Could you tell me the time, young sir?" "Certainly!" says Tommy, as he goes through the motion of looking at a pocket-watch. "The time is 'Pork-pie' time!" "'Pork-pie' time! How do you mean: 'Pork-pie' time?" "It's 'Pork- pie time because its: 'summat to eight'! Something to eat!" says Tommy triumphantly. No! I don't reckon much to it either. "If that's the best you can come up with, I am going back to sleep." "Sorry mate! Oh I do have a bit of news! We have got a new teacher to replace Miss Johnson."

"What's she like then?" "Oh mate! She's a cracker; she is gorgeous!" "What's her name then?" "It's Peggy and I bet that you will never guess her other name."

"Sorry Tommy! I can't be bothered." "That's alright mate! Here have another swig of barley water." "Thanks!" "You're welcome! Her name is Peggy Love." "Peggy Love?" "Yes! Peggy Love and she's got smashing legs. I call her 'Leggy Peggy'." "Not to her face?" "Course not! And she's very young." "Tommy! What are smashing legs?" "Well! They are legs that are err... Well! They are sort of... if you know what I mean?" "No! I don't know what you mean." "Well! When you get back to School, have a look at the other Teacher's legs and then at Peggy's." "Right! I will." "And I will tell you another thing." "What?" "She shows a bit more of them than the other teachers do." "Awe right!"

"How are you now? Do you want to go to sleep?" asks Tommy. "No, I am feeling a lot better." "Good! Have another swig." "Thanks mate!" "You're welcome!"

"Peeter! Do you want another powder?" "No thanks Mum! I am feeling much better since Tommy came to see me." "Would Thomas like some cocoa?" "Yes please Mrs. Jackson!" "And a couple of doorsteps?" "Thank you Mrs. Jackson!" "Me too Mum!" "Coming up shortly then."

"Oh Plug! Do you remember when you had Scarlet Fever and the fever van came?" Yes! I will never forget it." "Do you remember me telling you about being careful because you don't always come back and they did experiments or something?" "I certainly do!" "Well! Do you remember the driver:" "Pretty well." "Who did he look like then?" "Well! Err it was a long time ago." "I know it was but think! Peak cap; little moustache! Think!" "By gum! He looked like Hitler!" "Now what you don't know is that he is Hitler's brother." "Pull the other one!" "No straight up Plug! He is his brother: in fact, he is Hitler's twin brother!" "Well! He did look a bit like Hitler! But his brother! I don't know about that!" "Well! He is! Now listen! He dyed his hair and moustache to look different, and when did you hear him speak?" "Never!" "Exactly! And did he ever take his cap off? Did he?" "No never! But why would taking his cap off give him away?" "Why? Why? Because all Jerries have got square heads." "Are you sure, Tommy?" "Of course I'm sure! They call them 'Squareheads' and 'Krauts'." "Have another drink." "Thanks, mate!"

"How did they get on to him then?" "They were a bit suspicious of him; they arrested him and took him to the Cop-hole (Police station). One of the coppers asked him riddles and got him to do puzzles and answer trick questions. He got so fed up because being a Kraut he couldn't do or answer them. He took his cap off and they saw he had a square head and so he must be a Jerry." "They had got him then?" says I. "They sure had!" said Tommy, "But just to be sure they asked him what the pigs do in Pudsey. He got that mad; he threw his cap away and shouted 'Achtung'!" "What <u>do</u> the pigs do in Pudsey?" "Well! According to my Dad, they fly backards (backwards)." "Awe right! I suppose he would be shot or hanged if he was a spy. Was he spying then?" "Well! Sort of! You remember that day when he took you to the Fever Hospital?" "Too true I do!" "And I told you to watch out because they did experiments and things." "Yes you did!"

"Well! He used to make the lads do exercises and things. Those that passed he drugged them and sent them to Kraut land so Hitler could see what they were would be made of when they grew up, and what he would be up against. When Hitler had had a good look, they were re drugged and whipped back, and quite a few died in the Fever Hospital and nobody cottoned on why."

"Here's your bread and cocoa, Tommy." "Thank you! Mrs. Jackson. "How's the patient?" "Fair to midlin, Mum!" "Good! Good!" says Mum. "They must have hung him then?" "No!" says Tommy. "They sent him back in an 'Annie' (An Avro Anson aeroplane.) on a leaflet raid and dumped him in a parachute over Berlin." "Why did they let him get away with it Tommy?" "Well! They gave him a note for his twin brother." "Hitler?" "Yes! Adolf Hitler!" "And I suppose you know what it said?" "Of course I know what it said!" "Go on then!" "Right! I will go on then! Here goes!"

Dear Adolf,

Just a few lines to let know we have cottoned on to what your brother has been up to. Well the kids what your twin brother sent over to Germany were poor, sickly ones, and we bet you thought your lot could beat our lot.

Well! Hard luck Adolf! Because we have loads of unsick ones over here.

Yours sincerely,
His Majesty
Mr. Rex.
PS, Why don't you come over for a holiday sometime?.

Peeter? "Yes Mother!" "Do you want another Perry's powder?" "No Mother! I feel a heck of a lot better since Tommy came. I am going to get up and come downstairs for a couple of hours." "Oh! Good boy!" calls Mum. "Cheers Tommy!" "Cheers Plug!"

I am twelve years old and I am in love. She (I don't know her name yet.) has beautiful blonde hair and sort of green eyes. She wears a white top and a greenish skirt; white ankle socks and her shoes are always clean and shining. When it is cold or wet she wears a green gabardine and a green hat, I think she smiled at me once. I haven't found out that her name. I follow her to her billet. I follow her at lunchtime. Everywhere she walks I follow her. I have loved her for two whole weeks. My heart aches. I wash instead of a cat -lick. I wish I had a smarter pair of shoes. For weekdays, I can only wear my best for Saturdays, Sundays and Holy days. I have considered wearing a tie but perhaps knot- err not! She may think that I am stuck-up! The local talent knows that I am not stuck-up or stuck-to any body or anything, so I can get away with a tie.

"Tommy, I need your help." "Any time mate! Any time! What's the problem?" "Well you know that blonde girl who is billeted on Bridge Avenue?" "Yes! The one who is always with her sister." "How do you know it's her sister?" "Because I fancy her, and I have found things out!" "What!" "The sister clot! They call your bit of stuff Peggy." "Peggy! That's a beautiful name Thomas! Err Tommy! Absolutely beautiful!" "It reminds me of a Peggy-stick," says Tommy.

For all you that are dedicated followers of short-term memory: a 'Peggy-stick' is like a small stool with four or five short legs. It has a wooden shaft and a double-handed handle across the top. A 'Peggy-tick' is used in a wash-tub and spun backwards and forwards, or, forwards and backwards- take your pick. In fact, it was an old time agitator, old time agitator. That reminds me of a 'Sometimes Mum'. If you <u>aren't</u> a dedicated follower of short-term memory and still could not tell me what a 'Peggy-stick' is, I can only conclude that you must have skipped some pages in this book. Shame on you!) "Don't spoil it, Tommy! Don't spoil it!" "O.K. mate! It's the best name ever!" "Thanks Tommy!" "You're welcome!"

Peggy! Oh lovely Peggy is an evacuee from the other side of Leeds. All parents have the option to evacuate their children from likely bombing targets to the comparative safety of the countryside.

"Mornin Plug!" "Mornin Tommy!" "Is it still on with Peggy then?" "Of course it is, Thomas! Err Tommy! It's for life!" "Right then! This is what we will do." "Hello Blondie! Would you like a napple?" "No." "Tell me your name then!" "No!" "No! Is that your name?" "No, it isn't!" "Oh sorry! So 'No it isn't' is your name then?" "No!" "Is your name another name then?" "Yes it is!" "That's your name then? I like that! It reminds me of summat, but I can't think of owt at this moment in time." "No! It's not that!" "Well! What is it- if it isn't 'Yes' or 'No' or 'No it isn't' or 'Yes it is' or 'No it's not that'? Come on Blondie! Tell me your proper name... please!" "It's Peggy." "Peggy?" "Yes! Peggy." "Hmm! I don't like the sound of that at all, it reminds me of err..." "Leave her alone, Tommy! Just leave her alone!" interrupts I.

"And whose going to make me?" "I am!" "You and whose army? Not the Salvation Army!" "I don't need an army!" "Come on then!" says Tommy, "If you fancy your chance." "Right I will! Come on!" Tommy and I square up and scuffle. On Peggy's blind side, I go through the motion of giving Tommy a whacking great thump in the guts. He goes down, writhing in agony.

"So your name is Peggy then! That's a wonderful name!" "You gave me some <u>stick</u> there mate," says Tommy as he squirms on the deck. I think for goodness sake Tommy! Be quiet! "May I walk you home?" "Yes! That would be nice," says my love. As we walk away, Tommy calls, "After all this, I hope you "Stick" to Peggy or vice versa." "What does he mean?" asks my beloved. "I haven't a clue!" says I.

Peggy! Oh Peggy! We have been together for six and a half weeks. I comb my hair and wash every day- no cat licks. Mick can't understand it, neither can Mum. I pay young Mick tuppence a week to clean my boots. Mum hasn't a clue but Mick is suspicious. He asked me if I felt alright and what was all this in aid of. I told him that Father Dean had told us altar boys that: Cleanliness is next to Godliness." That shut him up!

My world has crashed! I went to meet Peggy out of school. She wasn't waiting for me. "Where's Peggy? Is she poorly?" I ask. "No! She is fine," says one of her friends. "She has gone back home to t'other side o' Leeds." "She has gone back home to t'other side o' Leeds?" says I. "Yes parrot! I just said that!" "Sorry! When did she go?" "Yesterday."

"What <u>am</u> I going to do, Tommy? What am I going to do? How far is it to the other side of Leeds?" "About twenty miles I reckon." "Oh heck! I can't afford to go that far! I am just about broke!" "Women don't come cheap you know! Looking after her has brocken (Bankrupted.)) you." "In more ways than one," says I.

"Mornin Tommy!" "Mornin Plug!" How's the great lover this fine sunny morning?" "Not fine funny or sunny," says I. "Well! I've got an idea." "What idea?" "Get on a Leeds bus; tell the Bus Conductor that you are an evacuee, and, you are going to Leeds to try and find your parents because they have just been bombed out." "Idiot! There's been no bombing in Leeds, that's why Peggy's gone home." "Why don't you get her address off one of her mates then you can write to her." "That's brilliant!" "I know it is," says Tommy.

Two weeks have passed; four letters written- no reply. "Maybe they are all dead!" offers Tommy. "Oh thank you very much! You have cheered me up no end!" "Sorry mate!"

Another few weeks pass. One morning Tommy says, "I've got an idea." "What idea?" "An idea about Leeds." "About Leeds?" "Yes! About Leeds!" "What about Leeds?" "About Leeds and Peggy." "What about Leeds and Peggy?" Peggy and I had walked, talked and laughed together. We had shared our sweets; gone to the flics (Cinema.) and walked down the Park. They wouldn't let us on the rowing boats because we were too young, so we went on the motor launch. We never kissed or held hands. I never put my arm round her. Oh! How I loved Peggy! But believe it or not! I never think about her now and I cannot remember clearly what she looked like.

"Mornin Plug!" "Mornin Tommy! Ready for another school week then?" "I guess so." "I tell you what Tommy!" "What?" "I think Miss Love is a bit of alright." "What?" "I think Miss Love is a bit of alright." "A bit of alright! She is more than alright! She is all alright on the left side as well as the right! She is a corker! And Oh! Those legs!" "I will have to have a look when we get to school." "You mean to tell me that you haven't noticed?" "No! I haven't". "You've been that besotted!" "What's 'besotted'?" "I'm not sure but you have been!" "How besotted?" "You've been so besotted with Peggy Stick that you haven't noticed a real woman like Peggy Love! And you certainly haven't been living in the real world for quite some time." "Sorry mate!" "I should co-co! I should co-co!"

As we turn to go into the school gates Miss Love is arriving from the opposite direction. "Good morning Miss Love!" "Good morning Thomas! Good morning Peter!" How sweet our names sound! Even 'Thomas'! A tug on my shoulder: "What's up, Tommy?" "Shhhh!" he whispers and puts his index finger to the side of his nose, "Take a good look now mate! Take a good look at those pins! They are bloomin... er bloomin...! They are, err well...! They are a bit of all right! Don't you think?" I do look. They just seem to be another pair of legs to me.

Dad is home for a week from ferrying troops. He is a different bloke since his leg was cured. "I've been thinking," says Dad. "Have you got a headache then?" asks Mick. "No! But he will probably get foot ache!" says I. "Don't be cheeky! How do you mean 'foot ache'?" "Well you were a very good footballer when your leg would let you," "True! Very true!" says Dad modestly. "Well! Your brains must be in your feet! Mustn't they?" "Ha! Very good! I think they are starting to ache!"

"So, what's this idea Dad?" "Well! If we dig the lawn up, we could grow potatoes and vegetables and set seeds and things. The only thing is that I cannot do the digging because my leg may not be strong enough." "Don't worry, old man!" "Less of the 'old'!" "Only joking Dad! Mick and I will dig it for you." "Thanks lads! I thought you would."

"What do we do then?" "Well first we turf it off and put the sod..." "Is that swearing Dad?" "No, not when you mean 'grass-sods'." "Well! I would have thought a sod was a sod, was a sod, was a so…" "Whoa! Hold it, young Jacko! You are getting close to swearing now!" "Sorry Dad!" says Mick. "We pile up the sods, grass to grass, so that they will rot down and go back on to the garden." "That's clever!" echoes Mick. "Then we dig. Well! You two dig to two spades deep and take out any stones or whatever." And so we turfed, dug and cleared the soil of stones. We planted potato sets to break up the soil when they developed. As they progressed, we hoed up the soil to block out the daylight to stop them going green.

The first year, we planted carrots also. Dad showed us how to make a hole with an iron bar; fill it with sharp sand and plant the seed. I don't know whether this worked; whether it was the virgin soil or whether we had a bit of luck, but we had some flipping big carrots that year. We had so many carrots that Mick said he felt like a rabbit.

We would go 'Hoss-mucking'- following the carthorses armed with a bucket and shovel. There were quite a few fall-outs as several .buckets and shovels vied with each other over one pile of droppings. This was solved when all the interested parties agreed to pool the crap.

The kitchen garden was just under fifteen foot by twelve feet plus a bit that you can lose if you are careless when calculating the area- making it just under twenty square yards. (That saves you working it out.) We developed our garden and became proficient. It was a great boost to our table all through the war. I don't know why they agreed to have a war in the first place, nowt's happened.

I am in a spot of bother. Although we are in the top classroom, we have contact with Miss Love, or, as Tommy would say: 'Leggy Peggy'. We have to pass through her classroom as we go to and fro from ours. She is: very young: always smiling and has blond hair (Another blond Peggy.). I don't think she is the sort to let a bloke down. You can say things to her that you couldn't say to the other teachers. Yes! She has better legs than them! I think I have overstepped the mark. (The next letter is "G"). She must have complained to Miss White because I heard Miss White say that she would stop any insolence towards Miss Love, and would send a note to my mother- my sister Maureen could take it.

Sister! What sister? You may ask. You might say: I didn't know you had a sister. Yes! I have a sister. In fact, I have two sisters! Maureen is five years younger than I am and Maria is a baby. My mother called her 'Maria' because as she was being born, Gracie Fields was singing 'Ave Maria' on the wireless. (I think that was lovely.). You have kept quiet about them- you may say but sisters were… well err… sisters! You might ask: how do you mean? Well! They're alright to fill a chair at meal times and mend a hole in your sock- if you catch them in a good mood. They test their cooking on you, and some of it is lousy, but in all fairness, most of it is fair.to midlin.

Anyhow back to one sister and one note. Normally Maureen would be taken home with an older girl. I got to my sister first and took the note from her. Of course, she snitched. The next day, Miss White sent Maureen and her minder home, half an hour early. (The crafty old so… err Teacher.)

As I arrive home from school and go in the back door, a voice says: "What's all this about?" Mother is stood in the kitchen and she is rolling up her sleeves- a sure bad sign. "Tell me! What this is all about?" "What what's about?" "What this is about?" "What?" "This note from Miss White?" "What note?" "This note! Read it!" "Yes Mother!" I read the note. What can I do to get clear of the ca-ca. Here goes. "But I have told you about Peggy and what we say to her." "Yes! I know you have! I know you have!" "Well! If you know, why are you mad?" "Have you told me everything?" "Well! More or less." "What do you mean, more or less?" "Well! Less than more, but I still cannot understand why you are mad." "I am mad because I thought you were kidding me!" "But that would be lying Mum!" "I wish you had been lying!" "Do you mean to say that you wish I would commit sins by lying?" "No.!" "So by not lying, I told you the truth and…" Wham! Something thumps my left ear and a shrill voice shouts: "Up the dancers and don't come back down until I say so!" I think I may just have won that argument but lost the battle, but I am still up the dancers. The following day, Mother went to see Miss White and apologized to Miss Love.

Tommy as number one leader of The Crescenters (Cheers.) has called a meeting for Friday in Newall Park after tea. All Members must attend or pay a forfeit.

"Everybody here then?" "Everybody but steady Freddy!" says

a voice, "We will have to get him a watch." "That's no good! It would always be ten minutes slow! (Laughter all round.) "We will start without him. Listen everybody! I have an announcement to make." "Go on then!" "I am going on." "Going on what then?" "On your back if you don't shut up!" "Sorry Tommy!" "I should coco! I should coco!"

"Good gentle people! (That reminds me of Bill.) I have an announcement to make. Our Number Two Leader of The Crescenters First Class (Cheers.) is stepping down." (Cheers). "Now that's not very nice!" "Sorry, Tommy!" "Sorry, Allan!" "Why is he stepping down, and where is he stepping down from?" "He is stepping down from nowt." "How can he be 'stepping down' from nowt? How can he step down from summat (Something.) that isn't theer (There.)?" "Well he is leaving us! Now are you sat- isfied?" "I suppose so." "Now is that suppose so, a 'suppose' for a 'Yes suppose' or a 'No suppose'?" "It's for a 'Yes suppose'." "Now you're absolutely sure?" "I suppose so" "Well! I am glad that we have finally settled that! He feels the burden is too heavy and he is going to the Grammar School because he passed the Scholarship Exam." "Well done, Allan!" "It's a good job that he isn't a Catholic then!" says a lone voice, "Well if he had been he would never have passed! In fact he would not have been able to pass a tramcar go- ing t'other way (Going the other way.)." "Cheers mate!" "All the best Allan!" "Thank you one and all! But I will still be a member of The Crescenters First Class (Cheers.).

"Now listen good folks!" says Tommy, "We will have to elect a new Number Two Leader- any ideas?" "No!" "No nowt!" "I haven't a clue!" Etc., etc. "Well that's a big help!" says Tommy. "Could I say something?" "Of course, Allan!" "Well! When Bill knew he was going to leave, he asked you lot to elect Tommy and it was a good decision." "Too true!" says Tommy immodestly. "Well! He wanted Tommy because he always said that he had a good brain and was full of ideas." "That's true!" says a quickly swelling head Tommy. "And I will tell you something else!" "What?" "We don't swear as much since Tommy was elected! So if we get another Roman Catholic, we might stop altogether." "That's true!" says Tommy. "Well! I would like to nominate Plug Jackson." "Eh! What?" gasp I. "Who, me?" "Yes you! Unless you know of another Plug Jackson?" "No, I don't! Well not at this mo-

ment!" "Or in any other time or double time, I shouldn't wonder, right?" "Err right it is!" "That's settled then!" "That is what
Bill would have wanted had he been here to guide us on our way
along the harsh road of life."

"But that would be two Roman Catholic- number one and two
in charge, and both of them would be First Class at that," says a
solitary, moaning plaintive voice.

"So what! We still outnumber them! All in favour! Raise your
right hands! Err right hand! Freddy, not the other one!" "Sorry
Boss!" "I should coco! Err right, that's unanimous then! Plug is
elected Number Two leader, First Class. (Cheers.)"

"Why are we here then, Tommy?" "You are here because I ordered it. You are here because I propose that we go "Jerry" hunting tomorrow. (Cheers.) Meet here at nine o'clock sharp in the
morning." "Not nine o'clock blunt then?" queries young Mick.
"No! Learn to be quick and sharp and then you will be handsome!"
"Thank you, Thomas!" "You're welcome, young Michael! You're
welcome!"

Saturday morning, five minutes to nine. It's a beautiful day, the
birds are singing. There is a rookery in the trees, the rooks are
squawking and squabbling, just like some couples I know. Several
dogs prance around barking excitedly at nothing nobody knows
where they live but I suppose that they do- the dogs I mean, they
should know where they live, I suppose. "Everybody here then?"
"Yes, all here!" "Eh?" "All here!" "Are you sure?" "Sure we are,
why?" "But what, what about Steady Freddy." "All present and
correct!" "Is that really you Freddy?" "Yes, boss!" "Well, I never
thought I would live to see this day. Possibly pigs can fly back'ards
in Pudsi (Pudsey.). How did you manage it?" "Our lad gave me
his old watch and he said it kept perfect time, but the Church
clock has just struck nine and my watch says ten past." "Full marks
to your brother then, for having it ten minutes fast this time- and
any other time." "I suppose so!" says Freddy.

"Before we set off, you should have: a large pop bottle of
coloured water (Goodness knows what went into some of the bottles to colour the water! Better not to ask!); at least two doorsteps,
and, a napple. Any body who has not got a napple will pay a forfeit
or they can obtain said item from me on terms to be agreed right?
Have you all got your catapults? (A catapult has a "Y" shaped

handle with two lengths of rubber attached. A leather pocket joins the rubbers together. In the right hands, a deadly weapon! Let's not forget the <u>left</u> handers!) Has everybody got their ammunition then?" (This would be small stones or marbles. Probably this is where the term: 'Lost your marbles.' comes from.) "Yes!" "Yep!" "Got 'em!" "All correct Tommy!"

Tommy reckons it is about seven miles to Clifton (Probably about two.). We have been trekking about five minutes. At the top of Carr Bank, Tommy calls a halt: "Good weary travellers! We will stop here for ten minutes for drinks." "How will we know when ten minutes is up?" "We will ask Steady Freddy." "Oh, sorry Tommy! I forgot about the watch!" "You would forget your head if it wasn't tightly screwed on!" "Sorry Tommy!" "I should coco!"

I will have one good swig. That will leave plenty. It's nice here: the peewits (Lapwings.) are wheeling and diving with <u>that</u> plaintiff cry- as though they are sad and unhappy. Somewhere in the hazy blue sky, two skylarks are singing. Half a dozen miserable looking cows wander over to the fence to gaze at the weary travellers. One or two are making comments about us but I can't understand what they are lowing about.

I am shaken out of my reverie by... "The first to spot a Skylark gets a swig from all the other bottles," shouts Tommy. "Right!" "Done! "O.K!" "What if one person spots two Skylarks?" "What do you think?" "<u>Two</u> swigs then!" "Correct!" says Tommy. All eyes toward Heaven. Nobody's spotted owt so far. "How are we doing for time, Freddy?" "One minute to go!" "Well!" says Tommy, "It looks as if they have beaten us! Oh look! There's one of them!" "Where?" "I can't see owt!" "Nor me!" "Are you sure?" "Sure I'm sure! <u>Can't</u> you see it Plug?" As I turn to answer Tommy, he winks. "Oh yes!" I cry. "I can see both of them!" There is a lot of moaning and groaning but number one and two Leaders First Class got their swigs.

Clifton Lane End- another stop timed by Freddy. I will have another good swig. Ah, that's better! I have still got half a bottle left. "Right lads! Move off into the killing-fields!" We leap over the dry stonewall (Can you build a 'dry-stone wall' when it's raining?) and crouch on the other side. "Steady men! Be very cautious!" whispers our leader. "Enemy spotted Tommy!" "Where?" "Over that wall to the right." "They've gone!" "Gone where?" "I don't know!" "They must have spotted us!" "O.K! that's it then, break for grub and drinks."

This is great! Life in the wild and under an open sky with a full gut. Tommy orders anybody who wants a slash to go to the wall- and get it done with dignity. "Any member who needs to crap will go <u>over</u> the wall and crap with dignity- and decorum." I don't know what 'decorum' means and I don't think that Tommy does either. (I think that he must have been at one of his Mother's books again.) "But any gang member who does not crap with dignity and decorum will be in deep, deep ca-ca." (Whoops!)

The sun still shines. Peewits are giving us a flying lesson: wheeling and diving at us. They must have a nest near by. A skylark high in the clear blue sky, wings trembling and singing its heart out. Its full of happiness. "Look! There's a hare!" "Where?" "There!" "By gum! He's a big un!" "Look lads!" I cry, "There's a curlew beginning its glide in." "Where?" "There!" "Oh, aye! Now I see it!" The bird is on a long slow glide; it is calling 'Coor-wee'. As it nears the ground, its call quickens, and lengthens: 'Coor-wee! Coorweee! cooorweeee! It reaches terra firma. As it disappears amongst the gorse bushes, its call ceases. (I think that I have said something like this before. I think... Old age mate! Old age!)

Well! I have got just under a quarter of my drink left. Shall I save it? Might as well. Oh, I don't know! Glug! Glug! All gone! I thought it would have lasted all day. Ah well! "Everybody ready then?" All slashes and craps done?" "No Boss!" "What do you mean: 'No Boss!'?" "We are one Crapper short!"" "Who's missing then?" "It's young Mark!" "How long are you going to .be young Marcus?" calls our leader. "Only half a mo Boss!" "He's been over the wall for two minutes and twenty five seconds," calls Freddy, "according to my watch." "Is that allowing for it being ten minutes fast?" "Err hang on! Err, just give me a sec. (Second.) or two to work it out! Yes Boss! Just coming up to three minutes!" "I think Mark must be marking time! Get it lads? Marking time? Oh forget it!" "He is probably making his mark on the field," says I.

"Well! Glory Be! Here he is at last! Come on Slashers, and Crappers! Off we go!" We crouch by the wall. Tommy carefully raises his head to have a gander (No, not a 'goose' but a 'gander': a look.). "Wait!" whispers Tommy. "They are over this wall in the next field! When I give the order, we go over this wall and get at

'em! But mind you! Don't land in any crap left by certain members
of The Crescenters (Very muffled cheers- or may be groans.)"

The order comes: "Over the wall and at 'em! Go! Go! Go! Go!"
We go: guns blazing- well pop bottles blazing away. "We've got
'em! Round up the survivors!" "Are we going to shoot them or
take them prisoner?" says Basil, the gang's youngest member. "We
will vote on it. Young Basil! Keep 'em covered!" "Right Boss!"

Tommy climbs and stands on top of the wall. In a loud commanding voice he says: "Now men! This operation has been highly
successful. They have four dead and we have taken three prisoners. We will put it to the vote." "To vote what?" "What we are
going to do with these three?" "You're going to leave my ruddy
sheep alone!" shouts a very loud, gruff voice. Oh lor! It's Farmer
Longfield!

Tommy, true leader that he is, leads the route back to the wall-
avoiding the crap as he takes the wall better than any Derby winner. As he disappears, he gives an almighty 'Hoowerr!" I vault
the wall to see Tommy clutching his left leg- as he runs round
in a rough circle. "What's up mate?" "Av brock mi leg! Av brock
mi leg!" (I have broken my leg.) "You can't run with a brocken
leg!" "I can if I want! It's my blood... err blinking brocken leg!"
"Whoa! Stop! I think old Longfield has bugg... err gone." says I.
Tommy hobbles to where we are grouped. "You can't walk on a
broken leg, Tommy!" says Freddy. "Look mate! It's my leg and if
it's my brocken leg! I can do what I want with it, right?" "Right?"
"Right Boss!"

"What happened, mate?" "I knocked a stone loose as I went
over the wall, and it landed on my leg." "Lay still, Tommy!" "Yes!
Err yes, I will, Plug! You take over as number one leader." "Are
you sure?" "Sure I'm sure! Well, as long as you are sure?" "I am
sure! I assure you!" "Right!" says I. "Well! I am sure glad, we have
sorted that out." "Are you sure?" "Sure! I'm... Oh don't start that
again!" "Right Boss!" "I'm not your Boss! You are!" "Awe right!"

"Right!" says Tommy who has done some First Aid. "We will
have to splint it! You lot go find two branches or something."
Tommy's leg is duly splinted, bound by a belt and a pair of braces-
that leaves two gang members having problems in maintaining
their dignity and decorum. I won't tell you who they are but they
are not happy campers today.

"Right lads! Who's bogey is working?" "Err not mine!" "Our lad's got ours." "Axle's broken on mine." "Well! That's a great help! Not one workable bogey amongst the lot of us!" "Err, Tommy!" "Yes lad?" "My bogey is O.K." "That's more like it! Get off home and get it!" "Am not goin on mi orn! (By myself.)!" says Basil. "Of course you're not! Eeny, Meeny, Miney Mo! Catch a Kraut by the toe!" "Right then! Mark go with him!" "Off you go lads!" encourages our wounded, temporary ex-leader, "And don't be long."

What's a bogey? Some of you may ask. Basically, it's a plank of wood, mounted usually on four pram wheels, sometimes the wheels would be of various sizes- this could cause problems of varying degrees, if you see what I mean. The cross-piece at the front swivels for steering. It has a detachable box fitted so that groceries, coal, coke, etc, fish, and chips, and manure can be transported. You might ask: "Are you sure about the manure?" Sure I am sure! The bogey can be pulled along with a piece of rope or old clothesline, or propelled with one foot, whilst kneeling on the bogey.

"I've got an idea whilst we are waiting." "What idea, Tommy?" "Well, has anybody got any water left? Good! We will have a competition to see which tastes best." "That's a good idea, Tommy." "Yes, I know, and I will be the judge. I will give a napple to the winner." "Why should you be the judge?" "I should be the judge because I am wounded, right?" "Right! But you aren't the leader I am!" "Well I am taking over again! Right- O K.?" "I suppose so." "Is that 'suppose' a 'Yes' or a 'No' then?" "It's a Yes, Tommy!" "Are you sure it's a Yes?" "I suppose so!" "I declare the winner is err,,, myself." "Yourself! How do you make that out?" "Because mine tastes the best, any objections?" (Silence.) "I should coco!"

"How long have they been gone?" "Err, sixty two and a half minutes," says steady Freddy. "Is that allowing for your watch being ten minutes fast then?" "Err, hang on! Just give me a sec. to sort it out." "Come on then! How long?" "Err, about fifty two and a half minutes." "That's more like it!" says Tommy, "We have waited long enough! Let's make tracks!" We have gone about fifty yards. Tommy says "I can't walk with this lot on! Its hurting like Elephants! Let's get it off!" "How are you feeling now?" "Not too bad mate! Let's get to the road!"

We trudge down past Clifton Lane End. "Here comes the rescue party!" calls I. "About ruddy time too! Where have you been?" "You know where! We've been home! That's where we've been! So why are you asking?" "You've been a long time!" "I thought your leg was brock!" "It was!" says Tommy, "But the splints mended it." "Awe right!" "But as I am still wounded, I commandeer this vehicle, and elect Plug to be my minder! Right! Err right?" "Err, I suppose so! Err right, Tommy!" So Tommy and I take the bogey. We leave orders to meet at the Ivy Cottage with empty pop bottles. From Clifton Top to the Shop it's all downhill.

Finally the rest of the gang appears. We all get a penny back on each empty bottle. We pool the cash and buy sweets that are shared out as Tommy says: "Fairly and equally." Tommy gets first choice for being wounded. Something my Mother taught me:

> Up yon hill a long way off.
> The wind it blew mi billycock off.
> Ah picked it up an away ah ran
> Ter see mi Aunt Sar' Anne.
> Aunt Sar' Anne, she was not in
> Ah went tert barber for a pin.
> The barber said, "If thar's not off
> Al cut thi whiskers reet slap off
> Up in a balloon lads, up in a balloon,
> Mi Father kicked mi art o bed,
> Cos there wasn't room.
> Ah kicked mi Father,
> Mi Father kicked me,
> Reet intert pig sty.
> The pigs bit me,
> What dya think ah did lads?
> What dya think ah did?
> Ah upset cradle,
> Ant nearly killt the kid,
> Awer dogs belly ache
> Awer cat's deead.
> Awer dog'st belly ache,
> Reet tat top o hed.

"The cheeky buggars,! shouts Dad, as he listens to the wireless. "Language, Father!" chides Mum. It's May, 1940. Dad is working locally moving troops by bus and coach. (He can get home most nights.) "What's up, Father?" It's just been on the News that the cheeky bug... err blighters have gone round the Maginot Line." "What's the 'Maginot Line' then?" enquires Mum. "The 'Maginot Line' was built by the Froggies, err the French..." (Building started in 1928. It extended from Northern France to the French Alps in the South, as a defence against Germany and Italy. Briefly, it consisted of concrete and steel being sunk into the ground to withstand the heaviest artillery fire etc. Bunkers provided shelter from enemy attack. It was self sufficient for about a month.) "The Germans have the Siegfried Line haven't they, Dad?" "Yes! The bugg... err the blighters have."

We,re going to hang out the washing on the Siegfried
Line,
Have you any dirty washing Mother dear?
We're going to hang out the washing on the Siegfried
Line,
If the Siegfried Line's still there.
Whether the weather be wet or fine,
We'll roll along without a care.
We're going to hang out the washing on the Siegfried
Line,
If the Siegfried Line's still there.

"That doesn't sound fair," says Mum. "It isn't blood... err blinking fair!" fumes Dad. "You'd think the Jerries would have agreed to fight the Ma... the... the... Magi... the 'Maginot Line'." "Thanks Dad!" says Mick, "You would have thought that they would have agreed to fight there- so that the Maginot Line got used," says Dad. "Well!! Why didn't they move the line?" "Nay Mother! It's static." "What's 'static'?" "'Static' is electricity, Mum," says I. "Well! If they had a line and electricity, I don't see why they couldn't move it!" "Nay Mother!" "How much did it cost, this line then?" "Thousands! Err millions of pounds!" "Well Father! If it cost all that money, surely they could have had it on wheels!" "Well they didn't and they haven't! And the sneaky buggars have gone round it!"

This was the only time I heard my Father swear. Years later, I mentioned this. He told me he did swear a lot. (He was a very good footballer as a young man- when his leg would allow.) One day, he scored a goal and he celebrated vocally. The referee said to him: 'You've a ruddy good right foot that could take you far but you've a bad foul mouth that will get you nowhere.' Apart from the Maginot incident, he never swore again, as far as I know. Well! I never heard him- and that's the truth.

The Germans <u>did</u> avoid the Line and swept through France. A few weeks later as we sat down to tea, Dad says, "Things don't look too good lass." "Have you got the sack, Dad?" asks Mick. "No lad! It could be worse than that." "What could be worse than that? What could be worse than being on the dole?" Hail Mary! I start to recite mentally. As I get to: 'Is with thee.' Dad says: "Them Jerries have knocked hamlet out of (Given a good beating to...) our lot. Our armies are trapped on the beaches at Dunkirk." "That's in Scotland," says Mick. "How do you mean in Scotland?" "Well mum! We have had a Jog...err, Jog..." "You mean 'Geography'," says I. "That's right! We have had.... err, a what you just said lesson." "Geography." "Yes! Geography!" "Anyhow! What makes you think Dunkirk is in Scotland, young fella?" "Well for a start! Scotland must be abroad, because it said on the wireless, they were going to evacuate Dunkirk. Will we get a load of kids, err, evacuees, Dad?" "No son! They will be evacuating soldiers. But back to this Scotland business. How do you figure Dunkirk is in Scotland?" "Well! Miss Johnson showed us a map and I saw Dunbarton, Dumfries and Falkirk. I didn't see Dunkirk, but Miss Johnson says there are a lot of 'kirks' in Scotland." We now call Mick 'Thick Mick' or ' Wrong End of the Stick, Mick.'.

The successful evacuation of Dunkirk was a miracle thanks to boats large and small; service-boats and private vessels, and, their brave crews of Service and Civilian personnel

"Peter Jackson! Come up to the front of the class to receive your prize." "Yes Miss White!" We have been competing in the Inter Schools Athletics. I am the only prizewinner: a propelling pencil for coming first in the Hundred Yards Race.

"Give Peter Jackson a good round of applause for winning." Two or three pairs of hands are reluctantly brought together. "Come on! You can do better than that!" (I am stood like a spare-part-grinning sheepishly. I poke my finger in my left ear hole: funny now it's started to itch all at once- at the same time as my hooter (Nose.) "If you can't clap better than that, you will all stay in at play time and read." That's done the trick! The Victor receives his accolade.

It is not surprising, with 3 female teachers, we got no coaching whatever in Cricket, Football or Athletics. We had no sporting facilities or equipment: just a couple of old bats; a set of pivoted wickets for the playground, and, one football- usually flat at the bottom side. At play time, Tommy says, "I've got an idea." "What idea?" "We will have our own competition." "What sort of competition?" "I will tell you tomorrow. Pass it round! Everybody to come early in the morning and we'll sort it out."

Tuesday morning- quarter to nine. "Everybody here then?" "Everybody except Steady Freddy." "Well, he is always late! I thought he had a watch which is ten minutes fast." "He has lost it," says Mark. "I am not surprised! He would lose his nut if it wasn't glued on!" Steady Freddy as you may have gathered was not the world's best at time keeping. He had two gears: slow and stop. He was always about five minutes late for everything. "What's your excuse this morning?" Miss White would ask as Freddy, zombie-like, entered the classroom. Freddy had a list of excuses such as:

"What's your excuse today?"	"Ear ache, Miss."
"Late again?"	"Arm ache, Miss."
Ditto	"Couldn't find my boots Miss.
Ditto	"Clock stopped Miss."
Ditto	"Leg ache Miss."
Ditto	"Stomach ache Miss."

"And why are you late this morning?" "Heart ache Miss." "Tell me about it," says Miss White, "I don't know what you will be when you grow up!" "Maybe a clock maker," says I. "He would make a good Doctor," says Tommy. "Why a Doctor Thomas?" "Well Miss! He seems to know every part of the human body and what it feels like when it's aching. He would be very good at knowing how poorly people felt, and where." "Quite! Err quite! Now let's gets on!" Good old Freddy!

"Right then! I propose we have a competition of our own." "What competition?" "We will have a piss up." "A what?" I gasp. "Are you deaf? I said we will have a piss up." "We can't drink beer, Tommy!" I plead, "And I don't see the point."

"Miners can't drink beer either," says Mick. "Why not?" "Well it was in the paper that two miners had been caught with a bottle of Guinness and it was ill... err illee..." "Do you mean 'illegal'?" begs Tommy. "Yes! That's it!" "Well! Thick Mick! Or as some would say: wrong end of the stick thick Mick! You are talking about 'minors' who are kids but 'miners' are coalminers, right!" "Awe right!" says Mick. "That's summat else that arr have learnt terday."

"Who's talking about beer?" "You are!" "No I am not!" "But you just said 'Piss... Err ah! I think I know what you might mean: you're talking about 'slashing'! Right?" "By Jove! I think he's got it at last!" "Do we have to drink our own pee?" asks young Mick. "No! That's disgusting!" "Sorry Tommy! But I think they did in the Bible." "Well! Just because they might have, doesn't mean to say that us civilized lot have to." "Sorry Tommy!" "I should coco!" says Tommy. "Can we get on now thick Mick, or very thick Mick." "Yes Tommy!" "Thank you!"

"Tommy! Have you got a minute?" "What is now?" "I don't like you calling my brother 'Thick Mick' in public. (This is the first time I have really questioned the leader's authority. My throat is tightening; there seems to be a shortage of air and I think I am getting stomach ache.) I don't mind you calling him 'Thick Mick' in private but not in public," says I- gasping a little and already regretting the situation. "Tell you what Plug! I will make a public announcement." "Listen everybody! Before the bell goes, I have an announcement, a <u>very</u> public announcement." "Get on with it then!" "Right! I will." "Go on then!" "Right I will if certain people will let me!" "Let you what?" "Let me get on with what I want to get on with.... That's the bell! Meet here in the morning eight forty five am, right?" "Right!" "O.K. will do!"

Wednesday 8.45 am. "Everybody here?" "Yes! " "What everybody?" "Yes everybody!" "What you mean is everybody except Steady Freddy." "No! I am here boss!" What are <u>you</u> doing here?"

"Waiting for news of this piss up." "How did you manage to get here early? Have you found your ticker? (Watch.)" "No! My Mum got me up early and told me that I was late." "Well! I bet the pigs are flying backwards in Pudsi this fine morning! Anyhow! Glad you could make it." "Thanks Boss!" "You're welcome!"

"Well! I am glad that's settled. Now we don't want to waste another morning. First: this very public announcement. Ahem! Hmm!" Tommy clears his throat. "Good gentle people, listen! In future, young Mick, known as: 'Thick Mick', or, 'Very Thick Mick' (Tommy is punishing me for challenging him,), or, 'Wrong End of the Stick Very Thick Mick'. In future Thick Mick can be known as: "Thick Mick'; 'Quick Mick', or, 'Slick Quick', or, 'Thick Slick Mick'." "Traitor!" I gasp to myself. "But in future, anybody calling Thick Mick, or anything Thick Mick does not want to be called will answer to me. Is that understood?" "Yes!" "O.K!" "Right!" "Yep!" "Right then! Thick Mick! <u>What</u> do <u>you</u> want to be called?" "Err, 'Young Mick'." "Right then! Thick Mick is now Young Mick." "Right Thick Mick?" "Right Boss!"

"Now about this piss-up! We will have a competition to see who can piss highest up the piss-hole wall." "That's not fair!" says Mark. "What's not fair?" "Well you and your mates are bigger than us and you can pee higher." "Point taken! Point taken young Mark! We will mark two lines on this wall here. Those below the bottom line are Group A; those between the lines are in Group B and anybody taller than the top line shall be in Group C. How's that sound? All in agreement raise your right hand. Right hand Freddy! Not the other one!" "Sorry Boss!" "I should coco! That's unanimous. We will have the competition tonight, after school."

"The rules are simple. You can drink as much as you want up to a quarter to four. The winner in each group will get a napple off the others. If there are six in a group, the winner will receive five apples, right?" "Right!" "O.K!" "That's fair!" "Yep!" "Any questions?" "Yes, Tommy! I have a question." "Spit it out young Mark!" "Well! Can us young ones call it a 'pee up' instead of a 'piss up'?" "You can call it what you want: a 'piss up'; a 'peanut'; a 'peacock'… Well! Maybe not 'a peacock'!" "I think we would all like to call it a 'pee up'." "Right young Mark! A 'pee up' it is." "That's the bell lads! In we go."

"May I leave the room Miss?" "But you have only just come in."

says Miss White. "Can I go for a drink of water Miss?" "But you have just drunk your milk." "I have left my glasses in the porch Miss." "Oh! Go get them." "Thanks Miss!" I thought she might have twigged but teaching different classes in one room is more than a full time job.

Lunch time. "Gather round," says Tommy. "What's up now?" "Nothing's up now! But I think drinking all this water is a waste of time." "Why?" "Why? Because we are drinking all this water, and we are pissing or peeing it, as young Mark would say. We are peeing it out before time, agreed?" "Agreed!" "Well! I propose, we only drink between three and four o'clock. All those in favour?... That's unanimous then."

There were two water closets; the urinal was open-aired. A trough and a smooth wall with a rusty pipe running the length of the troug. It would occasionally wake up: the pipe flushed as though it was very tired, and struggled into life about every ten minutes. "Right then lads! Young uns to go first!" "Why us first?" "Why you lot first? I'll tell you why you lot first." "Go on! Tell us!" "Right! I will then!" "Go on then!"

"Right! I will go on! You lot go first because if the tallest go first, we will wet the wall and then you young uns wouldn't be able to mark it, would you Mark? Do you get it, Mark? Mark 'marks' it? Oh never mind!" "O.K! We go first." "Thank you young Mark," says Tommy. "Right lads! Go! Go! Go!" "Some did; some couldn't and a couple wouldn't. "Come on you lot! Give them a big cheer!"

"Stop this at once!" says a very loud, almost shrieking voice. " Stop this at once I say!" "Yee Gods! It's Miss White!" (She has twigged or someone has snitched.) Some could; some couldn't stop; some tried to hide their embarrassment. "Everybody back into school! Immediately!" says one very irate lady. When Miss White is mad at something, she stands; leans forward- hands on hips and glares over her specs. When she walks, she still leans forwards and stamps flat-footed- like she is crushing eggs. As we troop across the playground, Miss White is certainly crushing eggs today.

We are made to stand at the desks in the top room. "All those under ten years of age and anybody who has not made their first Communion, go home. The rest of you say a prayer, and be ashamed of yourselves!" We stand and wait, nothing happens. Half an hour passes, still nothing. Miss White hasn't uttered a word to us. She whispered something to Miss Love, who put her hand and coat on and disappeared.

Some obviously wanted to go to the toilet but dare not ask. We try to relax and forget about pissing in any shape or form. "I think she is going to keep us in for an hour," whispers Tommy from the corner of his mouth. "I think you're right!" I whisper from the opposite mouth corner. "But I do not think that I can hold out that long." "Hard cheese mate!" says my very good friend.

"You two can stay behind for half an hour each day next week for talking." How the elephants did she know we were talking. She must have a gift. "And you will sluice the toilets each day," says this angry lady. Oh no! It can't be! A figure has just passed the window, the same window I slung the ball through and clobbered Miss White. Now I know where Miss Love went. "Did, you see that Tommy?" I whisper. "Yes! Shut up, or we will be kept in for the rest of this year!

In walks Father Dean. He is a tallish, thinish, oldish manish… err man dressed all in blackish… err black except for a whitish… err white Dog Collar. He always wears a high huge trilby hat, black of course, otherwise he could not be dressed all in black-ish… err black, could he? He reminds me of a Cowboy, (Wyatt Earp perhaps.). He carries a big walking stick, possibly it's a rifle in disguise, or a punishing cane specially grown to make it fit for purpose. Miss White leaves the room. Today, he and his stick, rifle or purpose grown cane, look a lot bigger. He slowly looks round the room, stops and gazes out of <u>that</u> window for quite a while. Slowly his head turns back to the centre and he leans back. He seems to be studying the ceiling. His lips are quivering- just like us when trying not to laugh. I think he is going to smile. No! I must be wrong because we are in deep ca-ca. I catch Tommy's eye. A slight shrug of his shoulders: a wry smile and a furtive thumbs up and then palms towards the heavens. Tommy seems to be tak-ing things quite well; I feel sick.

Father Dean clears his throat. I think he is looking at each of us individually. His gaze moves left to right, does a slow full sweep back to the left and works its way back to the centre. "Ahem! Mm! Err, every boy will kneel; bow their heads and put their hands together. Close your eyes and say after me: I must not abuse my bodily functions in an indecent manner. Say it now!" We hesitatingly comply. "And I am heartily sorry." "And I am heartily sorry." "Again! Louder!" commands Father Dean. "And I am heartily sorry!" "And again!" "We are heartily sorry!" shout the penitents. "You will now say: three Our Fathers; three Hail Marys and a Glory Be to the Father, and, make a good Act of Contrition." (Oh my God! I am sorry!) "And try to keep yourselves clean of mind and body."

Father Dean stalks out of the room. I still think he could manage a smile but I must be wrong. A sigh of relief spreads through the repenters. "That wasn't too bad, was it?" says Tommy. "Not too bad!" says I. "I'll tell you what," says young Mick. "What?" "I think it's a lot better idea to have a group confession rather than one to one with Father Dean." "You're right there, young Mick! You're right." "And, it would save him and us a lot of time and trouble." "I think I have heard something like that before! Right Plug?" "Right Tommy!"

"Oh Tommy!" "Yes!" "When we were waiting for Father Dean to punish us, or whatever, you smiled and gave me a thumbs- up. You did not seem to be too bothered." "Well! I wasn't bothered at all." "Why not?" "Just stop and think about it." "About what?" "Well! What was the worst thing Father Dean could have done?" "Err, well err." "Would he have hit us with his stick?" "No, of course not." "Would he kick you up the arse?" "No!" "Tell our parents?" "Well! Maybe." "If he did, what would they do?" "Well they would give us a clip round the ear hole. We would get the rounds of the kitchen and sent up the dancers. Oh! And they might dock our pocket money!" "Right!" says Tommy. "And none of that lot would be the end of the world, would it?" "No! I suppose you're right." "Course I am."

I learnt a valuable lesson that day: if things go wrong, rather than panic or react impulsively, if you stop and think about the situation what can be the worst scenario and can I cope? If you can say: 'Yes, I think I can. Things could be a lot worse and there are a lot of people a darned sight worse off then me.' Then you can cope. "Thanks Tommy!"

I think I am falling in love with Peggy, err Miss Love, but I must be very careful. I have been let down by one Peggy, or

Peggy Stick, as Tommy called her, but this Peggy is different. I am sure she wouldn't let a bloke down. Peggy, I must call her Peggy, 'Miss Love' sounds too far away. Well! My Peggy is a bit taller than me! She has lovely fair hair, as my Mum would say: "Not a brash 'Suicide Blonde'," (Dyed by her own hand!). Like that other Peggy person: she is very slim and has sort of green, blue eyes. She wears nice dresses. As Tommy would say, "She doesn't mind showing a little bit of leg." (I don't know what's the matter with Tommy: he seems to have a thing about Peggy's legs.) Peggy usually wears stockings with a line down the back and her shoes have higher heels than the other teachers. I have had a decko (Look.) at the other teachers' legs and some of them remind me of baby elephants. I think that Tommy could be on to something after all. I think she loves me but will not admit to it. When I catch her eyes they seem to sparkle and she sometimes gives me a little smile. It must always be our secret smile.

Christmas is approaching. We are decorating our classroom. We are not allowed to go up the stepladder, so my love, Peggy, has to climb up. I hope she will be very careful, and not have an accident. Three or four of us older boys, being gentlemen, take it in turns to hold the steps. I know Tommy does it to see a bit more leg, I don't know about the others maybe I am the only gentleman amongst us.

It's my turn again to keep my Peggy safe. I grip the steps tightly. A quick glance upwards to make sure she is alright. "Oh heck!" I whisper. "What's up?" whispers Tommy. "Nowt," says I. "There must be!" "No! There's nowt up! It's your turn Tommy." "But you've not had your full whack yet mate." "It doesn't matter! You take over!" "Please Miss! May I go to get a drink of water?" I want to get away and hide my red-hot flushing blushing cheeks.

Tommy calls next morning for school. "Now come clean, mate! Something upset you yesterday, didn't it?" "Err, yes, I suppose so." "Is that 'suppose so' a Yes or a No?" says Tommy with a big grin. "No! Don't joke Tommy! My 'suppose' is a Yes." "Come on then mate! Out with it!" "Well! If I do tell you, promise you will keep it a secret, promise?" "Course mate! Cross my heart! Spit on my right hand and wipe it on my shirt sleeve and hope to die!" "Right then! When I was holding the steps for Miss Love…" "'Miss Love'! What's gone wrong with Peggy then?" "I want to

call her 'Miss Love'! Right?" "All right then! When you were
holding the steps for Miss Love?" "When I was holding the steps
for Miss Love, I looked up to see if she was O.K." "But I always
look up all the time," says Tommy, "otherwise I wouldn't stand
there like a spare part!" "Can I go on?" "Yes go on!" "Well, when
I glanced up, I saw... err... err... I saw..." "Well! What did you
'saw'? A piece of wood?" "No! Idiot! I err saw... Well! I saw Miss
Love's pants." "Oh heck!" says Tommy, "You saw Peggy's pants?"
"No!" "But you just said you did!" insists Tommy. "Well yes! I saw
Miss Love's pants and it did not seem right. I felt a bit upset! Do
you understand Tommy?" "Of course I do mate! I would feel the
same if I saw her pants." "Not 'her' Tommy! Not 'her'! But Miss
Love!" "Right Plug! Miss Love it is. So what do you want to do?"
"Well! I want Miss Love to be treated with respect." "Right mate!"
says Tommy, "Leave it to me."

Next morning 8.45 am. "Gather round everybody! I have an
announcement to make. Hmm! Hmm! From today, it has been
decided that Miss Love, known as 'Peggy Love'; 'Peggy' or 'Leggy
Peggy', or, 'Leggy Peggy Love' will be treated with respect and
decorum. (There he goes again.)" "What's brought this on," says
young Mark. "You don't want to know, mate! You just don't want
to know!" "But I do want to know! Don't we lads?" "Yes! We
do!" "Too true!" "Yes!" "Come on out with it!" "Well! Hard
luck! You're too young to know and as your Leader, I order you to
forget it. Right?" " Right!" "O.K!" "You're the Boss!" "I should
co-co!" "From today! Miss Love will be called 'Miss Love' with
respect and decorum nothing else." "That's a long name," says
Mark. "What is?" "'Miss Love with respect and decorum, and
nothing else'." (Lots of laughter.) "Young Mark!" "Yes!" "Would
you like a knuckle-sandwich?" (A clenched fist punch.) "No!"
"Then shut your cakehole! (Mouth.)" "Yes Boss!"

"Tommy," says young Mick. "Could I have a word?" "Of
course," so Mick whispers into Tommy's ear. "Hang on! I have a
P.S." "Not another piss up!" moans Brian. "No! Not another piss
up! This is a P.S." "What's a 'P.S.'?" asks Brian. "It sounds very
close to piss to me." "It's a word with one eye and one ess missing.
So you're wrong! It's nothing to do with a piss up." "Well! What
does it mean Tommy?" "I don't know. "So you're going to tell us
about something you don't know owt about then?" "Err yes! Err

no!" "Make your mind up!" says Brian. "I still have a knuckle-sandwich left if you would like one." "No thanks, Boss!"

"Now listen good folk to this P.S. before the bell goes!" "Goes where?" "Shut up and listen! I have just been informed by young Mick, formerly known as 'Thick Mick', 'Slick Mick', 'Slick' or 'Quick Slick Mick', (Tommy's having another go at me!) or 'Wrong end of the Stick Thick Mick', he wishes to be known as 'Young Plug'. All who agree- raise their hand." "Which hand?" "Any blankerty hand you want! But only one hand each." The bell sounds. As we cross the playground Tommy calls out, "Are you happy not to be called: 'Thick Mick', 'Young Mick', or, 'Double Thick Mick'?" (He just can't help it, can he?)

As we finished School that teatime, we passed through Miss Love's classroom. We both said, "Goodnight Miss Love!" She smiled a lovely smile and a sweet voice said quietly, "Thank you Thomas! Thank you Peter!"

Tommy and I are still delivering orders: coke; fish, etc. and chips, and manure. Mrs. Pepper has given me a tin of pears and a tin of corned beef from under the counter. It was a case of 'who you knew' but we had to pay for them of course probably over the odds. We had a good basic diet and nobody needed to go hungry- but those little treats from 'under the counter" made all the difference.

Clothes and shoes were rationed; trousers lost their turn-ups. As Mum said, "They only harbour muck anyrode." Jackets were all single-breasted to save cloth. Clothes were called 'Utility, items. I recall I had a pair of new shoes. One Sunday night, I walked from a Cinema in Shipley, about four or five miles to Harry Ramsden's (A Fish Restaurant.) at White Cross, Guiseley- and my right sole had a hole in it.

> Who's that walking down the street?
> It's Mrs. Simpson and her sweaty feet.
> She's been married twice before,
> Now she's knocking on Teddy's door.
> Oh! Oh! Oh! Oh!

Just one week to Christmas. We will all get good presents this year: Dad is away ferrying troops and making good money. (Well it's all 'good money'- ain't it? Mum has a part-time cleaning job. She quit her first job because her employers expected her to supply: a mop; bucket; dusters and cleaning materials- and she was working for a pittance. Mum is only four foot summat but when upset or annoyed, her sleeves and dander go up. She told her first, very short-term employer, what they could do with their job and where to stuff their money! I wonder if it was 'arse' or 'bum'? Ah! I remember now! It was 'Gee...arr! Don't ask me where that came from. She is happy in her present job- cleaning for a widow lady. When she has finished her tasks, they sit, eat, drink and gossip. Mum says she is more of a companion than an employee.

So back to one week before Christmas then. "That's the ten to eight bus," says Mum, as the 'Newall Flyer' stops and starts and fades away round the Crescent- where the Tiger and spooked horses run and gallop. The horses do the galloping and the Tiger does the running. "Dad will be on it," says young Plug. "No, I am afraid not! Your Father is in Coventry, at least that where he thought he was going." "He must be lonely in Coventry." "Why Michael?" "Because no one will speak to him if he has been sent to Coventry!"

The front door slams; the room door opens and Dad barges in and knocks over the Christmas tree. The lights splutter and splatter, and, the fallen tree bursts into flames. (This year we can afford an artificial tree not an orphan from Farnley Wood.) Panic! "Switch it off!" "Be careful!" "I've got it! O.K. now!" Cries of fear turn to tears of joy- Dad's home! "How have you managed to get home, Father?" "Well! I got on a train then a bus and... Sorry only joking lass but I couldn't resist it! Well, Mother! I haven't been feeling too good for a week or two." "You never said in your letters." "Well! I did not want to worry you." "How long are you home for?" "About five foot eight I should think!" says Mick "Be quiet our Michael! And let your Dad get a word in edgeways!" gently scolds Mum, "Well! I am home until I am better." "That's very generous and trusting of them." "Yes it is Mother! But they know who's who and those that malinger." "Well Father! That is wonderful now we can spend Christmas together as a family."

We had very few holidays. Those we did have would be to stay with relatives. We never had a holiday with Mum and Dad together. If he was on the dole, we could not afford to. If Dad was working, he worked so long and hard. He never could afford time off except for Christmas and maybe Easter. One of the best holidays I had was with one of my Aunties. We spent two weeks on a farm in Suffolk with relatives.

"Are you feeling any better?" "Not much!" "Well I think you should go see the Doctor!" "You're right Mother! I will!" Dad toddles off. He is away about an hour and a half. As he enters the sitting room, Mum says, "What did the Doc. say then?" "Well Mother! He gave me this medicine and a Sicknote." "What does it say then?" "Well! It says I am 'idle'." "Idle! Are you sure? That can't be right!" "It says I have 'Lazyitis!. I have not got a lazy bone in my body! I can't understand it!" "Let's have a look Father." Dad passes the offending note to Mum. Mum reads the Sicknote; her head goes from side to side: "Ha! Ha! Ha! Ha!" and her eyes lift towards heaven. "What's wrong Mother?" "Nay Father! You are! It doesn't say 'Lazyitis'– it's 'Laryngitis'!" "Ha! Ha! Oh! Oh! Dad's home!"

Tommy and I decide to go the Park way home. We ride through the Park (Shouldn't do really!) and dump our carrier bikes (Both are Spitfires today!) on the path near the weir. Below is a large flat rock. By climbing over the low wall and hanging by the fingertips, one can drop onto the rock then use other stepping-stones to reach the riverbank lower down stream. Tommy goes first, unfortunately, he grazes his forehead on the stone wall as he drops. He lands on the rock- a bit bloodied.

"Are you O.K. mate?" "Yes!" "Can you make it to the bank?" "Yes! No problem! But I've nowt to put in!" "Put in what?" "I've no money to put in the Bank!" (Tommy can still joke.)"Join the club mate!" says I. Tommy reaches the river bank. "Let's have a look." There is a gash above his right eye and it is gently bleeding. "My mother will kill me!" wails Tommy. "No she won't! Well she won't! But she will get the old bu... err... the old man to execute me when he comes home." "No she won't!" "Why not?" "Well! Tell your mother that I accidentally pushed you, you fell and hurt your forehead." "That's a brilliant idea Plug!" "Yes, I know it is." "Thanks Plug! But... " "But what?" "You will have to confess to a lie when you go to Confession on Saturday." "No, I won't!" "Why not?" "Not if you confess to two lies." "You're learning Plug! You're learning!"

The war came a bit closer today. "That's a Dornier!" shouts Tommy. "No it isn't! It's a Heinkel!" argues Brian. "You're both wrong! It's a Gloster Gladiator." The plane circles lazily; drops lower and lower; the engine cuts as it disappears down towards the Mile Field- so called because it is a mile long. "Right lads! I think that the plane has forced landed. We will rescue the pilot." As we make our way to where we think the plane may have landed, Tommy asks, "How do you know it is a Gladiator?" "Well! It is a biplane and I can tell by the nose and the fuselage." "Anything else, brain box?" Well! It's painted silver and it is carrying R.A.F. markings." "But how do you know?" "I just do know because that's what a Gloster Gladiator should look like! Right?" "Right! I supp..." "Is that 'supp...', a 'Right' or a 'No!'" says I grinning. "It's a Right!" says Tommy grinning back.

We arrive in the Mile Field, so called because it's a mile long if you have forgotten already, Several people are gathered. The pilot has been rescued. Two lads are actually talking to him; he seems to be O.K. "Let's check the plane for damage!" orders Tommy. "Don't touch anything lads!" calls the Pilot. "No sir,we won't!" Every-thing seems O.K. Just some torn fabric under the fuselage.

"Hi Tommy! Hi Plug!" We turn- it's Monty. "Err... Hi Monty!" This individual can be a bit of a lad.

Eventually, an R.A.F. lorry arrives with a Corporal and two guards. We haven't had much contact with service personnel. They seem like people from another planet: this lot does not seem too bad and soon we are chatting to them. Suddenly, there's a ripping sound. Oh no! It's Monty tugging at a strip of loose fabric for a souvenir. "Hey lad! Leave that alone!" shouts one of the guards. Now if Monty had let go and run he might have got away but he gave an almighty tug and pulled the strip away from the plane- then he ran. One very fit airman caught Monty after about 50 yards.

"You let them catch you then?" says I. A dejected Monty says, "Yes! I let them catch me." "Why?" "Because I didn't want to leave you lot in the cart." That's not like Monty: I think he was caught fair and square. "You will be prosecuted!" says one of the guards, "And you will have to pay for the damage." "How... err... How much do you think that will be?" asks an anxious Monty. A silence; a ponder; a grimace; a look towards Heaven; a muffled clear your throat cough; a sly wink in my direction and… "I think it could be repaired for about eight hundred quid." "Eight hundred what?" ""Eight hundred quid." "Oh lor! Oh heck! Are you sure?" "What do you think, Corporal?" says a guard. "Nearer a thousand quid, I reckon!" "Oh lor!" gasps Monty. "What am I going to do?"

"I've got an idea," says Tommy. "If we go home and get our ration cards, we can pool our money and buy them some sweets and chocolate." "And I will bring some fags," says Mick. "That sounds fair! Have you got the strip of fabric?" "Yes Sir! Here Sir! Thank you Sir!" says an anxious to please Monty. "Three bags full, Sir!" whispers I. "Hand it over then and we'll settle for what you bring back." "Cross our hearts and hope to die! We will come back," says Tommy.

"Sorry mate! That's no good!" says the Corporal, "We will keep a hostage." He turns, winks at me again and says, "We will keep you until your mates return." I am a prisoner and a hostage. "Will you be O.K.?" "Yes Tommy!" says I bravely. "I will be alright, I won't tell them anything." Well! I think that I was very brave that day, at least very brave. Well! that's what the rest of the Gang thought. "Good old Plug! Keep your gob (Mouth.) shut! We won't be long!" The patrol trudges off towards home.

As they move out of sight, the Corporal says, "Do you want to have a good look at the Gladdy?" "Yes Sir! Thank you Sir!" "Call me John." "Thank you Sir John!" "No!" (They all laugh.) "Just call me John."

I wander round the aeroplane taking in details: struts, ailerons, etc., and I stop by the guns under the lower wing; they look like an ordinary tube painted black. I stand and gaze at the little black hole. Death and destruction can come from this tube. It does not care if it kills or maims men women or children. I give a little shiver; I feel the back of my neck tighten and my shoulders are cold. The black tube does not care! But Oh Lord! I hope the pilot does! I think war can be evil.

"Come on young un! Would you like to sit in the plane?" I am shaken out of my chilly daydream. "Oh yes please!" I want to get away from the guns and forget them. I can't believe it! I am sat in a Gloster Gladiator. "Switch on! Engine on! We are taxiing across the rough field open the throttle; stick gently back to hold the tail down; stick slightly forward, lift tail, ease joystick back, and off we go! We are airborne! I climb, bank, dive, roll. There's an Avro Anson! I could shoot it down but I won't. I have fallen-out with the guns. Time to land: throttle back; line up; glide down gently; nearly down; bring nose up; to flair out; touch down; cut engine. Brilliant!"

I am still sat in the Gladdy when I am surrounded by an in-credulous patrol. What a time I've had and as a bonus, Tommy has promoted me to Leader First Class Plus for one week for be-ing brave beyond and above the call of duty- and for keeping my gob shut.

We didn't have much contact with Monty- apart from School. He was always in trouble. He got a caning several times a week. After a particularly bad week and feeling very much aggrieved, he went to Tommy for ideas. For foreigners, that is anybody not being a gang member of The Crescenters (Cheers.) or St. Josephs (More cheers.), Tommy would charge a fee: for example, a napple, school milk, or ration book to be borrowed for sweets etc.

Monty had to take cod-liver oil and malt every day, supervised by Tommy, Brian, or myself. He hated it. "Tell you what I will do! I will have your malt and milk for a week." "Done!" says Monty, and done he was because Tommy loved cod liver oil and malt.

"Nip to Wood's Forge and get some horse hair, lay some across your hand when you're going to be caned." "I have tried that and it doesn't work." "Well! I tell you what I've got an idea. Why don't you hide or break the cane and smuggle it out of school?" "Well! If I do that Tommy, she will only get another." "Well! Keep on breaking them!" "But she will have another one." wails Monty. We called him Moaning Monty sometimes. "Regard it as a chal-lenge! We will help you to look for her hiding place. At least it will cut down your canings for a while when we find it." "I sup-pose so," moans Monty.

Although we searched high and low and back again, we never found Miss White's hiding-place. Several years later, I met Miss White at a re-union. She told me that she always kept her spare canes at home. "If you see Monty, tell him that's why he never found them." "Yes Miss! I will." "And you can tell Tommy, when you see him, that was one of his brilliant ideas that didn't work!"

"Mornin Plug!" "Mornin Tommy! Have you got your free boots

yet, and are you going to Beamsley Beacon for a holiday?" "Yep both!" says Tommy. "We got two letters this morning." "Same here!" says I. The poorer children of the Parish were given new footwear occasionally, and during the Summer Holidays were taken to Beamsley Beacon for a week's holiday.

Saturday morning then. "Mornin Tommy!" "Mornin Plug! All set?" "Yep!" We proceed to walk into town our belongings in a paper carrier bag: shiny black boots, held back and worn for the first time today. "How far do you think it is to Beamsley?" "It's a long way!" "Well! Young Plug says it's about thirty miles away and it's in Hot Pot Land." "What's 'Hot Pot Land' then?" "I think he means Lancashire... Lancashire Hot Pot." "Well! We will soon know," says Tommy.

Into Manor Square then. The coach is already there and about half full. "Get your hair cut, Plug!" "It's Monty," hanging out of a window. "I will lend you a basin (A basin you may remember or bowl was placed on the head and the hair below the basin was cut and shorn.)." "Same to you with brass fittings!" I reply. Amid banter and catcalls we board the coach.

In next to no time, we arrive at a big house near Beamsley. I reckon that it must have only been ten miles, and it certainly wasn't in Hot Pot Land. There is a huge lawn to the front and about a dozen bell tents have been erected. "I don't fancy sleeping on grass!" says Tommy. "Nor do I!" says I. "You don't have to!" says Monty, "I was here last year, the tents have wooden floors." "That's O.K. then."

"Right lads! Pick up a palliasse." "What's a 'palliasse'? It sounds very rude to me! I wonder if its something to do with giants being friendly?" "No! It's nowt to do with giant's arses," says Tommy "It's these bags that we will sleep on. I suppose we fill them with feathers or something."

"Right lads! Everybody got one! Right! Good! Follow me!" says this big bloke dressed in hunting gear and seemed to be eight foot tall (Well he was pretty big anyrode!) We troop round to the back of the big house and into an outbuilding. "O.K. everybody! Fill your palliasses with straw." Everybody wades in. Will there be enough filling for all of us? Well! I am going to make sure that I get my share- plus a bit. Everyone seems to be in the same mind, except Tommy, he is steadily filling his sack.

"All done? Right then! Back to the tents and each get a place."
Tommy with his lightly-filled palliasse is first back to the tent
nearest to the big house. "This way, Plug!" he calls. "Right mate!"
and into the tent I go. "Sorry this tent is full! No you can't come
in! "Let's have a look then?" "Would you like a knuckle sandwich?" "No!" "Well! Don't look then- and naff off!" Tommy has
done a wonderful job: he has filled the tent with Roman Catholics,
and, the tent is the nearest one to the big house.

"Well done, Tommy!" says I. "We will be first to the big house
for meals when the bell goes." "You're learning Plug!" says Tommy.
"Now what I suggest is that we all take our palliasses outside and
fill them all equally. One for all and all for one!" "That's brilliant,
Tommy!" "Yes, I know it is."

We did all sorts of outdoor activities that week: "Hare and
Hounds."; exploring streams, rivers, woods, etc. Everybody went
to the top of Beamsley Beacon, except those who didn't, and,
placed a stone on the pile there. The pile had steadily grown over
the years as this was a local tradition

One day, we arrived back at camp at about 4.30 pm. "What's
that smell?" Everyone wants to know what that smell is. "Search
me!" "The house must have been on fire." "Are the tents O.K?"
Nobody could christen the smell.

"Right lads! A quick wash and then it will be grub up." "What's
that smell Mister?" "What smell?" "That smell." "I can't see any
smell." "You can't see a smell, Mister!" "I can't hear a smell either."
"You can't see or hear a smell, Mister!" "He obviously, isn't going
to let on, Plug!" says Tommy. No! He ain't!" say I.

Into the Dining Room then. "By Gum! It's strong in here!
Something's happened!" but no one can decide what this invisible,
unheard of smell, is. Apple pie and custard for afters. Now the
mystery is solved! "This custard is burnt! It's horrible!" "I can't eat
that!" "It would have been better without custard!" "There's nothing wrong with the custard!" says the Cook (Who probably burnt
it.). "Then you eat it then!" "Sorry lad! I have already had mine!"
"Pull the other one! You can still taste some of ours!" "Sorry lads!
I can't do that!" "Why not?" "Well! I have had three helpings of
custard already and couldn't manage another spoonful." "Fibber!"
"Nedder!" "Liar!" He disappears towards the kitchen.

"Listen everybody!" It's the second in command. "We have a

game arranged for this evening and the prize is a pocket watch."
"Oh good!" "Hooray!" "I'll win it!" "No you won't!" "Yes I will!"
"Pigs might fly!" "Where?" "In Pudsi!" "That'll be the day!"

"Quiet now! That will only be the day if you eat all the custard!" "Bugger the custard!" says Monty. "Sack the Cook!" I say.
"Yes sack him!" "Put him on the dole!" "Make the cook eat all the
ruddy custard!" The chant is taken up. "Sack the Cook! Sack the
Cook! Sack the Coo…" Bang! "Silence!" The big chief boss stands
there in his hunting gear filling the doorway. A smoking double-
barrelled in his hand. "Sack the…" Another bang. "Silence! Now
then! Now then! The next shots won't be blanks."

"Those people who eat their custard and present an empty
bowl to me will be allowed to participate." "What's 'parti…' err…
'part…'? Err, what you just said?" "It means to take part or join in."
"Why didn't you say so then?" "That's enough of that young man!
You will eat an extra bowl of custard, as will any other insolent
boy." "Sorry sir! Sorry!"

Meal over; custard eaten- or slung away. About seventy clean
bowls presented- plus one (Mine). "What's the game sir?" "You
will all go straight to your tents and when you hear a gunshot, the
game begins. We have placed white markers in various locations.
Err, we have put sticks in different places." "Glad you said that sir!"
"Thank you, boy! You had two bowls of custard, didn't you?" "Yes
sir!" "A second shot will denote… err, will mean the time is up,
and you must cease… err, stop looking. Everybody understand?"
"Yes Sir!" "Understood sir!" "Fair enough, Sir!" etc.

"The boy who finds the most markers will receive this pocket
watch." The Gunsmoke Kid holds up a Mickey Mouse watch. It
has a picture of Mickey on the dial and a long and a short arm that
shows the time. "If you had to buy this watch, it would cost you
half a crown." "I feel sorry for the jeweller!" says Monty. "And
why is that?" asks Wyatt Earp. "Because no bugg… err- no bloke
here could afford one, sir!" "Another bowl of custard, son?" "Yes
Sir!"

"Into the tent then, I've got an idea," says Tommy. "What?"
"This is what we will do." Bang! Game over then. "Peter Jackson,
you have handed in the most markers. The prize is yours." Amidst
applause from the Catholics and the odd reluctant clap from other
denominations (Non- and percentage believers.), I collect the

watch.

That night in the tent. "Right Plug! How many markers did you find?" "Err, four Tommy." "Right Plug! I got three. Anybody else with three? No! Two then?" "I got two!" "Same here!" "And me!" "Right then! Plug gets to keep the watch for four weeks, then it's mine for three weeks. You two who found the markers will keep it for two weeks. You can toss for who has it first and then, who got one marker, gets to keep the watch for one week. Then we start all over again, right!" "Right!" "O.K!" "Fair enough!" "Yes that's fine!" "What about us?" "No chance!" "Why not?" "Why not? What did you put into the pool?" "Nowt." "Well! If you put nowt in, you gets nowt out. Right?" "Err yes."

I learnt a valuable lesson that day; that unity is strength and if you are not prepared to put owt in, or not work as a team, odds are you won't get owt out of life.

Home then. "Hi Mum!" "Hello son! Have you had a good time?" "Smashing! our tent won this watch. We get turns to have it." "That's good! Here's your tea." "Thanks Mum!"

Second day at home, Young Plug and I are sat by the hearth listening to the wireless and reading comics. We have just finished our mid-day meal. Mick seems to be restless and scratching his nut. Come to think of it so am I.

"What's the matter with you two?" says Mum. "Anybody would think you were lousy! Err… Oh lor! I bet that you have got livestock in your hair! Oh my God! Come here you two! Kneel down here and let me see. Oh Lord above! You are lousy… err bug… err ridden! Err you have both got head-lice as big as elephants!"

"Nay Mum!" "As big as Elephants I say! And nits as big as hen eggs!" "Never Mother!" "As big as hen eggs, I say!" "Yes Mother!" The prize watch wasn't the only thing I had brought home from Beamsley. "What are we going to do Mum?" say I, scratching my nut. "You are both going to get socks on your hands." "What for?" "To stop you scratching, of course!" "Sorry Mum!" "Yes sorry!" says a nut-scratching Mick. "Right! Put these on. I want you to go to Mainprize, the Chemist, and get two bars of 'Durbac' soap and a toothcomb." ('Durbac' - it could have been 'Derbac' was a coal-tar soap guaranteed to get rid of head-lice- even the size of elephants!). The toothcomb was a very fine comb, designed to scoop and loosen nits, and prevent elephants slipping through

(Hang on Readers! I will have to stop writing to rub my nut!).

"Right you two! Get a bath! And when you are ready, I will do your hair with 'Durbac/ Derbac'. I will pop up to see Thomas's Mum and have a word."

"Right Mum!" Hair duly washed and dried. "Right then!" says Mum, "Let's see what we have got! Come and kneel here Michael!" "Are we going to pray that the lousy bug... err lice as big as Elephants will bug... err... naff off then?" "No! We are going to face up to things! Fight the little so-and-sos!" "But Mum! I thought that you said that they were as big as elephants!" " Well may be not as big as Elephants! But near enough! Peter, you come and see if you can see anything. I will lay this newspaper on the rug." Mum starts to comb Mick's hair. "Look Mum!" I cry. "They are dropping out and running wild. We haven't copped em all! Well! What I mean is: we haven't killed all of the little/big lousy lice!" "Quick! Hit them then!" "Righto Mum!" "Oh hec Mum! I will have to stop trying to clobber them?" "Why?" "Well! Every time I hit the paper, it tears and they drop through on to the rug." Probably that's where the saying "As snug as a bug in a rug." comes from.

"Oh lor! What are we going to do?" "Get a bu... bu... bucket Mum," says Mick, "and then we stand a chance of killing them." And so, dear Reader, Mother pretty well cleared our heads of intruders. Mick and I killed them by pressing Dad's cobbling knife handle and wood chisel handle hard down on to them. The nits were removed and cracked between two thumbnails. (I hope you have finished your meal!). The rug was duly disposed of and sent to the tip. That was the only time we were infested. Mum saw to that: armed with comb; 'Derbac/ Durbac'; bucket, and, Dad's tools.

Tommy and I are checking the school-windows to make sure the material is still stuck to the glass. This prevents broken glass flying during an Air Raid thus causing injury. We work it so we are in the porch ready for the bell. It rings! We are out first, collect our carrier bikes/taxis cum Spitfires and dash into Crow Lane. Oh Lor! Peggy's down (We call her 'Peggy' in private- just Tommy and me.) "What's the matter, Miss?" says Tommy. "I have an appointment at four fifteen. I finished early. I was dashing and I tripped over the kerb. I have hurt my ankle."

"You could be dead in Crow Lane and nobody would know."
"You're right mate!" says I. "Stand back, you lot! I will get a chair
into the porch. Can you walk there Miss?" "I don't think so."
"Right, Plug! You will have to carry her." "Who me?" "Yes you!
You can't expect the leader of The Crescenters to do it- and anyrode I am in charge." whispers Tommy from the right hand corner
of his mouth on Peggy's blind-side. He certainly has perfected a
non-type talking technique that nobody can see or hear except
the chosen one. I am one of the tallest lads in the school and I
know I am pretty strong. Tommy has said many times: "He does
not think Peggy will weigh six stone, wet through."

Peggy is tallish and very slim as you may have guessed by now if
you have been paying attention- as Miss White would say. I bend
down. At the second attempt, I scoop her into my arms. Good
Lord! She doesn't seem to weigh anything! If she weighs six stone
they must be an extra light six stones. As I carry my beloved across
the playground towards the cloak room, I am in Heaven. Peggy
is in my arms and she has hers round my neck. Its like a dream!
We seem to float across the playground- I wish it were fifty miles
long! (Tommy says afterwards it must have been the Adrenaline.) I
hope I have some more Adrenaline saved up somewhere.

"Quick! Sit down Miss!" orders Tommy. "I will go and get
some gear. How are you feeling, Miss?" "A little better Thomas."
Thomas doesn't sound half bad when Peggy says it. I wish I could
think of something to ask her then she could call me Peter- 'Peeter'
that would sound wonderful.

"Could you take your stockings off, Miss?" "Yes, Thomas, I
think so." Oh Lor! Oh heck! What can I do? I can't hide! I look
at Tommy; he raises his eyes; turns his head sideways. I finally get
the message: he wants me to stand behind the chair. Good thinking, Tommy! He dashes off and I quietly move behind my love.
Off with the stocking! Peggy has a nice leg! I think I see what
Tommy means: she probably has two nice legs. Oh! How I ache
to touch her. I close my eyes and gently place my hands on to the
shoulders and whisper, "Sit back, Miss!"

Oh Lor! I open my eyes; my hands seem glued gently to my
beloved's shoulders. I have never been so close to my Peggy before. Her hair is rolled upwards above her neck. Oh my! She has a
lovely lovely neck! I want to touch it. I am suddenly brought back

to reality when a sweet voice says, "I am fine now, Peter," and my hands are gently removed from her wondrous shoulders.

"What's happened?" enquires Miss White. I proceed to tell her. "I am in very good hands," says my love. Peggy's voice is music in my head. Just think! I got up this morning and I have had a normal day up to four o'clock and now my whole world has changed in the blink of an eye! I am in Paradise or pretty close anyrode. Here on Earth, I am guarding and looking after my beloved! My sweet sweetheart! She is depending on me and I suppose on Tommy as well. Well! More on me at this moment. Oh! This wonderful moment! I wish that it could last for ever- and then some. Tommy returns all too soon, I think that he could have been a bit longer (Not taller.) but I think that he could have taken more time. I bet he has dashed back because he is jealous. He is carrying a bowl of water, bandages and towels. "Are you sure you will be alright?" asks Miss White. "Yes! I will be fine with these two gentlemen looking after me." I don't think I woke up this morning a 'Gentleman'- things can change you know.

"Right then, Miss Love! I will close school down for today." "Thank you, Miss White!" Tommy kneels and oh so gently cradles her wonderful foot and lightly touches her gorgeous ankle. "Does that hurt Miss?" "A little! Thomas." "I'm very sorry! Miss." Is this my gang-leader who is supposed to be very tough. I can't believe it is but it is. Tommy bathes Peggy's foot (That wonderful foot! And just to think, she has got another on the end of her other ankle!). Oh so caringly! I wish I had learnt First Aid when Tommy had wanted me to. Ah well! Tommy expertly bandages my beloved's foot, that wonderful foot (No cracks about a foot being about twelve inches here!). "How does that feel, Miss?" "Much better and very comfortable." "Thank you, Miss!" "You look after Miss and I will go for a Taxi." (Take your time Tommy; take your time.).

Tommy dashes off on his carrier bike, I am left alone with my Peggy. I can't think of anything to say but I start thinking: I wonder if Tommy loves Peggy. Is she his secret love? Does she love him? I have not told him I love her and I think she might love me, so he isn't telling me anything either.

There's a queezy feeling in my stomach. My wonderful day is cracking-up: I have been a rescuer; a saver and a guard (I became a 'Gentleman' at five minutes to four.) and a lover. I bet my best mate, the bastar...! Well! My mate is going to do the dirty.

My evil thoughts are shattered when a sweet voice says, "Thank you, Peter, for all you have done." "Yes Miss!" I feel a lot better, course she loves me more that that bast... err mate. Here's the taxi. It managed to get down Crow Lane then, closely followed by Tommy. My love is whisked away.

A few days later, we dash out of the playground on our bikes up Crow Lane (Where people can die and nobody would know.) Tommy shouts, "Did you see that Squaddy (Soldier.) at the gate?" "Yes!" says I. "What's he in?" "I think he's in the Tank Corps and I think he is waiting for Peggy." "Are you sure?" "Well! He's been waiting every night this week." "It's not fair! It's just not fair!" "What's not fair?" "It's not fair for him just to turn up each day and for Peggy to go off with him." "Why are you so upset?" "Err... Oh hang on! You are in love with Peggy!" "Yes I am! And so are you!" "You what? Not a chance Mate!" "Why not then?" "As leader of The Crescenters and St. Josephs, I don't have time to fall in love with anybody! And anyway, I think it's soppy!" "Well! You could have fooled me!" "You can be a Gentleman without being a lover, you know!" "Sorry, Tommy! I have got it all wrong." "That's alright mate! She's all yours and the Squaddy's!" "Well! I hope he gets killed and then I could comfort Peggy." "You mean like David and Bathsheba in the Bible." "How do you mean?" "Well! David sent Bathsheba's bloke into battle to get killed so he could have her." "The rotten so... err so-and-so! Well! Err, not like that! I hope he gets wounded." "Well! All you have just said isn't a Christian attitude." "Well! David did it!" "Yes! I agree Plug! But two wrongs don't make a right!" "You're right Tommy! I hope they split up then." "<u>That's</u> more like it mate! Why don't you pray for that? All's fair in Love and War!" "Who said that?" "I just did."

A few days later, Tommy says, "Do you want the good news, or the bad news?" "Oh blimey, Tommy! Let's have the good news first." "Right then! You know the Squaddy?" "Yes, course I do!" "Well! He wasn't waiting for Peggy at all! He is young Wilkin's father and he was home on a week's leave. He came each day to collect young Damian."

"That's wonderful news Tommy! I hope the bad news is not as

bad as the good news is good, if you see what I mean." "Course I do mate!" "Go on! Let's have it." "Did you see the 'Brylcream Boy' (R.A.F.) waiting at the gate last night?" "You mean the Navigator bloke." "Yep, that's him!" "Well what abou...? Oh no! Don't tell me! He was waiting for Peggy!" "Sorry mate!" "But how do you know if she loves him?" "I know mate! I just know!" "But, how do you just know?" "Well! I was a bit late out last night. I was in the bog collecting my bike. I heard her run across the playground and I heard enough, sorry mate." Surely Tommy my best mate and leader wouldn't 'ned' (lie to) me. Right then! Tonight I will wait in the bog and see, or hear, what happens.

Footsteps tripping across the playground. The Brilli says, "Hello my darling!" My sweetheart replies, "Hello my love!" Life's not fair! Another dream shattered! I know I have lost everything. How do you know you have lost everything you might ask. I did not see either of them but there was something about the voices that told me. I had lost my true love. I hope he doesn't get killed, wounded or captured and they will live happy ever after! So Lord can I take back all those Prayers and use them for something else? Thank you Lord!

Not longer after, Peggy and John became engaged. She left to get married and they went to live in Devon. The day she walked out of my life, we said goodbye. Her eyes seemed to twinkle as she said "Goodbye Peter." I think she must have loved me a little.

The War came closer today. Bill, our ex-leader has been killed, He joined up and went into the Navy: his boat has been sunk with all hands. I will always remember the gentle giant I once called Sir Bill. I think that this is turning out to be a lousy War.

."Mornin Tommy!" "Mornin Plug!" "Did you hear the planes last night? Do you think the were Jerries?" "Yes, Tommy, I do! You can tell by the up and down drone of the engines." "Do you think they may have dropped some bombs?" "They did drop some incend... err incen... err firebombs on the top of Chevin." "Oh Plug! You mean 'incendiary' bombs?" "That's it! Yes!" "How do you know?" "The postman told me this morning. He said they were looking for 'Avro' and Yeadon Airport." "Tell you what Plug!" "What?" "Let's go up Chevin on Saturday afternoon and have a look, right?" "Right!"

For those of you who have forgotten what the Chevin is: its a hill-just-short-of-a-mountain to the South of Otley. It runs from East to West, or from West to East whichever you fancy. It's quite level. In fact, it's very level. When I lay in bed and sight the bottom of the bedroom window-frame with the Chevin, they line up. Well! Just about anyrode.

'Avro' is a semi-underground Aircraft Factory to the South East of the Chevin. It is owned by 'A. V. Roe'- hence we call it 'Avro'. The roof is painted green and brown etc. Wood and fabric cows stand on the roof. It's called 'camouflage'. It's designed to fool the Jerry aircrews, but I think that wouldn't have tecken (Taken.) much doing anyrode. It's situated quite close to Yeadon Aero Club. Aeroplanes are towed from Avro to the airfield for testing and flying to wherever.

Friday lunchtime. Tommy has called a meeting. "Hmm! Right! Is everybody who matters here? What I mean is: are all St. Joseph's Gang Members present?" "Yes!" "Here!" "Present!" "Here boss!" etc. "What about Steady Freddy?" "Oh! He left early." "What!" "He left as the bell was ringing." "You're trying to tell me that he <u>actually</u> left early to go somewhere?" "Straight up, boss! He's probably hungry and nipped home sharpish." "Well! I'll tell you something!" "What will you tell us?" "The ruddy pigs in Pudsi must be knackered!" "Hear hear!" "Right lads! Let's get on! I have called a meeting of The Crescenters for six-o-clock tonight. I propose we go up Chevin on Saturday afternoon to see what the baskets (Bastards.) have done and, <u>any</u> St. Joseph's Pupil will be welcome to join." "But will The Crescenters let us go with them?" "Don't worry! I will sort that lot out." "Let me know by School tonight. Members who decide to go, bring usual provisions: a big bottle of coloured water and at least, two doorsteps, right?" "Right!" "Just one more thing!" "What?" "Somebody tell Steady Freddy." "Right, boss!" "And tell him to be on time and give those pigs a rest." "Right boss! Will do!" I can't remember Freddy ever joining The Crescent Gang officially, he just seemed to turn up- late of course, and he was well just accepted.

Six-o-clock Friday in the Newall Park. "Quiet! Quiet please! Err quiet one and all! And that includes you young Marcus!" "Sorry boss!" "I should coco! Are you all here? It doesn't matter about Steady Freddy. He will have been filled-in (Told.) at School this afternoon." "What's it all about, Tommy?" "What's it all

about? I will tell you what it is about! I propose The Crescenters
and St. Josephs go up Chevin on Saturday afternoon to see what
the bug... hmm the bast... the err... the Boche have been up
to." "What's 'Boche' then Tommy?" "I haven't a clue! But Young
Marcus says that, that's what they called them in the first World
War. Isn't that right Marcus?" "Well that's what our old man says."
"Respect! Respect Mark! You have done nowt for your Country
and you get called 'Mark' or 'Marcus' respectfully, so I think that
your 'Old Man' err Father what probably nearly laid down his life
for his Country and disrespectful offspring's deserves better! Don't
you think?" "Sorry Boss! Shall I call him 'Pater'?" "No the worst
that you should refer to him is by his Christian name." "O.K.
boss! If you insist." "By the way, what is his name?" "Ebeneezer."
"What?" "Ebeneezer!" "Well I think that your old Man was born
unlucky, so carry on as you were." "Thanks boss!" "You're welcome!" "What did the bas... err... the Boche call our lot then?"
"That's one thing I do know?" "Well what was it then?" "They
called our lot 'Tommy'." "Oh! Just like you then?" "Yes! And the
Scotties were 'Laddies'. Err no! They called them: 'Ladies from
Hell.'." "Why did they call them that then?" "Well if none of
you can figure that out, I will not dignify that ignorant question with an intelligent answer, but in this case I will take pity on
you ignorant lot. Kilts idiots! Kilts!" "Awe I see what you mean!"
says a lone voice. "Well educate the rest and then we can get on!"
"Will do Boss! Will do!" (I notice that when Tommy is with The
Crescenters, it sometimes can be bugg... in full and bast...in full
but when he is with the St. Joseph's gang, it is no worse than
'blighters' or 'baskets'.). "All those in favour."

We are all assembled Catholics and Protestants raring to go.
"Just a minute!" "What?" "Just a minute! I hope you don't want
us to become converts?" "Course not, idiot! I know what I would
like to convert you to! Do you really want to know?" "I suppose
not." "Is that a no?" "Err yes, err I mean no."

On the top of the Chevin then, we locate where the bombs
have dropped in the heather. People on Chevin say that Avro and
the airfield are O.K. No damage. When we have swigged our water and scoffed our bread, we set off home. "Halt!" cries Tommy.
"I've got an idea." "What idea?" "We could set up Ack- ack (Anti-
aircraft guns- known as Triple A today: Anti Aircraft Artillery.),

(The German acronym is 'Flak'.) and a Searchlight Battery before the Army think of it. We could defend Avro and Yeadon." "That's brilliant, Tommy." "Yes, I know it is," he replies immodestly.

"All you lot meet in the Newall Park at five o'clock on Friday and we'll go to Weston Woods for the guns and we will go up Chevin next Saturday afternoon. Right?" "Right!" "O.K!" "Sure!" "Yes!"

Saturday, two-o-clock, we have just arrived on to the top of the Chevin. We have used Mark's bogey to transport the guns etc. We have: two lengths of 2" diameter fall pipe about six feet long and two about four foot long- scrounged by Mark off his Dad. In addition we have: two straightish branches with a fork at one end about six foot long, and, two about three foot long. We have an old dustbin lid, a spade and a lump hammer- also scrounged by Mark (A lump hammer has a heavy head and a short shaft. If you get clobbered by it, it can sure raise a whacking gert (Big.) lump but I don't think that that is where it gets it's name from.) and an axe.

"Right lads! We will have one gun here and another over there," says Tommy, indicating the two sites about five yards apart. "Dig two holes at least, at least fifteen to eighteen inches deep, and drop a stone in the bottom." "What's the stone in the bottom for?" "It's for the upright pipe to rest on, so it doesn't sink into the ground, right?" "Awe right! That's a good idea boss." "Yes! I know it is. Bung the longer pipes in and fill the holes but knock some stones into the holes round the pipes to make them firm." "Right boss!" "O.K!" etc.

"What do we do now then?" "What do we do? We trim two branches with the axe, so they will drop into the pipes and turn." "Right boss, will do!" "Right." "O.K! Somebody hold the up-rights, upright." "Right! You want the uprights holding upright, right?" "Right! "I think you mean 'plumb' Tommy," says Mark. "Yes, that's right Mark! I want the uprights holding upright and plumb, right?" "That's funny!" says Mark. "What's funny?" "Well! when my Mum talks about anybody who is iffy or do-lally she says that they are 'not plumb'. Isn't that funny, Tommy?" "Yes very funny, now can we get on?" "Yes boss! Right boss!"

"Right then! When the uprights are upright and plumb, hammer in some more stones to hold the uprights upright, and plumb right?" "Right!" "Now we wedge the branches into the back end of the barrels. The forks will fit the gunner's shoulder and we rest the gun barrels into the upright forks that are in the pipes, that should be upright and plumb, then tie them off. Presto! We now have two Ack-ack guns!" (Do you think that you need a diagram? If you do let me know.) "We will put the searchlight on Mark's bogey." The Battery is now operational.

We have two anti-aircraft guns; they traverse 360 degrees and elevate, up and down. The dustbin lid is our searchlight. When clobbered with the lump hammer that's the sound of the guns firing. All this clobbering causes a problem for the searchlight operator to hold it steady. "Right lads! Take a break, you've earned it."

"Listen!" says Mark. "Listen what? I can't hear owt." "No shush! Listen!" (Silence.). "Ah! I can hear it now! It's a plane!" "Right!" shouts Tommy, "Let's see who is first to spot it." The droning gets louder. "There it is!" "Where?" "To the East." "Are you sure Tommy?" "Sure! I'm sure." "Where then?" "Over there!" "Where?" "There!" "That's not East! It's West." "No! It isn't! It's East!" "It can't be!" "Why not, know all?" "It's a 'Henschel'!" calls Tommy. "No! It's a 'Westland Lysander'!" "Are you sure, brain-box?" "Yes, I am! A 'Henschel' and a 'Lysander' <u>are</u> similar." The plane is making a slow approach to our battery. "When or if it comes close, you will be able to see a short wing on each wheel, they carry three small bombs." (I think it is three.)

"Right lads! Plug says it's a 'Lysander' but we will pretend it's a Jerry. Open Fire!" The guns swing into action. Two members hit the dustbin lid, for rapid fire. The 'Lysander' passes overhead; waggles its wings and starts to circle to make another approach. This happens twice. As it circles for the third time, I say to Tommy, "I think he's looking for Yeadon." "You could be right! Which way is Yeadon exactly?" "Over there!" "Are you sure?" "Sure I'm sure!"

The plane passes over and begins another circuit. "Right lads! At the next approach, everybody point the same way as Plug. Here he comes lads! Everybody point and wave towards Yeadon." The 'Lysander' approaches; turns to the right in the direction we are pointing; waggles its wings and disappears. "You did well there Plug! Three cheers for Plug!" "Hip hip!" "Boo!" "Hip hip!" "Boo!" "Hip, hip! Hooray!"

"Right Plug! Let's sort this East and West out." "O.K!" "Who's got the Mickey Mouse watch?" "I have." "Right Brian! What time is it?" "It's half past three." "And where does the sun set?" Everybody says West- except 'Doubting Thomas'. "Well mate!" says I. "Do you still say the sun sets in the East?" "No, not really! But I can't understand it! When we have 'Jog' (Geography.) lessons, East is towards Ilkley Moor- which is to the right, but up Chevin when we are turned the other way round it is still to the right- but it can't be!" "Got it!" thinks I. "Tommy!" "Yes!" "When we have Jog lessons which way are we facing?" "We're facing... err well... we're facing... Err where are we facing?" "We are facing the Gasometer South, right?" "Err well! I have always thought that it was North." "Well you are reading the Atlas facing South and looking at its North at the top." "Yes! That's right!" Well you <u>need</u> to be facing North to read it correctly." Tommy's no mug and he cottons on. "You're right Plug! You can learn something new every day."

Our activities were swiftly brought to an end the following Saturday. We arrived to find that the Army had set up Ack-ack guns and searchlights. When the Officers were absent, the Squaddies allowed us to sit on the guns and pretend to work the searchlights.

Mark, Tommy and I are shovelling coke in the school-yard. It cannot be tipped into the storage area so it has to be moved by hand. We three have volunteered to do this task to get out of lessons. One day Tommy says, "This is all wrong." "What's all wrong?" "This is all wrong." "Why is it all wrong?" "It's all wrong because we are sweating and working hard." "But we are missing lessons." "What's all wrong?" "This is all wrong." "Why is it all wrong?" "It's all wrong because we are working very hard and sweating very profusely." "What does that mean then?" "I haven't a clue! But I have heard it somewhere or other." "Yes, I agree! But it's still wrong!" "Why is it wrong?" "It's wrong because we are not being paid. We should receive something for our labour. We are like slaves." "You're right!" says Mark. "What do you think, Plug?" "I think, you've got something there, Tommy. I think you're on to something. What shall we do?" "What shall we do? I will tell you what we will do." "What then?" "This then." "What?" "We will stop work now and stay out in the playground until one of the Teachers comes looking for us."

"Hello, Plug, Mark!" Here she comes. Miss White stamps across the playground, she's crushing eggs again. "What's the meaning of this? You should have been back in School half an hour ago and why have you not cleared the coke?" "Miss," says Tommy (No 'Please Miss'- just a straight 'Miss'.) Tommy may be afraid of heights but when he fixes his mind on something, he has no fear. "Well! What is it?" "We have had a meeting (No 'Miss' even now.) and we have decided that we want paying for our work. We will withdraw our labour until it is rewarded." "And what brought this on?" Miss White's hands are on her hips and she is glaring over her specs. (Two ominous signs.) "Well in the Bible, the labourers in the vineyard were paid for their work and the Good Lord said this was fair and just. We are labourers in the coke-yard and we should be paid our due." "Well, you are due in the Classroom in two minutes with clean hands!" says Miss White and she stamps away, still crushing eggs.

"That's it!" says Tommy. "I propose we strike." "Strike what?" says Mark. "Go on strike, idiot! We have stopped work and we will refuse to go into lessons. We will put it to the vote. All in favour?" "Err, yes!" "Count me in!" "That's unanimous then!"

We troop into Crow Lane (Where you could be dead and nobody would know.). Tommy says, "No surrender! Whatever happens." "Nar (Now.) then lads! What's up?" It's Old Bob, the odd job man. Tommy tells him what has happened. "Hard luck, lads!" says he, stroking his stubble and off he goes into School.

About ten minutes later the egg crusher appears; she stands there- feet apart hands on hips and glaring over her specs. Not a sound! Not a word uttered! We shuffle out of dead man's Crow Lane, across the playground and into the cloakroom. A very angry voice the likes of one I have never heard before commands: "Now get your filthy hands washed!" Here endeth our first and last strike! We were kept in after school for three nights. We lost the job of course. Old Bob, the any old odd job bod (Man.) got a bob an hour. I think that she overpaid him just to spite us poor labourers /slaves.

Otley was a garrison town: the military camps were to the East. "Have you got that Tommy? To the East." The prisoner of war (P.O.Ws) camps were situated to the West. News would circulate that the trains carrying the prisoners were due. They usually arrived at the weekend: Sunday afternoon or evening. The prisoners were lined up in railway goods yards. They were then marched down Station Road along Kirkgate over the river Wharfe; along Weston Lane to the camps. Some marched proudly- heads held high, singing and defiant; others subdued- heads bent forward looking at the ground. The poor blighters must have been through a lot; they must have been apprehensive. What does that mean? I'm not sure either. The poor sod... err soldiers must have been wondering what their fate would be- but they must have been very relieved to be out of the War. Sometimes I would feel some pity towards them but on more than one occasion I have had a shiver down my spine, because some of them looked fierce and dangerous- and there never seemed to be enough guards.

"Mornin Tommy!" "Mornin Plug!" "Did you see the prisoners last night Tommy?" "No I missed them! Was there a lot of them then?" "There must have been millions! Err well... thousands! Anyrode there was a heck of a lot of them!" "Did you know that Mark's Father was a P.O.W. in the Great War then?" "No, I didn't know that!" "So you haven't heard the tale of when he was a prisoner then?" " No! I haven't." "Well! When we get to school get him going then and I am sure that he will fill you in then." "Right! I will do that small thing."

"Mornin Mark!" "Mornin Tommy!" "Mornin Plug!" "Did you see the prisoners last night, Mark?" "Yes, I did! The camps must be just about full now." "Tommy tells me your Dad was a P.O.W." "Yes! He was!" "What did he do then?" "Would you like to know?" "Yes! I am interested in all prisoners," says I, as I wink at Tommy. "Hey young Plug!" "Hey yourself Tommy!" "Would you like to hear about Mark's father when he was a prisoner in the Great War?" "Yes! That sounds interesting!" "Come on over!" calls Tommy. "Right, I will!"

"Right then young Mark! Fill us in!" "Right I will! Here goes! During the first World War, my Father was a sniper and he killed a hundred and forty seven Jerries in France and Belgium." "That's funny!" says young Mick" "What's funny?" "That's funny!" "Why is it funny?" " " Well Tommy! It's funny because that is the biggest score that you can get at snooker." "Well that's the best bit of useless information that has been imparted to me today!" says a sarcastic Tommy. "Tommy!" "Yes?" "Have you been reading one of your Mother's books again?" "How did you guess Mate? How did you guess?" "They are abroad," says Mick." "What are?" "France and Belgium are." "Everybody knows that!" says Tommy. "I know they do but I thought I would say it." "Are you sure he killed so many?" "Sure, I'm sure! If you don't believe me, ask him!" "Oh! Oh! I am a believer! I believe you!" says I. "Can I carry on and proceed now?" "Sorry Mark! Proceed and carry on." "Thank you."

"Well! He shot so many Jerries that the Kaiser got worried that they wouldn't have any blokes left to fight the War." "What's a 'Kaiser'?" "A 'Kaiser', young Plug, it means he is the Leader." "Awe right!" "What happened?" says I. "Well! He sent some agents to capture him. They told my father that they knew a good spot to shoot some Jerries. When he went, they drugged him and took him to Krautland, that's Germany for those what don't know." "That's cheating!" says I. "Course it is! But all's fair in love and war." "Who says that?" I don't know but somebody did."

"Well! He was brought before Kaiser Bill." "Why 'Kaiser Bill'?" "Well Plug! It's short for 'Villhelm' or something." "Awe right!" "He said to my Father that he had been rotten for knocking off so many of his lads. My Father, being very brave and possibly a little stupid, said that he was aiming to shoot a thousand Krauts. Do you get that?" "'Aiming'! Aiming to shoot! Get it?" "Yes, very good!" says I. "Aiming to shoot! Yes! Very good!"

"This made K.B. very mad and he said that my father and the other prisoners were to be shot at dawn the following morning." "Well! They couldn't be shot at any other time if it had to be dawn, could they?" says young Mick err Plug. "If you are going to be like that, that's it!" "Sorry young Marcus!" says young Plug. "I should coco!" says young Marcus to a younger Plug. "Not coffee then?" "That's it then! That is it!" "Well! If that is it I don't reckon much to it. Sorry Mark carry on! I will keep my big gob shut!" "Tightly?" "Yes tight tightly!" "Well thank goodness for that small mercy! Well! As they marched away, my Dad started playing 'God Save the King.'" on his penny whistle that he always carried." "What's that?" says Bill. "What's that music?" "It's that rotten British sniper playing a whistle." "Well! He may be rotten! But he plays that whistle very well. Bring him back to me." "Very good sir," says this kraut General. "Hey you musician! Come back here!" "You play very well," says the Kaiser. "Yes, I know I do," says my Father. "Where did you learn to play?" "My father taught me but I practiced a lot when I was waiting for one of your lads to stick his nut out. It was probably the last thing they heard." "Well! I am sure they died happy!" says Bill. "Course they did!" says Dad. "Err Fred," says K.B. (He called everybody Fred.) "Do you think you could teach me to play that whistle as good as you can?" "Course I can! But it will take a long time." "Can you teach me to play in German?" "I can teach you in any language." "So my Father taught the Kaiser to play "God Save the King." in German and nobody cottoned on." "But how did he go on when he got to playing in English? They would have got on to your Dad." "Well! He decided to leave playing in English to the very last for that reason, but the Kaiser was so pleased, he did a deal with my Father: he said he would set him free as long as he left the whistle and promised not to shoot any Jerries." "How did he go on?" "Well! He kept his promise; he taught other soldiers to become snipers and he played a new whistle as they shot the Krauts- so they all died happy!" "Course they did! Course they did!"

Third time lucky then. I have fallen in love again. I never thought I would. No her name isn't Peggy. I have been let down by two Peggy's and that's more than enough. I always thought that only blonde was beautiful but Janette has dark hair, almost black. She has deep dark blue eyes. She is a couple of inches shorter than me and I suppose as Tommy would say, she has a nice pair of pins. She will be my secret love. Mum is reading a book called 'Secret Love.'. She hides it when Dad is about. On the cover, it says: "Passions run high!" Mick says it is probably about rivers flooding- sometimes I wonder about that boy. Anyway, mine must be a secret love. I will make up a code and when we get to know each other, we can pass notes in School by classmates and nobody will know what they say.

My code is prepared, I will test it out on Tommy. "Mornin Plug!" "Mornin Tommy!" "Err, I would like you to have a look at this and see if you can fathom it." "Sure mate! Lets have a dekko (look)." I give him my first secret love message: "H KNUD IZMDSSD VGHSD." Tommy looks at the message; turns it over and looks at the back; turns it to the front, upside down and right

way up. "What do you think to it?" "I think you're bonkers!"
"Why bonkers?" "Why bonkers! You're bonkers! Because you say
here that you love Janette White." "Well! I do! But I want it to be
a secret." "Well! With a code like that, you might as well put an
advert in the local rag!" "Well! Keep it between you and me then."
"Right mate!" It would take a long time to write letters in code
anyway, I will only pass letters by people I can trust.

"Tommy! I need your help." "Sure mate! Anything anytime- as
long as it's not money that you're after!" "Well! I'm after Janette
White!" "Why not be <u>before</u> Miss Janette?" "Only kidding mate!"
"I would like you to teach me to dance in time for the School
Christmas Shindig." "No problem mate! Come to our house after
tea on Saturday. My Mum and Dad will be at the flicks, (Cinema.)
that will give us a couple of hours practice." "Oh thanks, mate!"
"You're welcome! You're welcome!"

After several Saturday evening sessions, Tommy says: "I think
you should dance the part of the man, it's called 'leading'. See
you next Saturday!" "Come in kind Sir!" calls Tommy in answer
to my knock. He is reclining on the sofa wearing a red dress,
dark stockings, silver high heel shoes and a bright red headscarf.
"Is that lipstick and powder you have got on?" "Yes." "What are
you wearing a headscarf indoors for?" "To cover my curlers so
you can't see them." "Awe right! Are you feeling alright Tommy?"
"Please call me 'Miss'! Kind Gentleman!" says my friend- flutter-
ing her... I mean his eyebrows. "Are you sure you're O.K?" "Yes!
I am fine! I thought it would help you if I dressed the part! Don't
worry mate! All this will come off when you leave. Shall we get
started?"

"I tell you what Tommy," "What?" "There isn't much difference between boys and girls is there?" "No! I suppose not. Right
then! Let's get cracking!" "Right mate!" Tommy puts a record on.
'Dancing with my shadow' gently fills the air. Tommy and I float
round the sitting room. This is great! I have got the rhythm. Oh
Janette! My Janette! When we finally get together, we will be in
Paradise- but still here on Earth (That's got to be the best of both
worlds.). "That's been great!" says I. "No charge young sir!" says
my partner. I hope he isn't getting into the part too much! No not
Tommy! "I will call in the morning for Mass." "O.K. Miss err...
Thomas... err Tommy! Thanks again!"

Tommy never turned up. After Mass, I went to his house. Nobody at home! He never called for school on Monday morning; Tuesday; Wednesday, no sign- not at work; Wednesday tea time, young Plug comes in and says: "Hey Plug! Have you heard about Tommy?" "No why?" "Well! They have taken him to see a Drain Doctor." "A 'Drain Doctor'?" "Yes! A Drain Doctor!" "You probably mean a 'Brain Doctor'!" "Yes! I probably do!" "What's he gone to see a Brain Doctor for?" "I don't know, but it will be a waste of time." "Why a waste of time?" "No brains!" "Nay! Mick!" "Only kidding!" "I should coco!" "Oh! And another thing! They are going to take him to the Circus." "The Circus! The lucky so-and-so!" "Yes! Mark says he is going to see a 'Trick Cyclist'!" "That should be fun!" says I.

"Dad." "Yes son!" "Err Tommy is going to the Circus to see a trick cyclist. Can we go? Can we go?" "No!" "Why not?" "Why not? I will tell you why not! There isn't a Circus on!" "Well! I heard his Mum say they had taken him to the Doctor and he had sent him to a Sike... err... a Si" "You mean a 'Psychiatrist' Michael!" "Yes Dad! S... Si... err... a Sike... Err yes what you just said!"

Rumours abound at School but still no Tommy. "Dad." "Yes son!" "What's a 'Pufter'?" "What's a what?" "What's a 'Pufter'?" "What's a 'Pufter'? Well it's... Err it's a... Why do you want to know?" "Just something I heard at school." "Well! It's err... hmm! It's somebody who smokes too many fags! O.K. son?" "O.K. Dad." That's funny because Tommy has never smoked. "Well what's a tran... err... a trans... Err a... ?" "Do you mean a 'transom'?" says Dad, who used to drive a wagon for a building firm. "No! That's not right!" "How about 'transport'? You know a transport worker?" "No! It isn't that either!" "Well son! You have got me beat!" "No Dad! It's something like 'vest tight'." "Oh! I think I know what you mean! I think it is a 'Transvestite'. A 'Transvestite' is a bloke... Well! It's a sort of chap. It's err... Tell him mother!" "Who me?" "Yes! You!" "Well it's a bloke... it's a bloke that wears tight vests and changes them every day- not just on a Friday night like you!" "Awe right!" Now I am puzzled because Tommy doesn't wear vests and he's never smoked.

"Mornin Plug!" "Mornin Tommy! Everything alright?" "It is now! Well! When you left on Saturday night, I was going to

change but I fell asleep." "You fell asleep?" "Yes I just said that!"
"So you did! So you did!" "Yes! And well! I was still asleep when
my Mum and Dad came home from the flics." (Cinema.) "Don't
tell me they found you in your girlie outfit?" "They sure did!"
"What happened then?" "Well my Mum started screaming and
couldn't stop. My Father disappeared and returned with his walking stick. He ordered me to lift my dress and take my panties
down and bend over. I closed my eyes and braced myself for many
whacks. Suddenly the screaming stopped and no whack! I opened
my eyes. My Mum had fainted just in time to save me a beating."
"What happened then?" "Well Plug! My Father couldn't send me
dressed as your loved one to the Doctor. Eventually, Mum came
round and started screaming and crying again and my Dad shot
off to the phone box. She was still screaming a bit when the Doc.
came but she had to stop, because she was knackered and was just
about out of breath. The Doc prescribed a sedative." "Did it do
you any good?" "No! Not for me, you idiot! It was for my Mother!"
"Well did it do her any good?" "No! It was a ruddy waste of time
because it set her off again worse than ever and she gave me a clip
round my earhole. The Doctor turned to me and said: 'Now then
young Thomas! What have you been up to?' After a few questions,
he told Mum and Dad not to worry, but just to clear things up, he
would send me to see a Psychiatrist." "Why didn't you tell your
parents what we had been doing?" "What and let my best mate's
secret out! No chance! (That's Tommy.)"

"Have you been to see the Trick Cyclist then?" "Yep!" "What
did he say?" "Well! He started to ask me some stupid questions.
After a while, I said: 'Can I speak?' 'Of course you can, young
man!' says he, "Feel free to say anything that comes into your head.'
Well!' says Tommy, " I asked him if he knew about Confession
and that the Priest could not repeat anything that was said. He
told me that he fully understood, so I said that what I would tell
him would be a secret. He said forgetting about Religion, my
words would be safe with him." "What did you tell him then?" "I
told him the truth, the whole truth, and nothing but the truth!"
"What did he say then?" "Well! When he stopped laughing, he
asked me if he could call my parents into the room and that I
could trust him." "O.K. says I, "Call them in."

"The Trick Cyclist told my Mum and Dad that many young

boys went through a phase like me; he guaranteed that my behaviour was a one off and it would not happen again- but he did say that it was safe to let me play an ugly sister if ever the School put on Cinderella." (Thanks Tommy for keeping my secret. 'You're welcome Mate! You're welcome!") Janette and I never did get together and sadly I let my dancing lapse.

I have got a brand new carrier bike (it can be a taxi/Spitfire/ etc). It's not like Tommy's with a small front wheel making his carrier bike, top heavy- even before it is loaded with orders. It is much faster than Tommy's lumbering machine. As I approach the junction of Weston Lane to Billams Hill, Tommy passes on his 'Junkers'. Good! He hasn't seen me! So I peel in behind him; down Billams Hill on to the Bridge (Where giant eels lie in wait <u>under</u> said bridge.); on to his tail then: "Tack! Tack! Tackacktack!" "Gotcha Mate! You're shot down!" "Nay! Plug! You don't shoot your own Mates down!" "Tack! Tacker! Tack-tack-tack! Gotcha Hans! You're shot down!" "O.K! It's a fair cop!" says Hans. I bank left, along Titty-bottle Park, so named because it is shaped like a baby's feeding bottle.

School's out; another day done. "That's a smashing bike, Plug!" "Yes! It's very good and it can't half motor." "I wish I could get a new one. Do you think if I could crash it into the river? I would get a new one." "No!" "If I buckled the front wheel?" "No!" "Why not?" "Why not? They would only get a new wheel. That's why not!" "Ah well! I will think of summat." "You do that small thing!" says I.

A couple of weeks later as I fly up Bridge Street: "Tacker! Tacker! Tack! Tack! Tack!" I turn! It's Tommy. "You are well and truly shot down Fritz!" "O.K! O.K! I am shot down!" I stop; Tommy taxies alongside. "So you got a new one!" says I. "How did you manage it? You didn't make a hole in the river did you?" "No!" "Well! How did you manage it?" "Well! I thought if I prayed to the Apostles, they might show me the way." "Which did you pray to then?" "All of 'em!" "Well! It seems to have worked! What happened?" "Well! You know that tight corner at the bottom of Charles Street?" "Yes." "Well! I left it in the gutter there." "But you don't deliver that way," says I. "So what!" says he. "Anyrode! This ruddy great tank went over the bike and the tracks chewed the old bike up. I cried my eyes out when it happened. The tank crew clubbed together and they gave me a couple of bob but I got a brand new one like yours because the Army paid for it." "Well! You jammy dodger!"

"Knock! Knock!" "Who's there?" "Tony." "Tony who?" "Tony bloke what does any work around here."

Saturday morning, I have just had my breakfast. It's a lovely morning- not a cloud in the sky. A warm gentle breeze caresses all the people who have fought a warm bed; won the battle and are lucky enough to be out and about. Two swans fly overhead; necks outstretched; wings beating the air. It's blooming marvelous! How an up and down movement can drive them so fast and strongly forward. They are probably going to land on the river.

I feeling wonderful: life is a good; my pocket money is in my pocket- where it should be. I will get more tips as I deliver orders. What could be better? Work done! Lunchtime! "What are you going to do this afternoon?" "Well Mum! I am going to meet some of the lads at Woollies (Woolworths.). We will go to the Milk Bar and probably go for a walk in the Park." "Good! I am going shopping. Don't forget to change!" "No Mother!" "Is Tommy going with you then?" "No Mother! He is going shopping with his Mum. He will be waiting at Woollies when I get there." "Oh right! Well make sure you get a wash not a cat lick- and comb your hair!" "Yes Mother!" All ready then! A good wash; hair combed with 'Council Hair Oil' (Water.) and a drop of Dad's Christmas after-shave (A rare thing in those days.). Out of the front door to greet this wonderful afternoon. I have already said: 'Hello!' to the morning and now I want to greet the rest of the day. Off we go then! Light of heart and a spring in step- maybe two springs.

About halfway to town and half a mile to go, I am walking, not springing along; my body seems to have lost some of its zip. I am beginning to have thoughts- sober thoughts. 'What sort of sober thoughts?' you may ask. Well! I have been thinking about Death. 'About what?' About Death. 'About death?' Yes! About Death, are you 'death'... Err deaf or something? 'You mean real live Death?' Yes! Real live Death and if you don't shut your gob, you could be one of the people that I am thinking about but I will fill you in (Tell you.). 'Sorry.' you may say, or you should say: 'Carry on!' Right then! I will! I have been thinking about age and people being old. You know childhood soon passes and we get into our teens and life probably goes by far too quickly. 'Quite the Philosopher aren't you?.' Yes, dear reader, if I knew what Fil... err... Filos... err... What you just said meant. I probably am.

Along Kirkgate then to Woollies- nobody waiting: they must be inside. I am a bit early. Through the doors: "Hiya Tommy!" "Hi Plug!... Snap!" "Snap yourself!" Tommy is wearing his first pair of long trousers also. "What's up mate? You look as though you have just lost a bob (Shilling.) and found a tanner! (Sixpence.)" "Sorry Tommy! But I just felt a bit down." "And I know why." "Why Tommy?" "It's these long gray flannels; they make you feel that you are getting old." "Yes! That must be it!" says I, "Things were fine until I came out in these long 'uns!" "Well! Look on the bright side!" says he. "How?" says I. "Well! For one thing! You don't have to wash your legs and knees, do you?" "No! That's true!" "And you have no need to wear garters to keep your socks up." "Well! Most of the time your socks are down round your ankles anyrode!" "Yep! You're right but you needn't wear socks at all!" "I don't fancy that!" "Nor do I! But you would have the choice: it's called 'Freedom to Choose.'" "Yes! I suppose it is!" "And you can always polish your boots, or shoes by rubbing them on the back of your trousers! That's better than trying to do it on your socks!" "Yes! I agree! Especially when yours are always down!" "And! I will tell you another thing!" "What?" "Well! When you want to be older wear these long 'uns. Then just think, when you take them off and put on your shorts, how young you will feel." "Do you know Tommy? I am feeling better already! You seem to sort things out and make the best of them." "Yes I do! Don't I? I must be a Philosopher." "A what?" "A 'Philosopher'." "That's funny!" "What is?" "That is! It's the second time I have heard that word today." "Who said it then?" "Oh! Just somebody reading a book out loud." "Awe right!"

Well, dear reader! You may want to know how the War is going. I don't listen to the News on the wireless. Mum says War news is for grown ups and children should not have to worry about things. So, in answer to your question: 'Nowts happened.'

July, l940, I have "Joined up." Well! I have become a member of the local Air Training Corps (The Fighting 279 Squadron.). All able-bodied teenagers l6 years old or more are required to join some organization such as: the Air Training Corps (A.T.C.); Army

Cadets or the Messengers (These were runners who carried messages for the Fire Service.). Girls joined the Girls Training Corp (G.T.C). Everybody has to be in something. As Tommy would say: "Everybody has gotta be somewhere doing summat (Something.)."

I am a tall thirteen-year old and have been accepted without any awkward questions being asked. I think quite a few blind eyes have been turned. Two lads at school have promised to report me for being under age. I have promised to thump them and give them a knuckle sandwich (A clenched fist.). This applies to any other brave soul contemplating suicide.

Crew and Ground Staff Courses are available. I have joined Air Crew because I want to fly. Any Air Crew position will suit me. I would like to be a Navigator though.

'What are you going to do when you leave School?' says the Notice on the Board, 'You could become an: Engineer; Plumber; Bricklayer; Joiner; Decorator; Butcher, etc. Interviews Friday evening. Ask your parents to attend.' Well! There's one thing for sure! No one reading the Notice will be a Doctor, Solicitor, Chemist, Bank Manager, Stockbroker, etc., because we all failed the Scholarship.

"What would you like to do when you leave school?" says this big bloke with a big brown case and big brown boots. "Err... Well! I err..." "Go on! Tell the man what you want to do when you leave School." "Well! I am not sure." "I thought you wanted to be a Joiner like Mr. Granger!" "No! I haven't made my mind up yet! I would like to know more about other jobs." "That's what I am here for!" Says the big brown boots. "Take these leaflets and if you are interested. We can arrange tours around works, factories, and the like." (Say thank you to the man.) "Thank you, Sir! (Brown boots.)" I whisper.

Of course, I <u>want</u> to be a Joiner! Tommy wants to be an Engineer, but as he pointed out to me: "If we don't tell them what we want to be, we can fiddle quite a few half days off School- and it should be interesting anyrode!"

So Tommy and I went to all the available jobs. I am glad we did because it helped to convince us both that we were making the right choice. The only thing was though, Tommy got his job but by the time I said 'Yes', Mother said: "You're too slow to catch a cold all the joiner jobs have gone and there's nowt left."

Good old Dad! He is home for a week. One of his colleagues
from Burley-in-Wharfedale has told him that a firm in Burley are
looking for an Apprentice Joiner. "But it is a Bound Apprenticeship
until twenty one?" says Dad. "What's that mean?" says I. "Well
son! We sign papers and you stay with the firm until you are
loose." "Loose from what Dad?" "Well it means that when you
are twenty one, you are no longer bound to the firm and you
can leave but you will probably be kicked out anyrode." "Why
Dad?" "Why? Because it is a small firm and they won't want to
pay you a man's wage." "Well who will then?" "Most big firms I
expect." "Awe right! I see! But it seems a bit daft to me." "What's
daft?" "Well to train me up all those years and then let me go." "I
agree son! But that's how it is! Anyrode! You haven't got the job
yet!" "No Dad!"

"Hi Dad!" "Hello Peter! Good news! We can go on Friday afternoon to Burley and let them have a look at you." "That's brilliant! Thanks Dad!" "You're welcome, Son! You're welcome!"

On the Bus Station waiting for the ten to two bus from Leeds:
it goes through Burley on its way to Skipton. "Here it is, Dad!
Can we go upstairs?" "Course we can." I haven't had many bus
rides and I think that I have only travelled upstairs on a double-
decker a couple of times. Ding! Dingggg! Goes the bell. Off we
go! There's only one bloke on the top deck apart from Dad and
me.

"Hello Walt! What are you up to?" "Hello Clive! I am taking
the lad to Burley to see about a job." "What sort of job then?" "I
want to be a Joiner." "Well! You could do a lot worse; you will
always be able to make a bob or two!" ('...And model aeroplanes,'
thinks I.)

Ding! Ding! Clive punches two tickets: "That's one and a half
to Burley return." Clive collects the other fare and with a cheeky
grin, disappears down the steps. "Dad?" "Yes." "You didn't give
him any money!" "Sshh!" says Dad. "Us transport workers must
stick together. You will find in life, it's not always <u>what</u> you know,
but <u>who</u> you know." How true those words proved to be.

Off to Burley then! I begin to feel queasy: my forehead is warm-
I am not breathing easy. Dad is chatting away to help me feel at
ease: "Now so! If there is anything you are not sure about ask. If
you're not happy about the job, don't take it. The choice is yours."

"Right Dad! Thanks Dad!" "You're welcome!"

"Here's where we get off." "Thanks Clive!" says Dad. "Thanks Mister!" says I. "You're welcome and Good Luck with the job young un!" "Thanks!"

Ding! Dinggg! The bus pulls away towards Skipton. "You see that road to the left?" says Dad. "Where?" "That part where it goes narrow" "Yes I see." "Do you know what they call it?" "No! I haven't a clue! What do they call it?" "It's called the 'Bottle Neck.'" "Why is it called the 'Bottle Neck' then?" "Well! Just have a little think!" "I have had a little think and I still haven't a clue." "Well Son! Think of a bottle." "Right!" "And what's the narrow part called?" "The 'neck'. Err... ah, I've got it! Narrow neck! Bottle neck!" "Right in one!" says Dad.

'John Mann & Sons' is at the bottom of North Parade on the right hand side- the two end houses of the row. It was built to be a couple of houses but it has always been a Joiners' Shop.

Through the big old batten door then: "Hello!" No reply. "Hello! Anybody there?" Still no reply but we hear tapping, saw-ing and subdued voices murmuring. We wander through to the back yard and outside to the right is a wooden open staircase and a handrail. This isn't a bit how I thought it would be. Where are the people waiting to greet and welcome me? We are stood in a yard at the bottom of these steps and it's starting to rain and that cold wind has turned icy. I give a shiver- more like a shudder. My forced high spirits are steadily becoming unforced and are rapidly moving downhill to low spirits. I grip my Dad's hand. "Steady Son!" he says, "I know just how you feel." "You do?" "Course I do! It's all new to you and it could be a big decision." "Come on son! Let's..." Just then a door opens outwards on to the landing (I always thought that that was a little bit stupid because that door could have knocked anybody off the landing.) and a voice en-quires: "Mr. Jackson?" "Yes!" "And Peter?" "Yes!" That sounds a bit better: he knows my name; he has at least remembered it.

We climb the steps. An old man is stood at the top. He has gray hair; a gray moustache and wire spectacles. He wears a gray/blue apron with a big pocket and dark blue trousers with turn-ups and black boots. He has a pencil balanced on each ear and a length of tape like material hangs from his apron pocket. When I look back, this could have been the man who made Pinocchio.

"Come on in! Come on in! I am Uncle Smith," says he looking over the top of his glasses. 'Uncle Smith,' thinks I that's a funny name, I know one or two Smiths, but I have never known or called anybody called 'Uncle'- apart from relatives.

"Come on then!" says my new Uncle. "Come and get warm by the stove." The stove is about three foot high and maybe eighteen inches in diameter. It glows red round the bottom; its certainly chucking some heat out. Uncle Smith pulls his apron round to his front and stands with his back to the stove. A big gluepot gently simmers on top of the stove. Uncle Smith takes it off and places a huge kettle in its place. "First things first, tea or cocoa?" "Tea," says Dad. "Could I have cocoa?" says I. "Course you can!"

To the right of the stove, there is a huge piece of Hessian, or sacking, about eight-feet square, one corner is lifted and a small man appears. "This is John," says Uncle Smith. (Do I call him 'Little John' I wonder?). "Hello! Hello Peter!" says he. "Err hello! Err, err…" "Call me John!" says John. This is very strange: I have never called any adult by their Christian name. Oh lor! I have got that long-trouser feeling again: I am hurtling towards old age!

John is balding at the front. He wears wire specs; has a moustache- gray like my new Uncle; a pencil on his right ear; a spotless white apron; navy-blue trousers with turn-ups and brilliant, shiny, black boots.

"Here's your cocoa, Peter," says Uncle Smith. "When we have finished I will show you round. Your Dad can have a natter (A talk.) with John. By the way! I have another nephew called George, he is in Birmingham directing a Funeral."

As we drink our tea and cocoa, Uncle Smith tells us about the business. It was founded by John Mann. He had three sons. Smith Mann was the surviving son. John, George and Ernest (Ernest is Uncle Smith's son.) are the third generation and they are cousins. Ernest was currently working at the A.V.Roe Aircraft Factory adjacent to Yeadon Aerodrome

Uncle Smith showed me round the Workshop. In the room where we stood by the stove are three work benches about ten feet long. A broad piece of timber runs full length- front and back on a base, leaving a trough up the centre. There is a big woodworker's vice attached to each bench. There are holes drilled into the workbench top, apparently at random. What struck me as peculiar was that there were no ceilings, just the timbers and big stone slates. A single lonely light bulb hangs over each bench. There are wood shavings everywhere!

"Come through here!" says Uncle Smith. (I have already taken to him, and I feel that I have just become a new nephew.). "Come here!" He lifts the sacking and we walk through. It's cold in here, there's no stove, I give a shiver. My Uncle notices: "Yes! It's colder through here," says he. "We use this room to assemble bigger things and lower them down into the back yard through those double doors on the right." "Oh yes! I see!" says I. "Now! To your left, we have: a wood turning lathe; a band saw, and, grinding wheels." "How do they work, Uncle Smith?" (There I have called him Uncle Smith for the very first time.). "They all work on belts and pulleys. You see that big broad belt hanging down and through the floor?" "Yes I see!" "Well! Downstairs, there is a big gas engine. The big belt can be fed on to a flywheel when the engine is working and it is eased off just before the engine stops. Do you know what this machine is for?" "Yes! It is a mortise machine." "And what does it do?" "The chisel cuts slots in wood called 'mortise slots' and tongues or 'tenons' are fit to slide into them." "Well done Peter! How did you know that?" "Mr. Granger is a retired joiner and one day, he took me to the Workshop where he used to work and he let me have a go." "Good for you!"

"Come-on! Let's go have a look downstairs." We go out on to the wooden steps. It's a bit different going down! I am very careful and grip the handrail tightly. On to the ground floor then. "That's the Circular Saw; that's the Spindle Moulder and this one is the Planer and Thicknesser," says Uncle Smith. "Why do they call it that then?" "Well! You plane a piece of timber on one side and one edge to straighten it, and then open the table like this." Uncle Smith bends, puts his hand under, turns something, and slides the table open. "Why do you open the table then?" "To let all the chippings come out when the timber passes between the bed and the under side of the table." "Awe! Right!"

"If we machine a piece of rough, three by two timber, it becomes three by two P.S.E. Well actually it becomes err... two and seven eights by one and seven eights." "What's P.S.E. then?" "P.S.E. means: 'Planed Side and Edge'." "Why not P.A.R. then?" "P.A.R. What do you mean 'P.A.R.'?" "Planed All Round," says I.

"Ah, very good!" says he.

"Come and have a look at the gas engine then." He opens a narrow door and we go into the Engine House. It is divided off from the Machine Shop and measures about eight feet by eight feet- or sixty-four square foot, take your pick.

Basically, the Gas Engine is a horizontal cylinder with a huge flywheel at one end attached parallel to the cylinder. Attached to this is another wheel about a foot wide and about eighteen inch in diameter. The big belt from upstairs hangs along side this wheel. There isn't much room between the belt and the wall.

"This big lady," says my Uncle, "Powers the machines, six in all. Each machine has a fixed, and a loose pulley, so they can be turned on and off." "Would you like to see it going?" "Err well! Err…" "Don't worry son! It's quite safe." "Err, err, all right then!" "Stand back in the doorway and I will start 'Sally' up." "Sally! That is my Mother's name! Why do you call her 'Sally'?" "Is it your Mother's name?" "Yes!" "Well I will be blowed! We could call her any woman's name but we call her 'Sally'." "Why?" "Because she's always 'gassing'! Gassing! Don't you get it? Always gossiping and talking!" "Ah yes! Very funny! Just like my Mother! I will have to tell Dad that!"

Uncle Smith lifts a big, dull, metal thing off a peg on the wall. "This is the starting handle," says he. It has a big, broad, hook at one end; a shaft and a handle at right angles to the shaft. I now notice that the handle part is very shiny- probably kept so by years and years of use and by many hands. Uncle Smith fiddles with a couple of things. I can't see what from where I stand. He moves a lever on the wall and tells me he has just turned on the gas.

"I am now going to engage this hook part into the slot on the shaft, like this. Come and have a look!" There is a shaft about six-inch diameter in the centre of the eighteen inch wheel. It has a slot cut into it. The hook fits into the slot and wraps round the shaft. "Stand back! Here we go!" Uncle Smith bends and slowly, very slowly, starts to turn the huge wheel. Phftt! Then phftt! And then phftt-phftt! Splutter! Phftt! Phftt! And we're airborne!" Uncle tells me that when the engine picks up speed, the starting-handle slips out of the slot.

I wouldn't like to be standing where he is. The huge wheel is hurtling round faster and faster: phftt! phftt! phftt! I can smell gas! A blue haze gently surrounds the machine and I can smell something. I didn't know what at the time but it was burning oil deposited accidentally during maintenance.

I catch Uncle Smith's eye; He motions me into the corner. "Oh heck! I don't know!" thinks I, "I don't fancy that!" Uncle beckons reassuringly. "Come on Pete! Don't be a coward." Gulp! Here goes and I gingerly step into the corner with the palms and back hard pressed against the rough, stone wall.

The flywheel is turning clockwise. Uncle Smith holds the hanging belt in his left hand and he eases the belt on to the broad wheel with his right hand. It seems very simple and easy to do. "Can I have a go?" shouts I. He nods his head sideways. "Not until you work for us!" he shouts back. "You will be taught and trained how to do it correctly." "That sounds hopeful," I think. He is speaking as though I will be working here.

"I am going to stop Sally and shut her up," he shouts and grins. He moves the lever. "Gas off!" he shouts. The engine falters, splutters: phftt! Phftt! Splutter! Phftt-phftt! Phftt! Slower and slower, and she realises that the battle is almost lost. Just before it stops, Uncle Smith levers the belt off the wheel with a round wooden pole about three foot long- rather like an over fed baseball bat. As the belt comes off the driving wheel, he steadies and stops it with his right hand.

The engine has decided it has lost the fight: it splutters one last gasp the huge wheel slows down, stops turning, reverses direction slightly and stops. There's a hiss and a sigh, as though it is saying: "You win!"

"How did you like that?" says Uncle. "Smashing!" says I. "You will have to look after Sally: fill the oil pots and empty the old used oil out of these troughs." "Awe right!" "And keep her clean." "I think she needs a good clean!" says I. "She certainly does!" says he.

I would like to mention here, that most of the time that I worked at Manns I suffered from boils and abscesses- ugh! When I was twenty-one, I got the push of course. Four years later when I had had plenty of experience I was welcomed back with open arms. Lo and behold! The nasty boils revisited me! It took quite a time to discover that I was allergic to oil- especially dirty, old Gas-engine oil.

We walk through the Machine Shop into the back yard and under the steps. He opens a door about a yard wide and says, "This
is the Furniture Shop." The Furniture Shop is quite a large room
with a huge window at the far end made up of small glass panes
about twelve inches by nine inches. Dust is gathered on the win-
dow-ledges and the glass could do with a good wash- not a cat
lick! Oh heck! There are coffins stacked against one wall: some
with lids and others open. They remind me of a bus queue lean-
ing against one of Tommy's 'lazy' North-winds. They are all
anonymous but someday they will all have names and identities.
Why am I thinking of Charles Dickens's books? I now know how
'Oliver Twist' must have felt when he was sold to the Undertaker!

A sofa stands in one corner; dining chairs stand along one wall
with and without seats. The missing seats are stacked on a bench
close by the window. Various items are piled against the other
wall: some gathering dust; other items are covered with sheets and
there is that solitary light bulb again- hanging from the ceiling.

"We repair furniture in here and make pieces to order. This
is my department. I upholster sofas and chairs etc., and through
that door is the Polishing Room. Would you like to have a look?"
"Yes please!" Through another door and: "Oh heck!" "Why 'Oh,
heck?" " "Well there is a coffin all finished. I have a funny feeling
that it could be occupied."

The coffin on the trestles has a wonderful grain and is highly
polished with gold coloured handles and a gold nameplate. Six
gold square-headed screws hold the lid down. "Would you like
to have a look inside?" "No!" says I. He grins and says, "There's
nobody at home! And anyway! This is for a nice old lady who
never wished or did any harm to anyone! Still 'No'?" "Err well! If
it's empty, alright!" "Here you are!" He gives me a spanner and a
piece of cloth. "Wrap this round the screw heads so as not to mark
when you loosen them with the spanner." So, I did my first task
for J. Mann & Sons." (Unpaid.).

"Right! Go to the foot and we will lift the lid off." As we did so,
I ventured a look and I must say, I was surprised: the main body of
the coffin (If you will excuse the pun.) was just like a pink dressing
gown. A pink lace border ran all the way round the coffin. From
under the border at the head were a pair of beautiful embroidered,
silk curtains. Uncle Smith lifted them to show a gold pillow and

gold padded sides. I am really taken aback and I give a little gasp. "What do you think of that then?" "It's the nicest thing I have ever seen!" I feel the pillow and the pads, and say, "It looks very posh and comfortable." "Well! I haven't had a complaint yet!" says he with a wicked grin. "Ah! Err yes! Of course not!" says I.

"Follow me Peter and I will show you our Polishing Shop." As we enter, I notice that there are <u>four</u> light bulbs hanging from <u>this</u> ceiling; everything is bright and sparkling; it reminded me of Mum's sparkling kitchen after each visit from the coal man.

The Polishing Room has been divided off from the Furniture Shop with a partition. The window in the Polishing Shop extends to form almost one wall of the area. The window frame is divided into three large panes of glass. The windows sparkle: no dust on the ledges- in fact, no dust anywhere as far as I can see. Three shelves run along one wall and three rows of pigeon holes along the other. There are jars, bottles, tins, pots, jugs, funnels, etc., all stacked neatly. On the top shelf are coffin linings and dress sets. A notice says: ' Everything has a place and there is a place for everything." In two pigeonholes there are jars with all manner of brushes with their clean bristles showing. I wonder how they manage to keep them in this perfect condition.

"Well you have seen most things here young man. Would you like to come and work here then?" "I certainly would!" "Then the Apprenticeship is yours if you want it, but you will be on three months' probation." "What's 'probation' then?" "Well! It means that if we like you and your work is satisfactory you can stay with us." "Well thank goodness for that! I thought it was what you got when you break the law and that." "Well! If you think about it that's sort of the same: behave yourself for a certain length of time and you are considered to be fit for civilized society." "But what about the others?" "If I say I like you and think you have got potential that's it." "What's 'potential' Uncle Smith?" "You will find out as you go along but I think you have got it." "Thank you Uncle Smith!" "You're welcome Peter!" says he. "Let's go back upstairs and have a cuppa and get warm."

"I thought I had lost you!" says Dad as we enter the workshop. "We <u>have</u> been a long time, but I have got the Apprenticeship." "That's marvellous! When can he start work?" "After the Christmas Holidays," says Uncle Smith as he grins and winks at me. If you get the ten to eight bus in Otley, it will get you here just in nice time, and there is a bus back at ten past five. Is there anything else you want to know?" "No! I don't think so." "Well! Goodbye then!" "Goodbye Uncle Smith! Goodbye John!" I really am getting old: two Christian names in one day. I know! But I dare not call my father 'Walter'- so probably, I am not as old as I think I am, if you see what I mean.

Back to the Otley bus stop and wait for the bus. I hope it's a Double-decker. "Daaard!" "Yes Son!" "When Uncle Smith told us about the bus times, you didn't say owt and I know you know them all." "Well Son! It always pays to listen; sometimes you can learn a lot. Never say that you know when you start work, because if you do, the odds are that nobody will tell you owt." (What a valuable lesson I learned that day!). "Yes Dad!" "I think you will be alright there," says Dad. "The only problem I can think of, is that you are the only apprentice and you will be working for three bosses." "How's that, Wal... err, Dad?" "Well! You could be at their beck and call and you might have a job pleasing them all at the same time." "Awe right Dad! I see!" "Don't worry Son! I think it will be alright." "I hope so! I wonder what George will be like.

On the way home I tell Walt... err, Dad what and why they call the Gas-engine 'Sally'. He laughs and says, "Very good! But don't say anything to your Mother." "No Dad!"

Knock! Knock! Knock-knock-knock...! Knock!" "That's Tommy at the door!" calls Mum. That's another knocking code she has broken. I know she reads spy novels such as: 'The Broken Chain.'; 'Crooked Cross'; and 'Patriot.' etc. I wonder if she is in the Secret Service and has been trained to break codes. No! I can't see that! Not my Mum! But Tommy says the best spies, don't look like spies at all. They can look like mincepies; custard pies, or any sort of pies. Sometimes, I wonder about him! Anyrode he says: 'Everybody gotta be somewhere, doing summatt.' I still can't believe Mum is a spy! But if she isn't, she should be, because she is a brilliant code-breaker.

"Hi Tommy!" "Hi yourself! How's tricks then?" "Oh! Fair to midlin!" "How did you go on then?" "Fine! It was very interesting." "Well! Fill me in then." So I told Tommy of my experience and about my new Uncle. "Didn't you feel a bit funny calling him 'Uncle Smith'?" "Well! I did at first, but by the time we left,

I couldn't imagine calling him anything else." "Did you go on alright then Tommy at the Engineering works?" "Yes! It was very good! I know they have different ways of doing things but I suppose that some of it is like woodwork anyway. They plane, drill and mill, whatever. Yes! I am sure I will enjoy being an Engineer." "And me a Joiner!" says I.

Bonfire Night approaches once again. We have had a good time chumping any thing that will burn, and, raiding other bonfires. We have a bigger bonfire than ever thanks to the Oval lot and The Crossways gang.

Tommy has called a meeting for Saturday afternoon at 2 pm in the Newall Park to arrange a last hurrah (It must be more, or longer, than the normal three cheers I think!). All members must attend at 2 pm. prompt or pay a ruddy great forfeit. One of Tommy's 'lazy' winds is blowing: it's going straight through everybody! It's too ruddy idle to go round! Nobody knows what a 'last hurrah' is. I think he is arranging a friendly football match. The last time we had a friendly, we took on The Ovallers and The Crossways gang. It was a great fight: a few torn shirts and bloody noses. It could have been called a 'Punch-up' rather than a Football Match, but we all gave three hearty cheers at the end- and shook hands.

A few snowflakes are being gently tossed about on this lazy wind; they escape the old gently puffing man and make a perfect landing; from a beautiful snowflake they turn into an uninteresting droplet. A flake lands on my nose and I have a cold spot; another comes to rest on my right eyebrow- now I have two cold spots. Maybe Tommy is planning one last great punch up before we leave school. "Is everybody here?" "Everybody except the Boss and 'Steady Freddy'." "Here he is!" calls Mark "Where have you been Freddy?" "I have been here all the time! I was the first one here, Mark!" "Wel! I bet the pigs in Pudsey have had a busy time flying backards today! I reckon it will keep them very trim and the Butchers will be able to sell them as fat free 'Porkers'!" "Too true Mar! Too true!"

Tommy comes a trotting through the park gates. "Sorry I am late gentle sirs!" "It's not like you to be late!" says I. "No it's not! I think that this 'Mickey Mouse' watch is knackered!" "What makes you say that then?" "Well because it is all over the place! And I reckon it's about ten minutes slow" "Well! You could have allowed for that couldn't you?" "Sorry mate! It would have taken too long to work it out! I would have been later than ever." Maybe he is not just an ugly face after all. "This knackered watch wants kicking into touch!" "Lets vote on it!" says I. "Good gentle people! This knackered watch has run out of time. I propose that we stone it. All in favour? Err right then! That's un... err unnan.... err... We all agree. Fetch a couple of stones." Mickey Mouse is laid gently on a stone and crushed with the other stone.

> Mickey Mouse is dead,
> Some body squashed his head,
> He copped a mighty clout
> and now his time's run out.
> Rest in pieces, Mickey.

"What's a 'last hurrah' then?" says Mark. "Well! For all you igner... igner... err..." "Do you mean 'ignoramuses'?" "I suppose so." "Is that 'suppose so', a Yes, or a No then?" "It's what I want it to be! And if you don't shut up you will receive a knuckle sandwich free of charge! Well! For all you lot what don't know: a 'last hurrah' is doing something you want to do before it's too late to do it. If you don't do what you want to do until after the time to do it is past, then you can't do it because it is too late to do it- if you see what I mean." "Clear as mud!" says I "As clear as ruddy mud!" echoes Mark.

Another tired snowflake floats gently down and lands on Tommy's head. It's obviously lost, the flake I mean not the head. "Err Tommy?" says I. "In a sec. Plug!" says Tommy. "Let's get on with the business!" "Yes! Get on with it! It's ruddy cold standing here like brass monkeys!" "Especially us in short trousers!" says a lone voice. "Anyrode! What's this 'last hurrah' thing? And where did you get it from?"

Another orphan flake gently comes to rest on Tommy's cranium, like a petal discarded by some heavenly plant close to death. "Err Tommy!" "What is it now, Plug?" "You've got a snowflake on your nut." "Where?" "It's on your... Oh! It's not there! It's dropped off!" "Plug!" says an exasperated leader. "You have interrupted this vital meeting to discuss summat that's not there. Remember Charlie Chuck?" "Well! It were there a minute ago!

It's turned into a droplet and now it's dropped off." "It's 'meta-morphisted'!" says Mark. "Mark!" "Yes Tommy!" "Have you got headache?" "No! Why?" "Coming up with 'met... err 'meta... err what you just said." "'Metamorphised' Tommy!" "Yes Marcus Bighead! You deserve to have a headache coming up with some-thing like that! Anyrode! What does it mean and where did you get that from?" "Well Tommy! It sort of means 'to change'- err like a caterpillar into a chrysalis and then a butterfly. We had this in Biology and I like the word 'metamorphism'. You can roll it about in your mouth and on your tongue and I have been saying it ever since." "Well if you don't spit it out quick, you will get a headache soon, I am sure! Or maybe tongue ache!" "Yes Boss!"

"Boss!" "Yes Plug! What's up now?" "Well! I tell you what's up. If that flake was 'metosed' or what Mark just said on that large cranium." "Metamorphism!" "Yes Markus! Thank you!" "You're welcome!" says Mark with a sort of bighead look on his face, "You're welcome!" "Well Boss!" says I, "If that flake was metamorphosis into a droplet, do you think in the great universal plan of things, it will metamorphisise back into a snowflake and go on forever into infinity?" "Have you got a headache Plug?" "No Boss! Why?" "Well! Two more big words that nobody un-derstands crammed into one sentence." "But I know what they mean!" "You're t-only bugg... err... bloke who does then apart from Mark!" "Thank you, Boss!" says I. "And me!" says Mark.

"Now listen everybody! And listen good! Are we going to go from a mutu... err mutual, that's my clever word for today, soci-ety...? " "That's a clever word for you!" says I. Tommy places a languid hand to his brow, and says, "I feel a teeny-weeny headache coming on! Anyrode! Are we going to form a mutual society for the welfare and protection of orphan snow flakes or get down to some serious business?" "Get on with things!" says a lone voice. "Yes! Get on with it!" chorus the rest. "Right! Then I reckon we have wasted enough time! If Mickey Mouse was alive today he would have told us that we have wasted precious minutes. Long live Mickey Mouse!" "Yes! Long live Mickey!"

"Well! A blind bloke couldn't see what you mean about a 'last hurrah'!" says a lone voice from somewhere lost in the crowd. "Right then! If everybody will hold their water we will get on. This is what I mean. I read... Well! I looked at one of my Mother's books." "Do you mean the sort of book she hides from your old man?" says this lone lost voice. "Right in one, long lost voice!" quips Tommy "In this book, some people living abroad or somewhere were surrounded by cannibals and the odds were that they were going to die, so they got together in this building, and a lot of people what was normally sober joined in and they had a gert (great) big orgy up. They got stoned; they tried to smoke themselves to death (Because nowt mattered.), and, one bloke shouted: "One last hurrah everybody! For tomorrow we die!" "Ah tell thi wot!" says Mark. "What will you tell me?" "I bet they were planning to get their revenge on those lousy Cannibals, as well as having a good knees up." "How's that young Mark?" "Well Tommy! If they had all that booze and smoke in their bodies, when the bad-boy cannibals ate them, they would all get gut-rot wouldn't they?" "Course they would and they would deserve to die like their victims!" "Course they would!"

"But how does this effect us?" the long lost voice is still with us. "Well! For simple minds; lost voices, and, others, I propose that next Saturday we go to Western Woods and over the moors." "But how is that a last hurrah then?" "It's a last hurrah because we shall be doing something before its too late." "What's that then?" "Well! Us older blokes who wear long trousers some of the time or most of the time depending will soon have to wear them permanently when we start work, so on Saturday we will turn out in shorts." "Hoody Blel! " says a new lost voice, "I hope it's not as cold as this next week! We are like brass monkeys today!" "Well! If you get 'em frozzen-off this week, you will not have a problem next week will you?" "No I suppose not." "Is that 'suppose not' a Yes or a No then?" "It's a No." "Are you sure?" "I suppose so!" "Can us junior members who wear shorts all the time be excused?" "Of course you can!" says Tommy. "If you can find some long trousers short enough, you can wear them." "Thanks Boss!" "This is a democratic gang! That's what we are fighting a war for, isn't it?" "Course it is!"

"We will meet here next Saturday at two-o-clock. Bring usual grub and drinks. If we have snow, we could bring our sledges and have a go on Giants, and if we want, we can park them there and go to Weston Woods and over the moors. All those brave lads who are in favour, please raise their right hands! Good! There are no left hands or cowards then?" says Tommy as the last two hands are raised reluctantly.

By gum! That week has shot by. We are gathering in the Newall Park on Saturday. It's this Saturday, which is the first Saturday following last Saturday: the one that was after the Saturday the week before which is making it this Saturday- if you see what I mean. Anyrode! Here we are! It's a fine clear brilliant, sunlit morning, not a cloud in the sky. A very lazy wind is blowing straight through everything and everybody. We have about two inches of snow.

"Hoody Blel!" says Mark, "My knees feel as though I haven't got them. I'm not so bad to the bottom of my shorts and what my socks cover. But Hoody Blel! I wish my knees belonged to some bugg... err... somebody else!" "What about your goolies then?" "Oh! No problem! I lost them last week!" "Same here," says I. "It must be two o'clock." wails the lone lost voice, "It's time our leader was here." "Here! Here!" echoes these 'heres' amidst a swinging of arms across the body; stamping feet and blowing into cupped hands and the odd handkerchief being filled with heaven knows what. "If he doesn't come in the next two minutes, I'm off home! What do you say?" "Same here!" "Here! Here!" and "here" says a late wailing lost-voice voice.

"There's more ears here than a field of corn!" says Tommy as he hoves into sight pulling his very long sledge. The one he uses to give... well... sell rides for a napple, comics, marbles or anything worthwhile having. "I've been listening to you lot from round the corner and you should all be christened 'Mona'!" "Why 'Mona'?" says I. "Why 'Mona'? Why 'Mona'? You should all be called 'Mona Lot'- 'cos that's what you do. We can call it off and go home, you know!" "No! Not that! Let's do it!" "Sorry Tommy!" says a sheepish voice. "I should coco!" says our leader.

"All here and correct? Right then! Off..." Tommy is interrupted by two voices. One says, "Hey Boss! What are you wearing?" The others echo, "Yes Boss! What are you wearing?" "Wearing where?" ""There!" "Where?" "There on your knees!" "Oh there!" "Yes Boss! There!" "You are wearing a pair of your Mother's stockings." "Remember last time?" says I. "Don't remind me mate! Do not remind me!" "He is wearing a pair of his Mum's stockings!" shouts Mark "He cannot deny it!" "Course I can!" "How?" "Well clever clogs! I am not wearing a pair of stockings! I am wearing <u>two</u> pair!" "Well! Why are you wearing them then?" says one of the lost voices. "To keep my knees warm idiot!" "Well that's cheating!" "Course it is!" We still have at least two lost voices with us. "It's breaking the rules!" "How can it be breaking rules what don't exist?" queries Tommy. "Because you have covered your knees and that's not fair and its cheating!" "Can anybody tell me the number of this broken rule then?" A long loud silence smothers the protesters. "Well it's not fair!" wails Mark "Course it's fair cos its not snowing or hailing or pissing-down! So it must be fair!" chortles Tommy. "Clever clogs!" "Yes! Clever clogs!" chorus the rest including <u>all</u> the lost voices. "Well! I still think it's unfair!"

We have a new lost voice! By gum! He has only just made it and avoided a forfeit. "Why is it unfair then?" "It's unfair because you are wearing both stockings <u>and</u> socks." "Well! I could always take my socks off and show you a very shapely pair of legs!" "Tommeee, remember!" says I. "It's OK Plug! Everything is under control!" "I sincerely hope so!" "Your sincere hope is duly noted." "There's no problem." "Well Amen to that then!" says I . "Yes folks! I can show you a better pair of pins than 'Leggy Peggy', Lana Turner or Betty Gable!" "Oh no! I don't think so!" says I. "Well! You are probably right!" concedes Tommy. "He is right!" agrees all The Crescenters including <u>all</u> the lost voices.

"Now listen everybody and learn a lesson! We have had our fill of school and lessons for years." "And years!" "I just said that." "Sorry Boss!" "I should coco!" "Well! This lesson is one that could do you a bit of good as you traverse…" "What's 'traverse' Boss?" "Well! As you walk on the rocky road of life." "You've been at your Mum's books again haven't you?" "I sure have mate!" "Well! Be quick then! And then we can get mobile." "Right then! Here goes! Here starteth the first lesson:"

"What's eight times twelve?" "Err seventy six." "No! It's eighty six." "More like a hundred and six!" "Well! You're all wrong!" "Well! What <u>is</u> It then?" "It's ninety four." "Are you sure, Tommy?" says I. "Sure I'm sure! Otherwise I wouldn't have asked." "Awe right!" says I. (Do you know, dear reader, I always thought it was ninety eight or something.)

"After that wonderful effort, that's not the lesson. I was only kidding." "Oh, for crying out loud! Let's have it!" "O.K. peasants! Here goes! If you are going on an expedition to the desert, or into brass monkey country." "Like it is here?" "Yes Jake! Like it is here!" "If you have to go where it's ruddy cold, or for instance, if you were in the Army and you were going to be sent into arc-tic conditions, they would tell you what equipment you would need. Right?" "Right!" "Right! Well! Suppose they supplied you with what shirts or socks, or whatever, boots, coats and the like that you had to wear. If you wanted to buy something better, that would keep you warmer, or wear two vests and two pair of socks or a thicker jacket, or two pair of a lady's stockings, as long as they conformed." "What's 'conformed' mean then?" "Well! I err... it err... it means that if the boss says it's O.K. then it's O.K." "Like you then?" "Yes Mark! Like me!" "I still don't get the point, Tommy." "That's because you are not sat on it and also because I am not giving it to you my friend," chortles Tommy. "Awe come on, Tommy! Explain!" "Well! Whatever you are ordered to do, if you use your loaf and still conform, odds are you can do it a lot better and have a lot more comfort and benefit both for yourselves and your mates. Keep the bosses and those in charge happy, be-cause they all like to think that they have got you by the short and curlies and the rocky road of life will be straighter, leveller and smoother." I think I know what he means, I think.

"Well! Conform or not, if you don't take them stockings off, or if we aren't moving in a couple of secs I'm off home." says Jake. "Here!" "Here!" "Here!" "Here!" and "Here!" echoes one of the long lost voices. "What's that I hear then? All these 'here's', it re-minds me of Ruth." "Who's this bird called Ruth then?" "Ruth is a piece of poetry! Ruth! Ruth! She stands amidst the corn, or maybe it's amongst the corn, I am not sure which, but she is stood there like a spare part." "But I still don't understand!" says I. "Well! It's like this! This bird is standing in the middle of this gert (very) big field of corn right?" "Right!" "Well! She is surrounded by ears, corn ears, the only difference between she and I is that I am stood in the middle of this desolate snowfield, and I am sur-rounded by ears and more ears, the only thing that's missing is my dear friend Ruth."

"Right then! That's it! I am off home!" says Jake. "And me!" "An me anorl! (Also.)" "All those in favour show hands! That's it then!" "Where have all the 'Heres, heres' and 'heres' and 'here and here' gone then?" asks our leader, "If it's going to upset you lot, I <u>will</u> take them off," "Go on then!" "Get on with it!" "Yes get em off!" "I bet you say that to all the young ladies!" says Tommy with hand on hip, legs slightly bent, and a wicked flicker of his eye lashes. "No only to Pufters!" shouts Mark, "and them others." "What others?" "You ruddy well know what others." "What he means Tommy is what everybody thought you were." "Oh you mean a 'Transvestite'?" "Yes! A 'trannie'," says I. "So come on my darling! Get them off or I will take them off for you!" "You have talked me into it, young Gentleman! But nobody can look! Everybody turn round and no peeking!" "You're kidding!" says I. "No! I'm not!" says she... err he, "if all you lot don't turn round I will bugg... err beggar off home, and no bug... err beggar will receive a napple."

I never discovered where he got his apples from, but he seemed to be able to lay his hands on them all year round, so we do our turn, and Tommy does <u>his</u> turn without an audience. "You can turn back round and have a good look! The lady... err... the lady... err the laddy is decent."

We finally troll out of the Park gates, the Newall Flyer (Bus.) passes- it's twenty past two. Past the workhouse then, I wonder where old Albert is, I hope he is O.K. probably tucked-up somewhere; maybe he is dead- either way I bet he's pretty warm. Along Parker's Lane and up Giants, it must have been brass-monkey weather during the night: the snow is crisp, and, the sledging track is <u>very</u> fast. We will wine and dine. Well! maybe not much wine! It's too ruddy cold and as Tommy says: "Too much to drink and we shall all be leaking like colanders."

We sledge for about an hour. "Right my bonnie lads! Off we go to the Woods! Anybody complaining of cold knees then?" scowls our leader. "What no raised hands? No 'Here Here's'? No takers? No lost voices then? Who's enjoying this short, short trip? You all are? Yes?" "Yes! We all is... err are!" "Come on lads! Let's be off!" "Off with what?" "Off with any thing you like! But I bet anybody what does will be the coldest brass monkey on parade."

"Right lads! Before we go to the woods then." Tommy calls a halt. "These are your orders for today. If we come across any snickles, and there's nobody about, you know what to do right?" "Right!" Tommy has certainly civilized the gang. They have compassion for living creatures; only two still smoke and very few swear. It's surprising what one person can achieve for good- especially if that person is a born leader (Adolf take note!).

"Tell you what lads! If you want to leave the sledges here, we can put our gear on mine, it will save us carrying it." "How much?" "No charge Jake! Not to my mates!" Tommy's sledge had two sides and a back at the rear end. The front piece fitted into a slot to make a box, this front piece could be removed when carrying personnel.

The sled is loaded and off we go over the back of Giants, across Long field and into Weston Wood. "Right lads! Spread out! You know where most of the snickles should be. Check nobody is about and yank em up!" "Right Boss!" "Will do!" etc. "Off you go then!"

So we set off snickle hunting. "Quick! Over here!" calls a voice. "Over where?" shouts I. "Over here! Where I am standing!" "Where are you standing, Steady Freddy?" "I am standing here!" "Where's 'here'?" "Where I am! That's 'here'!" "Well! If you move, I might see where your 'here' is." "If I move, it will mean I have moved from here to there." "For crying out loud! Just move to there." "Where's 'there'?" "'There' is where you will be when you leave your 'here' right?" "Right!" says Freddy emerging from amongst the trees. "Quick over here everybody!" "Not 'over there' then?" "No! Forget 'there' and come over here!" I am first to arrive at Freddie's 'here' and he quickly takes me to his <u>ex</u> 'there.'

"Look at this poor little sod... err so-and-so! It's caught in this snare." Tommy and the others arrive. "What's up?" asks Tommy. "That's what's up!" "Oh! The poor little bug... err bunny!" cries Tommy. "What can we do?"

The rabbit must be in pain and terrified. Its right leg is caught and there is dried blood on its fur. It must have been here for quite a long time. I don't think it is long for this world. "What can we do?" wails Tommy. Usually he tells us what to do but not today. "Well! There's only one thing for it: it will have to be killed. Killed... err... killed! I can't do it! Any volunteers?"

A heavy silence pervades (Another clever word.). No charges of cowardice from our leader. "Can you do it Plug?" "Err yes! I will do the honours because this little chap is in a lot of pain, and when

I do it, it will fall asleep and wake up in Bunny Heaven." "Quick get it done and over with!" "Right Boss I will!"

I ease the wire loop and gently remove the leg, before Tommy and this motley lot can blink or say 'murder', I have Bunny hanging by its hind-legs in my left hand and I give it the chop with the edge of my right hand, namely my little finger. I have seen my Uncle do this many times when we have been poach... err... rabbiting with ferrets. One blow is enough to see Mr. or Mrs. Bunny on their way to a land of taller, greener grass and deeper burrows. A heavy silence envelopes the area; no birds sing; the sun has disappeared; only a mournful wind struggles to find it's way through the trees.

One lone voice, possibly a lost voice whispers, "Do you think, that that wind is lamenting?" "No, it's blowing," says a whisper. Another whisper being a bit more of a whisper, than the whisper before, whispers, "Aye! And it's a goollie-breaker at that!" A brief silence; a muffled giggle; one nervous laugh. Suddenly the enveloping silence is splintered into thousands of minute silences, so tiny that if they <u>could</u> be heard you would never hear them. "Sorry mates! I will have to go for a slash," gasps Tommy, and he disappears amongst the trees.

"What are we going to do with the rabbit then?" "Yes! What <u>are</u> we going to do with it?" "Shall we put it to the vote then?" says I. "I tell you what!" says Mark. "What?" "This what?" quips Marcus. "Seeing that Plug killed it, he should have the say what's to be done, all agree?" The gang agree unani... err unan... err... everybody raises their right hands, except the left handers.

"What are you going to do with our late bunny friend then?" "Well Jake! I am going to... err... Hang on! I need a slash first!" "What is it with you Catholics? Have you all got weak bladders or is it something to do with your Religion?" "No! Nowt like that! But sorry lads! I will have to dash in a flash for a slash!"

"Oh! We have got a poet and he doesn't know it!" says a returned lost voice (Heavens knows where it's been!). As I make my way to Tommy's trees, I am thinking that he <u>has</u> been a long time, it must be a very big slash that he is splashing about. Finally I locate him, and guess what, he is crying like a baby, and sobbing his heart out, but doing it <u>very</u> quietly so that no bu... err... so that nobody can hear him. This is the very first time that I have seen our leader cry since we drank our milk together in the 'Infants'.

"What's up mate?" says I (I know what's up, but it's the only thing that I can find to say.). Tears are streaming down both cheeks; his shirtsleeves are wet through, so I offer him mine. I wish I hadn't because he blew and cleaned his snot… err… soaking nose out.

"Wots going on ovver there?" calls an unknown voice. "Nowt's going on ovver here!" shouts I. "Wel that nowt's tekking (taking) a lot of doing! Can we come ovver and spend a lot of time doing nowt?" "No you can't!" shouts I. "Well! What's this nowt that you are doing or not doing then?" "Err…well! Tommy is saying a Bunny Prayer for the rabbit and contemplating." "Well! If he gets his body back here we can <u>all</u> pray and cont… err… conter… Well! What you just said. If you Catholics will teach us to pray and what you just said." "You mean 'contemplate'!" "Err… yes… err… contemp… as long as it's not in Latin- or some weird lingo."

Tommy quickly wipes his nose and eyes on his shirtsleeves in that order; a final wipe across his eyes he turns to me and says: "Let's go!" "Oh! At last the record-slashers and pray-ers have decided to return then!" says Jake, as we appear on the scene. "Well! What <u>are</u> you going to do with this body then?" "Well Jake! We could flog (Sell.) it, or we could build a fire, gut the rabbit and eat it, then I could teach you to say Grace Before Meals." "And the Boss could say Grace After Meals," says Jake. "If you don't shut up, <u>all</u> the Prayers will be for you!" "Sorry Boss!" "I should coco!"

"Now listen! One and all and listen good! As your beloved leader, I exercise my perr… err… perrog… err… I exercise my power to decide what happens to the poor little bu…err… bunny." "Well! Decide then!" "Well Jake! I have already decided." "What have you decided then?" "I have decided that, as Plug killed the poor little sod… err… so-and-so, he should agree with me that Mr. Bunny should be buried with full honours." "No Latin, incense or holy water then?" "No Mark! Just a simple, honourable service. Well Plug! What dosta (Do you.) say?" "O.K. by me Boss!"

"Right! Jake and Freddy go to the woodman's hut and bring a pick and a spade. He always leaves it open." "What's an 'open spade', Boss?" "The <u>door</u> should be open, <u>not</u> the spade, idiot!" "Well! It takes one to know one!" says Freddy. "Watch it, Mate! Watch it!" "Can't do that, Boss!" "Why not?" "No watch, Boss!

No watch!"

"We shall ignore, whoever has not got his watch. Jake! If you see the Woodman ask him if we can borrow the said items. If you don't see him, don't ask him. Got that, Freddy?" "I think so! If I don't see him, I shouldn't ask him, and if I see him, I err... Well! I should ask him." "By Jove! I think he's got it! I think he's got it!" says Tommy with a barrow load of sarcasm. " So, I now go in search of the missing Mr. Woodman?" says Freddy. (Yes folks! His name was Mr. Woodman.). Young Mick would call him 'Mr. Woodbine'.

So we buried our late lamented friend and Tommy said his prayer. "Out of the depths, etc." He got some special timber from Mr. Granger and he made a headstone, or a woodstone. (Take your pick but not the Woodman's pick!). He wrote the inscription:

HERE LIES THE SOUL OF MR BUNNY
WHEN HE DIED IT WAS NOT FUNNY.
NEVER EATEN OR FORGOTTON,
HE WAS KILLED BY SOMEONE ROTTON.

PS. NOT BY PLUG JACKSON HE WASN'T.

And so dear reader, if ever you are in the North West Corner (Tommy's South East) of Weston Woods and know where to look, the headboard is still there but Tommy's sentiments have long since disappeared:

MY MOTHER TOLD ME
I NEVER SHOULD
PLAY WITH THE GIPSIES
IN THE WOOD.

"To the moors! Gallant lads!" says our, a bit upset gallant leader. "What are we going up onto the moors for then?" "Well, Jake! We might see some sheep in distress and we could rescue them." "But it's starting to snow and it's a ruddy lazy wind. I'm off home!" "Hang on! Hang on! Let's put it to the vote! Will all moaners and cowards, against going on, please show? There will be no sled rides or apples for cowards or moaners. All those in favour! That's unanimous then! Right, my gallant fellows! Forward!"

We set off and trek up the track to Clifton Village, across the road, taking it in turns to be hauled on the sled. Over the five-barred gate- it's locked with a padlock and chain. We make our way diagonally across the field towards the duck-pond; it's probably frozen, with brass-monkey ducks wandering about on it.

"Keep your eyes skinned for Farmer Longfield 'cos he warn't (Wasn't.) too happy when we shot his sheep and took some prisoner." "I don't think he will be out and about a day like today," says Freddy. Now Freddy very rarely spoke and his mate, 'Barnabas' never did speak. He could nod his head sideways, up ways and down ways, in fact, all ways, so we knew that he knew that we knew, that he knew what was going on, so as I write, I can assure you that Barnabas agrees, or disagrees or abstains. 'How does he abstain?' you may ask. He uses two fingers.

"Well keep a look out for old Longfield! He may be small, but he's a wiry, little, tough so-and-so and hard as nails." "Like a Yorkshire Terrier," says I. "Yes Plug! Like a Yorkshire Terrier." "Stop!" shouts Freddy. "By gum! He is doing well today! He will probably sprain his clacker (Tongue.)." "What's up Freddy?" "What's up? That's what's up!" "What is?" "That is!" "Well what's the 'that' that is up then, that is?" "Listen! There's a dog barking." "Not up the wrong tree, I hope!" "No Boss! Straight up! I can hear a dog barking."

For all his faults, Freddy must have bloomin' good hearing because nobody else can hear it. "Move forward men! And be quiet and careful!" "Yes Boss!" "I can hear it now," says I. Soon everybody, even Barnabas who is down on all fours and barking silently and vigorously, wagging his head up ways, down ways and sideways, if he had had a tail it would be moving like a fiddler's elbow, but it is obvious that he can hear some thing. I used to wonder about Barny: it turned out that there was something wrong with him. I never did find out what: he died when he was seventeen years old. May be it was a blessing, I don't know, but one thing I do know, his Mum and Dad really loved him and they must have missed him as we did. I remember when someone cruelly asked him how he came to be born, he wrote on a piece of paper: "My Mum and Dad had a little Barny." Hey Ho!

As we troll over the brow of the hill, the black and white sheep-dog is barking and prancing excitedly; chasing its tail and rearing up against some old sacking or something, against the dry stone wall, which isn't dry cos it's sleeting and snowing. If ever you're out on the Yorkshire Moors when it's sleeting and snowing with a lazy wind blowing- don't be! (If you see what I mean.)

"Be careful!" says Jake. "That dog is a nasty little so-and-so. It went for me once when I was at the Auction Mart with mi Dad." "Do you mean that it went for an errand for you then?" "No Tommy! It didn't actually go anywhere for me- it stayed where it was." "Well! If it stayed where it was, how could it go any where for you?" "No Tommy! You don't und…" "Yes I do Mate! I am only pulling your leg." "Awe right!" As we approach cautiously, the sacking moves and gives a low groan. Tommy holds his right hand aloft and orders us to stay where we are. He steadily walks towards this exciting barking, probably frightened, dog that can go for you, without actually moving. "Be careful Boss!" "Yes be careful!" "Tommy slowly turns, motions us lot to stay where we are and be quiet. He turns to face the beast; raises his right hand and as he slowly, oh so slowly drops it, he gives a long, low whistle. (If you ever saw Donald Sutherland in the 'Eagle has Landed.' you will know what I mean.) Anyrode it worked: the barking ceased. This very excited, upset canine crouched and crawled on its belly towards Tommy, whimpering quietly.

Meanwhile Tommy is muttering something to his new found friend that none of us can hear. He bends down and gently strokes the animal's head. "How did you do that?" I ask. "Magic! Pure magic!" says Tommy. He did tell me afterwards that his Grandfather, who came from Ireland had taught him, but he would never tell me what he said to the dog.

The sacking moves and groans. "Hey up! It's Farmer Longfield! What's the matter then? Have you had an accident?" "Aye lad! I have," whispers the good farmer. "I have slipped on the frozzen pond and twisted my right leg, it could be brokken."

Tommy may have been upset at the demise of the rabbit but he didn't show it now. Some are born leaders and others are born to be led. The orders come thick and fast. "Is the barn unlocked, Mr. Longfield?" "Aye lad! It is." "With all the usual gear in?" "Aye lad it is!" "How do you… err…?" "Yes lad it's all in there." "Off with your coats lads and cover him up! Plug! Jake! Freddy! Down to the barn; teck (take) your coats off first and cover Mr Longfield.

I want old sacking, anything to keep him warm. Is the saw still in the barn, Mr?" "Aye lad! A couple." "Plug! You cut a piece of fence-rail about a yard long, when they come back. Have you got the key to the five-bar gate?" "Nay lad! It's at home." "Right Jake! When Plug has finished with the saw, cut the rails from the gate leg." "Which leg?" "The one that's chained, twit!" "Sorry Boss!" "Off you go then Freddy." "Yes! Sorry Boss!" "Come on then! Get on with it! You're too slow to catch a cold Freddy!" "Yes Boss!" "Oh! And see if there is any rope!"

Tommy organized getting Mr. Longfield on to the sledge. He placed the timber down the outside of his left leg and with his mother's stockings; he tied both legs and the splint together above the knees and clear of the ankles. "Right lads! Get our jackets back and cover him with sacking. Are you fit to move off?" "Aye lad! I am fine." Yes! He must be a tough nut! Thinks I. An extra length of rope to pull the sledge and off we go. The sawn off gate is wide open. The rescue party trolls through on to the road and the gate is dragged back into place. About three inch of snow has fallen, it's stopped and it's a clear fine day. (You may remember that it is downhill all the way into Otley from the Clifton Lane end.) Another length of rope is attached to a rear hook under the sledge to hold it back.

Tommy's orders flow again: "Freddy! Go to the farm and tell Mrs. Longfield and stay with her until we sort this lot out." "Right Boss!" "Plug! You take the front rope to steer." "Will do!" "The rest hang on to the rear rope to hold the sledge back." "O.K. Boss!" "Yes right! Will do!" "Thanks lads! I will stay alongside Mr.Longfield and see that he is O.K. You alright Mr. Longfield?" "Aye! I am now and I am a bit warmer." "Ready to go then?" "Reet ladi Ready to go."

Off we go at a fair lick (Pace.) down the first hill; down a gentle slope; down the next hill; past 'The Spite' pub (So called according to local legend because there was great rivalry between the 'Spite' and the pub next door- hence the names 'Spite' and 'Malice.'): "How's it going Mr. Longfield?" "Aye lad! I'm enjoying it! I've never had so much fun, sin ar war a lad (Since I was a lad.)." "Good!" says Tommy, "Join the Club!" "Aye lad! Ar think ar will." (Yes lad! I think I will.)

It's a fair long downward slope to the top of Carr Bank Hill.

This is quite steep; past Parker's Lane End then turn right into the
hospital entrance. Mr. Longfield has a bad sprain but in view of his
age and exposure, they decide to keep him in overnight.

"That's a job well done!" says Tommy. "Now one last thing."
"What's that then?" "Well! I want one volunteer to go back to the
farm with me. Plug! How about it?" "Sure!" says I. "No problem!" Tommy thanks the gang members and off we troll hauling
the sledge to the Farm to fill Mrs. Longfield in (To reassure her
and tell her what has happened. After mugs of cocoa and warm
buttered scones, the butter runs down each side of our chins- a
quick swipe of a coat sleeve removes the dribble. Mrs. Longfield
convinces us that she will be alright so we make sure she has
plenty of coke and wood on the hearth. We say our goodbyes and
leave a warm, cosy kitchen with a roaring fire and that special
smell of new baked bread. "Oh! Yum! Yum!"

From Clifton to Otley in a few minutes. Tommy, Freddy and
myself sit one behind the other- digging our heels in the snow to
brake and steer. It's quite dark! The normally quiet roads are even
more silent. Not a vehicle to be seen! In fact, we haven't seen any
on the road all afternoon; not even a horse and cart. They would
have been fighting a losing battle anyrode. Down Carr Bank and
left into the "Crescent"; heels dig in; we slide slower and come to
a halt, where several members of the gang are grouped under the
gas lamp- actually it is an electric lamp, but we always called them
gas lamps, don't know why.

"Thanks lads! See you for Mass tomorrow." "Hang on Tommy!"
"What is it Freddy?" "Well! Mrs. Longfield asked me for all
our addresses and she wrote them down." "What for?" "What
for?" "I don't know what for, do I?" "Well! Didn't she say owt?"
"No nowt! Well! She did say not to buy a bird or a joint for
Christmas."

A few sceptical households on the 'Crescent' took a bit of con-
vincing but, eventually, they complied with Mrs. Longfield's re-
quest and the parcel they each received contained: a duck, a pork
joint, and, a dozen eggs.

When we are up near Clifton Village, we call at the farm and
say 'Hello' to our newfound friends- Mr. and Mrs. Longfield.

"Go on Mum!" "Yes, Mum! Go on!" "I don't know! It could
be a nuisance you two. Anyway! I would have to ask your Dad."

"Oh! I am sure he will say it is O.K!" says I. "Yes! O.K!" says Mick. "But he won't be here will he? And I am sure it will all fall on me!" "No it won't Mum! We will sort it out! Won't we, Mick?" "Course we will!" "Oh yes! I have heard this sort of tale before." "Cross our hearts and hope to die!" "Both of you?" "Yes Mother!" "All right then! Off you go!" "Yippee!" "Thanks Mum!" "You keep your promises then?" "Yes Mother!" "Of course Mum!"

"Hello Mr. B! (Bradley.)" "Hello you two! What can I do for you?" "Well! Mum says it is O.K. and we can sort it out because she thinks Dad would agree." "That's fine! Then come through into the kitchen." "Thanks Mr. B!" says I. "Yes thanks Mr. B!" echoes Mick.

"I like that one!" says I. "Well! I like em all!" says Mick. "Well! You can't have them all! We are lucky to be getting one!" "I know that! But it doesn't stop me liking all of em, does it?" "No! I suppose not." "How many are there, Mr. B?" "Err six, two died." "Oh! I am sorry Mr. B." "Well! It was just as well: they were sick." "Oh! I am sorry to hear that! I err... We will say a prayer for them won't we Mick?" "Course we will!" "Tell you what!" says Mr. B. "I will make us a mug of cocoa, whilst you choose." "Right then!" says I. "Let's have a look at this lot." "O.K." says Mick. "Let's look and choose."

My fancy is drawn to one of the puppies immediately. "I have chosen!" "So have I! " says Mick. "That was quick Mick," says Mr. B as he comes with three steaming mugs of cocoa. "Have you both chosen? Because you can only take one." "Which one is it Michael?" I close my eyes; say a very quick prayer; open them and I say: "I like Sandy!" "That's the one I want also!" shouts Mick. "Thank you Lord!" breathes I.

So Sandy, called Sandy because he is sandy coloured, came to live at the Crescent. "Where's he going to sleep then Mum?" "I have cleaned out the bottom of the cupboard and put in a basket for him." "Thank Mum!" "And when he gets bigger, he can sleep in the coal hole (Coal house)." Yes, 21 The Crescent had an inside coal house also. We had never used it for coal. Mr. Granger had put a wooden floor in, level with the kitchen. Before he did this, there were two steps down on to a concrete floor.

"Hi, Dad! Welcome home! When do you go back?" "Nay lad! Let me get in't (into the) house and get mi coat off." "Sorry Dad!

What I meant was: how long are you home for?" "I know what you meant lad! I am home for two weeks. Where's this tripe hound that you've got?" "Nay Dad! He is called Sandy. Why did you call Sandy a 'tripe hound'?" "Didn't you know? Your Mother refers to all dogs as 'tripe hounds'." "Awe right! I see Dad!" "I haven't a clue lad- why, but there it is."

"Let's have a look then! Oh aye! He's a little beauty! Pity I won't be able to train him." "That's what I want to talk to you about! Will you teach me to look after him and things?" "Course I will, Son! Course I will!" So Dad spent quite a lot of time showing and telling me what to do and how to progress as Sandy grew to manhood... err 'doghood'!

Sandy is six months old. We have just been up Giants and we both are doing very well: along Parkers Lane then towards Carr Bank Road- better put him on the lead. When he grows up, I will be like my Father: I will never need to use a lead.

"Here Sandy! Here boy! Come on then!" Sandy stops; turns; looks me in the eye mischievously; turns again and bounds off. A squeal of brakes; a shout; a yelp: Oh no! Sandy has been knocked down. "Sorry mate!" says the cyclist, "I didn't have a chance. I hope it will be O.K." "It's not an 'it,' it's Sandy." "Sorry! I didn't know, but it wasn't my fault." "I know it wasn't," says I. "I was just going to put the lead on him, but he ran away." "Well! I hope Sandy will be alright." "So do I! So do I!"

Although I would not admit it at the time, Sandy started to go down hill. He seemed as though he could not hear properly. He would sit looking sort of vacant and sometimes, there was no response. "I am very sorry," said the Vet. "Sandy took quite a knock in the accident and had he been older, he would probably have been alright but I am afraid it would be kinder to let him go to sleep. He is in pain now, and it would not be fair to Sandy or you to let him live and be in constant pain." (Letter 'H' is next.)

So Sandy was put to sleep. I went home probably the saddest boy in the whole world- well in the whole of Yorkshire at least! Mum was quiet; even Mick was silent. I will be brave. "Come on son and have your tea!" "O.K. Mum! I am sad but I will be alright! I know how Dad must have felt when he took Nance to the Tan yard." "Yes! That was a very sad day but it had to be done just like Sandy today." "Yes Mother!" I sat at the table; we started our meal. "Here Sandy!" I started to say and then I realised Sandy was not there. I gulp and closed my eyes- of course he's sat there! I can see him, head cocked sideways and twinkling eyes, patiently waiting for his grub. I couldn't open my eyes because he would disappear. "Mum! Oh Mum!" I cried. "I dare not look down! Please take me upstairs." "O. K. son! Easy son! Come on! Up the stairs to your room and have a good cry."

That was a terrible day! I did not have a meal at the table for about a fortnight. I did not believe it at the time but Mum said time was a great healer and her words were proved true.

Christmas once more. The War still seems to be a long way off. All our news is on the wireless (No tele in those days.). As Dad says: "They only tell you what they want you to know." The air raid sirens sound quite frequently. At first we were afraid. I used to get a heaving stomach when I heard them, but it was amazing how we accepted them as part of every day life. We have heard the Jerry planes at night. We know they are the enemy by the up and down drone of their engines, but nobody that I know has actually seen any.

Tommy and I are going to Midnight Mass. There's something special about this Service. The Church is steadily filling; people are lighting holy candles; kneeling at the Crib for a few moments of prayer and peace. The aroma of burning incense spreads throughout the Church. Two altar boys are lighting the candles with tapers on long poles (Good Luck to em!). People are coughing nervously, someone sneezes, I get the whiff of tobacco, beer and spirits.

Yes, it's Christmas once again. We sing carols. The Mass is over. Father Dean wishes us: "A Happy and Peaceful Christmas!" and announces that we will sing: 'Silent Night.' It's my favourite carol. As the echoes die away, I have a wonderful feeling of happiness and peace. The organ starts to play 'Silent Night." Oh good! We are going to sing it again. What's this? It's the German prisoners singing the carol in German ("Stille Nacht! Heilige Nacht!). We don't have an official choir, but we get by. The German prisoners must have been practicing for a long time; they are absolutely perfect. Handkerchiefs come out; men and women are weeping. The carol comes to an end and the organ once more starts to play. The prisoners start to sing 'Silent Night' in English and we all join in.

That was the most moving experience of my young life.

Mass over then! We shuffle toward the exit. There's the German Officer. I will work my way towards him and touch him. As I did so, he must have felt me. He turned, smiled and whispered: "Happy Christmas!" "Same to you!" whispered I. I had touched the enemy who was to become my friend.

The cold Christmas wind blows in through the open door. Odd flakes drift in and settle; they are too late to hear Mass- hard luck! Their brief lives end as they turn into droplets, and to add insult to injury, shuffling feet snuff out any life remaining in them. Out into the night then, people are wishing everybody well. It has been snowing heavily, about an inch and a half covers the ground. Soldiers, sailors, airmen and members of the congregation are throwing snowballs. One hits the German Officer- he retaliates. Soon we are all throwing snowballs. Service men and woman are shaking hands with the prisoners and everybody seems to be happy.

There's something wrong about this War. These men are no different from us. They don't have square heads. They have come to see the baby Jesus in the Crib and tonight, they have become part of our congregation. I pray that tonight is the start of something good.

The prisoners of war have been escorted to Mass each Sunday for a few months. After Christmas if the weather was bad, they were brought by lorry and dropped off without guards and collected after Mass. If it was a half decent morning, they marched to Church and back to camp, always singing.

On Boxing Day, I told my Dad what had happened at Midnight Mass. He said that during the Great War, both sides stopped fighting at Christmas and they came out of the trenches to exchange greetings and small gifts. Some groups played football. "Who won, Dad?" "Everybody! Everybody won lad!"

"Good Heavens!" says Mum. "What's up?" says I. "The skies up!" says Mick "Shut up!" scolds Mum, "Which 'up' should I shut up?" "Shut up and belt up! Father Dean is coming! He is at the gate! Quick nip upstairs! Get a wash and not a cat-lick! Make sure Michael washes also." "Yes Mum!" "And comb your hair! Both of you!" "Yes Mum!" "Peeeterr!" "Yes Mother!" "Father Dean is here, he wants a word with you." "Right Mother! Coming!"

Father Dean rarely visited. He was knocking on and it was a large Parish. I wonder what he wants, as far as I know I have done nowt wrong. I will just keep my fingers crossed: "Morning Father!" "Good morning, Peter! How are you?" "Fine Father!" He seems to be in a good mood and still I can't think of owt I have done wrong. "Now then Peter!" "Yes Father!" "You have seen the P.O.Ws at Church?" "Yes Father!" "I understand you had spoken to one of them." Oh heck! That's what I have done wrong. I have fraternized with the enemy. I could be shot, but they would have to shoot that lot who fratted (Talked to etc.) with the Jerries at Midnight Mass also.

"You have spoken to the Officer, Willi." "Yes Father! He wished me a Happy Christmas and I said the same to him but I didn't know his name. "His name is Willi and he would like you to go to see him at the Camp on Weston Lane if your Father and Mother agree." "Well Father! I'm not too sure because he is a German after all." "Yes Peter, I agree! But we are all God's children and there are good, bad and indifferent." "What's 'indifferent' Father?" "Well! People who are not really bad or not very good." "Err well! Err, you mean normal people Father." "Yes, I suppose I do."

"What do you think Mum?" "Well! Your Father is away but if Father Dean thinks it is alright, you have my permission to go." "When can I go Father?" "Well! Willi has got permission for you to visit him on Sunday afternoon about two-o-clock." "That's fine! Tell him I will see him next Sunday." "I will! And now I must go." Father Dean makes the sign of the cross and says "Bless this house and family."

I went to see Willi. He was the only adult I had called by their Christian name. He never told me his surname. Willi was married with two young daughters. They were a family like us: Mum, Dad and the kids. He taught me German: "Was ist das?" 'Das' is 'der/die/das' whatever. We became good friends.

Eventually rules were relaxed and the P.O.Ws were allowed to visit. Willi was a regular visitor to our home. Eventually, he was repatriated. He found his family, miraculously all well. We exchanged letters for many years until he died. Other P.O.Ws stayed and married local girls. They had probably lost everything at home. I worked with a couple of 'Jerries' and we became good friends.

What do you remember about Willi you may ask. I remember his lovely smile and his beautiful brown, knee length boots.

It's a cold morning in January. Here I am trudging through the snow. I look back at my footmarks. At least there are other prints so I am not entirely alone: some other guy has passed this way and he must be somewhere in front of me. Into the bus station then. I have my brown, imitation wood-grained, tin lunch box under my arm. I don't know what's in my 'packing up' but I shall enjoy it. (I took packed lunches to work through the war and for many years after.) Once when we were reminiscing with friends, my Mother said that quote: "I never complained or asked for a change of diet ever." (Well done me!)

So I am sat here, then I am surprised how many people are awake and about, well they must be awake if they are about, maybe not all of them if you see what I mean.

A queue starts to form at the Skipton sign. People get up off the bus station seats and the queue lengthens. Should I get up and join it? It's warmer under here but the bus comes from Leeds. It will drop some passengers off for Otley but will there be enough room. Better not chance it so I join my very first travellers' queue.

"What's the time?" asks this bloke. "It's eleven minutes to." "Good! He will be here in a minute," says this other chap. He turns to me and says, "Is this your first morning young 'un?" "Yes Sir!" "Call me Jacob," says Jacob. "Right err... Jacob! I will!" I've got that old galloping old-age feeling again. "Tell you what!" "What Jacob?" says I. I may as well get used to being an adult. "By the time you count to sixty, the bus will be here, go on start counting slowly."

The bus pulls in. Good! It's a double-decker (It always was but I didn't know that at the time.) "What did you count to then?" "I got to forty six, Jacob." It still sounds a bit odd this Christian name lark but practice makes perfect. "There! I told you! It's always on time." (They certainly were very punctual as I was to discover as time and years passed by.) The queue shuffles forward. It's snowing heavier. Coat collars are turned down and snow brushed off by each queue member entering the bus. It reminds me of a big red dragon devouring a huge snake as the line of unknowns in front of me disappear in through the doorway.

It's my turn; collar down; snow brushed off with my hand. By

gum! It's cold! In future, I will leave the snow where it is. Up
the curved steps and on to the top-deck. There's a fare... err fair
amount of room. And Oh good! There's a seat right at the front.
I give a cough and blink my eyes: tobacco smoke has caught me
at the back of my throat. My eyes feel as though they are going
to water. Men are coughing and spluttering. As I walk down the
aisle to the front of the bus, I can see a bluish haze of tobacco
smoke flirting with the lights illuminating the top deck. One chap
is coughing and spluttering into his handkerchief, so much so, as
Tommy would say: enough to spew his ring up.

"Fare, young un?" No! It's not Clive. "Workman Return to
Burley, please?" Good lord! That does make me feel ancient! "That
will be thruppence (Three pence.)." Ping! (From the ticket machine.) "Here you are son." "Thanks, Mister!" Dingggg- Dinggg!
Off we go! I am driving this monster. All the passengers are in
my charge; I will get them safely to Burley and then my Assistant
Driver can take over. The snowflakes hammer silently as they attack the front window. They realize they are fighting a losing battle: some fly off and away; others splatter the glass and silently turn
into droplets- they slide defeated down the window. Surviving
flakes form a narrow white band along the window ledge and
make a pattern as they settle up the left hand side of the glass and
along the bottom (Persistent little devils aren't they?)

Time to get off then. The bell rings once to stop the bus;
two rings tell the driver to move off. I hand the bus over to my
Assistant Driver. Along the aisle, down the steps. What's coming
in through the doorway? It's God's cold, clean, fresh air, accompanied by dancing pure white snowflakes. That's the last time I
travel upstairs on a ten to eight workmens' bus.

Down North Parade then clutching my Jock-box (Sandwich-
box.). By gum! It's ruddy cold! The metal handle is so cold it's
burning my hand. "Tuck the tuck-box under your arm, idiot!"
"Right! I will do that small thing." I must get myself a haversack
and a cap. Snowflakes settle onto my hands and face as they melt,
each tiny pinprick of cold nips the spot but as Mum would say:
they have given me a healthy glow. But by gum! It's a ruddy cold,
healthy glow.

So I trudge in the darkness; pass under the solitary lamp-post.
It's struggling to be seen through the darkness and swirling fog. I

can just make out a few snowflakes dancing like moths around the glass. By gum! It's cold! A silent figure passes under the sick looking lamp on the other side. Can this be the ghost of North Parade? It, or he, or she, produces a muffled cough; a glow of a cigarette and a hoarse whispered "Good morning." Well! That's no ghost and it's a lousy morning but better be civilized. "G-good morning!" says I, as the non ghost disappears into the darkness, coughing, spluttering and probably glowing.

Here we are then. What's this? The whole place is in darkness. Nose pressed against the glass, I attempt to look through the window, shading my eyes from nothing really. Everything is inky black. It's snowing and blowing or blowing and snowing, I haven't decided which yet. I'm shivering and stamping my feet to warm them up. I bet Tommy would have worn two pair of socks. By gum! I will tomorrow.

Hang on Pete! You passed a passage a few yards back. At least I will be able to get out of this lousy weather in there. As I turn into the shelter, the Daddy of all cold winds, well it's more like a breeze really, lazily goes straight through me. Ye gods! I will be better out in the open. Thank goodness! A figure trudges into a tired pool of light cast by the street lamp. The voice calls, "Good morning, Peter! I am sorry I am late!" It's my new Uncle.

The key turns in the front door lock. Through the machine shop to the back door. I unbolt it. "Be careful up the steps! When we have lit the stove and had a cuppa, you can clear the snow off them." "Yes, Uncle Smith! Err... where's err... John, this morning?" "Oh! He is in bed: he has a chill." I wish I was in bed- with or without a chill! "George won't be in today: he is tied up with a funeral."

To the right of the stove is a box of chopped wood. On the other side a larger box with a lid. Uncle Smith lifts the lid. The box is full of wood shavings. "Never move these boxes nearer to the stove because it gets very hot." "No, Uncle Smith!" "First we clean out the stove from the bottom here." He swings an iron door up and it rests against the stove. "We don't leave it lit overnight. It would be too dangerous." "Awe right!"

So I rake out the stove. The smell reminds me of the Gas House yard. I drop shavings and then firewood into the stove; light it and when it is burning nicely, I tip about half a scoop of coke into the flames. "Here we are!" says Uncle, as he appears from between the hung sacking from the other room with two steaming mugs. "How did you manage to boil the water before the stove got hot?" "Magic!" says Uncle. "No, I am only kidding! We have a gas ring through there."

So Uncle Smith and I, sat on two wooden saw-stocks (Trestles.) and he told me tales of when he was a lad and an apprentice joiner. He told me that he was seventy two years old. Ye gods! That is old! At lunchtime, I did a calculation. He was born about 1870- now that is ancient. The stove really is radiating heat, we draw back a little. The stove can be regulated by sliding the bottom door open; almost closed, and closed. This determines the amount of air allowed into the stove.

It was one of the happiest days of my life. Uncle Smith was webbing, springing and re-covering: a sofa; four dining chairs and two easy chairs. He had had them brought upstairs where it was, as he said "Cosy and warm." He showed me how to tack, stretch, weave and fasten the webbing. I now twig it was webbing hanging from his apron the day I came with my Father. He scooped a small handful of tin-tacks (They have very sharp points.), and believe it or not, he tossed them into his mouth and proceeded to fasten the webbing using a tack hammer. He presented each tack head to the hammer with his tongue; most times, one blow was sufficient to drive the tacks home. This left his left hand free to work. He was proficient using his right or left hand. "How do you get the tacks to stick to the hammer, Uncle Smith?" He just put his finger to the side of his nose, winked, grinned and whispered: "Magic!" I don't know if there were magnetic hammers in those days, but I am sure his must have been. When he had emptied his tack-holder (Mouth.), he made me promise that I would not even think of copying him. I promised and there was no chance of breaking my promise. When Uncle Smith died, a length of webbing, some tacks and the hammer were buried with him. To give him some-thing to do, I suppose.

Uncle Smith stayed for his lunch: sandwiches same as me. He spun yarns of yester-year and spoke of his youth. I remember he told me a nice little story about the 'Big House'. When the young man came a courting the daughter, he arrived in a small bi-plane and landed in a field on the other side of the river. A rowing boat was always tethered to the bank, no not that bank, the riverbank. He would row across and woo his lady-love. Afterwards he would fly off into the sunset as they say. Even at my tender age I thought that it was very romantic – just like the flicks. Hey ho! It's a by-gone age isn't it?

Our dinner hour lasted about two and a half hours but that's how it was in those days at Manns: not like trains or buses working to a timetable, or clocking on or off at a Mill, or Factory. Time didn't seem to matter where I served my apprenticeship. If a job took longer than estimated, nobody bothered as long as it was done expertly and more important, to the customer's satisfaction.

"Here's your key," says Uncle. "It fits all the locks. You can let yourself in in the morning and sort the stove, first job." "How does one key fit all the different locks then?" says I. "Well, these are rim locks. They fit on to one side of a door. (These locks were made of wood and metal and were about 8" x 6". The key was about 5" long). Inside the lock around each keyhole are wards: these are rings, usually two or three. They prevent the key from turning unless it has slots in the right places to clear the wards. Are you with me?" "Yes, Uncle Smith!" "Well! If the key is cut or filed away to clear all the wards you can turn it in all the locks." "Ah, yes! I see! It's called a 'skeleton key' isn't it?" "Yes, that's right! But we still have to lift the levers into the correct position to allow the shoot to move in and out. That's what the slots on the bottom edge of the key are for. If we have a problem with the levers, we can cut away that part that is preventing the shoot moving, so that it has a clear run." "That's very clever, Uncle Smith!" "Yes, Peter! Isn't it!"

The day passed very quickly, like lightening, in fact. We had a final mug of cocoa and knocked off at four o'clock in nice time for me to catch the ten-past bus that comes from Ilkley en route to Otley.

So, here I am at the bus stop. I make sure that I have not lost or forgotten my return bus ticket home. 'Very good!' you may say. 'But haven't you forgotten something?' Err no! I don't think so! I have my jock box and my ticket home. Err... Oh now I see! No I didn't have to clear the snow off the steps: the sun did it for me. 'I still think there should be something else.' Well, reader! I can't think of owt! 'How much are you being paid?' Oh that! I am getting twelve and a tanner (62.1/2 new pence.) for forty four hours, eight a day and four on a Saturday morning.

"Hi Mum! I'm home! What's that smell?" "It's your dinner." "Yes! But what is it?" "It's rabbit pie. Mr. Longfield has given each member of the gang, two rabbits." "That's brilliant, Mum!" "You're early, anyhow! How have you gone on?" So I tell my Mother about my day between my sniffs of baking pie. "You seem to have had a busy day, have you learnt anything useful?" "Yes! Mum." "What?" "If you don't smoke, don't travel upstairs on a ten to eight Workman's Bus."

So I got a haversack for my lunch-box and my sister Maureen knitted me a thick woolly hat with side flaps to keep my lugs (ears) warm. Sisters can be useful occasionally.

Father Longfield and his wife seemed to take a shine to the rescuers. They had no children, apparently a son died from meningitis when he was about fifteen years old. Freddy wasn't leaving School until Easter. To pass time, he started visiting the Farm. He chopped wood and made sure that coal or coke was always handy- in fact, I reckon he had taken them under his wing. They were both in their mid-sixties I reckon. Anyrode! Farmer Longfield offered steady Freddy a job on the Farm, to which steady Freddy readily agreed. "How's your first week gone Freddy?" "Well, Plug! It's been brill! I didn't think I could be so interested in anything in my life, especially the animals." "Good! That sounds very good!" says I. "What time do you start in a morning?" "Six-o-clock." "What?" "Six- o-clock." "What?" "Six-o-clock every morning." "Well! I reckon that you must set off the night before to get there for that time, it's the middle of the night man! I bet you never get there at six!" "No, I don't!" "I bet you don't! What time do you make it for then?" "I get there for half past five each day." "Pull the other one!" "No straight up Plug! I am there on the dot! No effort! No problem!" "By gum!"

"Freddy! Those pigs in Pudsi will have to get up early to fly backards.today." "Serve em right, Plug! Serves em right!" says Freddy with a grin a mile wide. "Anyrode! I let myself in with a key." "Join the club!" says I, "I also have my own key." "Well, Plug! When I arrive in the morning, I make sure the fire is O.K. and then I take 'Ma' and..." "'Ma' who?" "'Ma' and 'Pa' that's what they want me to call them." "Like me with Uncle Smith?"

"Yes! Like you." "And what do they call you?" "'Son' just 'Son',"
comes a contented reply.

Have you noticed if you have to do something you don't like
or want to do, it's an effort and a bore, but if it's something you
like doing, or something you are interested in, it's a breeze. Freddy
worked and grew up on Longfields Farm. Eventually, they retired
and Freddy inherited the business. He became a happy contented
man. Just think if Mr. Longfield hadn't had the accident; if we
hadn't gone on to the Moors, on a lousy morning really, and if
Tommy hadn't taken his long sledge and Freddy hadn't gone to
keep Mrs. Longfield company, Freddy could have ended up in a
mundane job that he hated, and I bet he would have been late for
work every morning. Hey ho! It's a funny old life.

> As ah war gooin hover Rombalds Mooer,
> Ar met mi Uncle Billy
> He said nowt.
> An ar said Nowt.
> Nar dunta think tharts silly.?

"Hi everybody!" says Dad as he comes into the sitting room.
"Another week over." "Hello, Father!" says Mum. "Hi Dad!"
"Hello Dad!" from us. "Now Son! How have you gone on at
Manns." "Well, Dad! I still haven't met George. Both John and
George are in bed, it could be Flu, but I have had a great week
with Uncle Smith." I filled Dad in on my first week and I told him
about Uncle throwing tacks into his mouth and being able to use
either hand. "Well! You could call him 'ambi dextrous' then." "I
suppose so! But I prefer 'Uncle Smith'!" (Well reader! What are
you laughing at? I thought it could have been Latin for 'Uncle
Smith'!).

Second Monday morning then: the stoves lit; both kettles are on;
glue kettle on the stove; water kettle on the gas ring. John's back! I
don't think he should be. Three mugs waiting to be filled and one
in reserve for the elusive George. Thump! Thump! Thump! And
more thumps, as someone thumps up the outside wooden steps.
The door opens and three chins and two flabby cheeks under a tall
gray trilby-hat appears, all shaking as it thumps across the workshop. Two huge flabby hands envelope mine and from somewhere

between the two cheeks and three chins, a quick stuttering voice says, "Ah, P... P... P... Peter! I am gl... gla... glad to... to meet you." ("Th... th... this... mu... must be... be G... G... George!" thinks I.) He wore a long, loose raincoat; his gray trousers were several inches too short. They revealed a pair of blue socks and shiny, black boots with laces tied in large horizontal bows (I wonder what would happen if I could tie both laces together, thinks I.). I don't know why I thought this, but I did. I noted that the left trouser leg turn-up, was in need of a stitch. It was hanging down and stroking his ankle. 'What's a turn-up?' you may ask. Well! All long trousers had turn-ups around the bottom. These would be turned up about an inch to an inch and a quarterish. My Mother called them 'muck collectors'. It was surprising how much dust etc., that they did collect. I have wondered how many colonies of tics, mites and bugs lived therein- only to dash out for dropped food scraps when the wearer was sat down to a meal. Or whether they got by on the dust and muck steadily accumulating in their hidey-holes. Turn-ups vanished eventually when the War started. Trouser widths were reduced; pocket flaps disappeared all to save material and reduce labour. Oh I remember! Suits were all single breasted (The clothes we wore were called 'Utility Clothes'- requiring coupons from ration books.).

When he took his coat off, his trousers were tight round his gut. He had bellies to match his chins and cheeks. From the waist down he reminded me of Mr. Pickwick and from the neck upwards, he looked like an overfed bull-dog.

I did not have too much contact with George. He was often away on business or officiating at funerals and organizing the work. His wife did the book-keeping. Uncle Smith and John were both craftsmen and always seemed to be laid back; they were obviously contented, happy men who loved their work. George was so different: always in a hurry and bustling but I am sure that he was happy also in his own way. If he attempted to hit a nail in with a hammer he would invariably miss and hit his thumb or spoil the timber, or both, and this would be accompanied by his favourite exclamation ("D... Damn! Blast! and B...Bugger it!) I used to describe it as: Storm over the Nile. (Work that one out!)

So I settled into my 'prenticeship. I would accompany John to different jobs. I learnt how to pack tools into a Joiner's Bass,

(Tool bag.). This was oval in shape when laid out. It had two strong, rope handles covered with strong usually brown material. It was made of a Hessian-type material and was very strong. The trick when packing a tool-bass was to lay a hand saw or panel saw (Finer-tooth hand-saw.) vertically along one side and keep it in an upright position, teeth up, with other tools. This would fit comfortably across the back and shoulders. To carry a tool bass: the two loops or handles were brought together; a hammer, usually a claw-hammer with a striking head and a hook-like a claw for withdrawing nails etc., was inserted into the handles and lifted on to a shoulder and held cantilever like with one or both hands gripping the hammer.

On occasions when I went to do small jobs with Ge... Ge... George. He would thump! Thump! And more thumps up the steps; throw open the door and shout: "P... P... Peter! G....g... get a light b... b... bass to... together! An... and... w... we will g... go in f...f...five minutes." "R... r... right... B... B... Boss." (Now he has g... g... got m... me... d... d... doing it!) A 'light bass' by the way is a smaller tool bag containing basic tools. I could guarantee that when we got on to a job, the very first tool required would not be in the kit! (All hell would break loose and we all know what G... G... George says when he is not best pleased, don't we?) And I would have to go back to the Workshop to get whatever. He never learned! But I did as I progressed through my apprenticeship: I used to carry as many tools as possible. I would have taken the kitchen-sink had it been loose.

So I am settling into a routine. As it's still winter, there's not much outside work. If John requires help on the workbench or machining timber, I work with him. If there is inside work available, I carry his tools and timber. If the tools and timber are too much to carry, weather permitting, we have a hand-cart.

Tommy seems happy enough at his work as an Apprentice Engineer. "Hi Tommy!" "Hi, Plug!" "How's it going Tommy?" "Not bad! Not bad at all!" "Have you learnt anything useful then?" "Yes! I know how to make tea and cocoa for a lot of blokes." "Well! That will come in handy if you work in or own a café." "Yes! I suppose so, and I bet I could do well, because they all say that I am the best ever tea-boy that they had ever had." "They could be nedding (Kidding.) you- you know." "How?" "Well! If they keep on telling you that you are the best, you will want to carry on being the best and you will be giving them a good service, won't you?" "Well! The crafty sods! I never though of that! Tell me Plug! What can I use to sabotage their drinks?" "Sour milk or salt."

"I've got an idea." "What idea, Tommy?" "Well! You can get hold of loads of timber off-cuts and you can have the use of tools." "Yes! That's true!" "Well! There's a bloke at work who makes models." "Yes I see! But what's the point?" "The point is that he can make aeroplane propellers and wheels, and you can supply the wood." "Right! I am with you! I tell you what! I can make the shapes in my dinner hour and we can assemble then at home." "That's good! Very good! Now this is what we can do." "Shoot!" says I. Tommy points his index finger at my heart; cocks his thumb and fires. I fall, mortally wounded, "Thanks mate!" I croak and expire. "Come on Tommy! No pissing about! Fill me in!" "Well! We can buy one kit of each plane from Jack Hardy's Toyshop. This will give us the plans and we can reproduce any model. I have had a word with this bloke at work and we could do a three-way split. How about it? Are you on?" "On!" says I.

So we went into business making model aircraft: B-17's (Flying Fortress.); Westland Lysanders (One of my favourites!); Lancasters; Avro Ansons; Mossies (Mosquitoes.) and others. We could not make them fast enough for the youngsters in Otley. For a very small fee, Jack Hardy hung them in his Toy Shop and sold them.

Back to work then, as I have already mentioned I spent most of my time with Uncle Smith, we became very close. He taught me how to bring timber to a high finish for staining and polishing by using various hand planes, scraping and finally damping to raise the grain, which was leveled-off with very, very, fine glass paper, (sandpaper), rubbers were made for polishing. These were cloth pads filled with cotton wool. They had a tail so that as the polish was applied it tapered off on to the work surface. The polish was loaded into the inside of the rubber to avoid excess polish being applied to the work. The polish mixed with methylated spirit was applied with a circular rubbing action. As the work progressed the circular action became an elongated figure eight and the polish was gradually thinned with methylated spirit. The room was misted with water before the work commenced. The temperature was constant and woe-betide anybody who opened the door and let in a draught or dust when the sign said: 'Don't be a mutt! Keep me shut!' Some polished work could take months or even longer to complete: the work was allowed to rest and harden between applications.

Plane irons were also allowed to rest. There were spare blades all dated for reference. Many moulded timbers such as: skirting boards; architraves and picture-mouldings were produced by hand. There must have been about a hundred moulding planes at Manns. One I would like to mention was held in both hands and pushed away from the operator- it had an adjustable iron for depth. The blade projected from the bottom of the plane to make trenches (Square-cut grooves.). It was called the 'Old Woman's Tooth'.

Uncle Smith taught me how to make coffins. This was one of my favourite jobs. I got great satisfaction from taking a set of coffin timbers and in a short while transferring it into a beautifully lined, highly polished, waxed or matt finished product. Have you every wondered how a coffin side is bent? Well! Coffin timbers are bought in 'sets': a top; a bottom; two sides and two ends. The sides have a series of circular-saw cuts running across them at the 'shoulder' height- if you see what I mean.

A coffin side is clamped on to the workbench with a bench clamp. This consists of a round metal bar that fits loosely into a hole in the bench. At right-angles to the bar is an arm with a foot. This rests on the work. It can be tightened and loosened. When it is screwed down on to the work piece the rod binds in the hole and everything tightens up. Now you know what the holes are for in a joiner's workbench. (No! They are not worm holes!) If desired or required (I like that it rhymes!) a packing can be placed between the foot of the clamp and the timber to protect the work from being marked by fibre-compression.

So we have the side, securely clamped on the bench with a panel-saw each machined slot is sawn almost through. In fact, some have to be cut so deep that they can be detected at times on the outside of the coffin. So: it's saw; lift; saw; lift, and, bend etc.- until sufficient bend is achieved. Sometimes, gentle damping of the fibres helps. When the side is nailed to the bottom, glue is run into the saw kerfs (Cuts.) and coarse linen is stuck over the shoulder area to strengthen it (That's something else you have learnt today.).

All we need to make now is the lid. We rest it on the coffin and mark it all round. It is sawn just oversize on the circular saw; the edges are shot (planed) straight with a tri-plane (A very long wood plane.); the shoulder area rounded to suit (Maybe this is where the term 'round shouldered' comes from.).   Back to business then. A mould is glued and pinned round the edge of the lid to fit down the outside of the top edge of the coffin. And hey presto! Any holes are filled with coloured filler to match whatever stain and polish to be used. A final clean up and we are ready to seal the coffin. Hot wax is run all round inside; the head is held up and the assistant pours wax into the shoulder area, say the left shoulder; the coffin is tilted to the left; the wax runs down to the bottom; a further left tilt and it runs up the left corner at the foot end. A tilt to the right seals across the foot end and if there is any wax left; a further tilt seals the right corner. This process is repeated for the right side and then the foot end is tilted to seal the head.

Sometimes a raised coffin lid would be required by the customer (Well not the customer!) but by relations ordering the funeral. To make a raised lid, or as Uncle Smith would say: "Raise a lid and charge a quid." To make a raised lid then: the centre would be cut out about six-inch smaller all round than the original lid, and the edges would be shot (Planed straight.) and moulded. A moulded strip about four inches wide would be fit under the centre section projecting about an inch and a half all round, this was then glued and screwed from the underside to the centre section. The outside section (the original lid) was then glued and screwed from underneath to the two other sections thus making a lid with two moulded levels, and three sizes, a moulded strip was fitted round the outside of the lid projecting down below the under level of the lid and about an eighth of an inch below the top edge of the lid to show a quirk, as we say in the trade. I think that you could make a raised lid now, but I bet you a half a dollar, it wouldn't fit.

The only transport we had was George's car and the hand cart. We couldn't get a coffin into the car and we wouldn't carry a coffin on the handcart. So, if it was local, we carried the box covered in a purple and gold drape. For the first three months or so, John and I, escorted by Uncle Smith, would carry the coffin to whereever and then I would return to the Workshop, but this particular day, nothing was said and before you could say:

not for the feint-hearted, Mate! I had laid my first corpse to rest. Screw your nose up and keep your mouth open and you will be O.K.

I spent two very happy years with my Uncle Smith. He became ill and had to retire. He would pay us an occasional visit to 'keep an eye on us'. He died about a year later.

Easter then. The 'Open Air Baths' are open, well they are always open-air but at Easter they are open, what I mean is that they are open for business. We have got Season Tickets for the Swimming Baths. Because we are working, including Freddy, we don't need to sneak in. The next letter is "T."

"Tell you what!" says Tommy, "It's a lovely day! I fancy a dip in the river." "You know that we are not supposed to go topside of the weir!" says Jake. "Yes!" says I, "Our Mums would not be well pleased!" "What they don't know won't hurt them will it? What do you say Freddy?" "You can count me in!" "Right then! I will. That makes two of us. Are you two ditherers coming or not?" Jake and I exchange looks; shrug our shoulders and fall into line. "Good!" says our leader, "Let's be off!"

I must confess the river is more interesting than the Swimming Baths. Shoes and socks off and tied round our necks, we wade across to the main island. The water giggles and chatters as it flows around stones and larger rocks, pebbles of different colours show through the clear water. They are very smooth to walk on. The weir is running normal: water cascades over the top turning into frothy white ripples as it slides down the sloping weir; it turns into clear blue water reflecting the sky as it makes its way between the islands to rejoin the main stream.

There's plenty of cover on the island. Well! Enough cover to get uncovered and put our cossies (Swimming trunks.) on. The weir is topped by a concrete coping about twelve inches wide. Here we sit then: feet in the river and water cascading around our waists; it is all very pleasant. We chat and make an occasional dive. It has to be a flat dive: a belly flop in fact, because here near the weir it's quite shallow, but it falls away to be quite deep about four yards out. When the sun shines, it's pleasantly warm but when it disappears behind a cloud, the temperature drops and it causes one to shiver.

"Tell you what lads!" says Tommy, "Let's bum skate down the

weir." "Good idea!" says I. "Right let's go!" says Freddy. He really
is a different lad since he started going to Longfield's Farm- full
of vim and vigour. We used to say that he was too slow to catch
a cold, but now he is faster than the clock. The weir is covered in
moss and when it is wet, it is very slippery, all one has to do is sit
down, the moss and the flow of river does the rest.

"You lot go!" says Jake, "I am going for a swim." And he belly
flops into the river. Half a dozen skates later Freddy says, "Jake's a
long time." "He will be O.K." says Tommy. "He is the best swim-
mer in the School but we can make sure that he is alright when
we get back to the top of the weir." "Where is he?" says I. "Don't
know!" says Tommy. "Can't see! Oh! There he... Goodness! He is
very close to Garnetts Mill!" A half-raised arm; a faint shout and
Tommy's away- cutting through the water like an otter, doing the
crawl. Jake disappears. Tommy goes underwater; a splash; a shout.
Tommy has surfaced with Jake. He has got behind him and he is
supporting and dragging him back towards us.

Freddy and I jump in; Tommy pulls Jake closer to the weir and
we've got him. "Quick!" shouts Tommy, "Slide him down the
weir and on to the island!"

Jake doesn't look too good to me, I think he could be uncon-
scious or worse. I begin to panic. "Quick! Lay him face down,"
commands Tommy. He proceeds to practice what he has learnt
at the Life Saving Classes. I wish I had gone to First Aid and the
Life Saving Course when I had that chance. A cough and a splutter; Jake gives a low groan and moves his head. To me, it is like a
miracle, like raising Lazarus from the dead. "Take it easy, Mate!"
says Tommy. "You will be O.K." Thankfully, Jake did recover,
apparently, as he put it, he had had a touch of cramp, had gone
under and swallowed some water. Tommy swore to us that he had
seen a hole in the River Wharfe where Jake had drunk more than
his fill.

Tommy saved a life that day. We swore each other to secrecy:
"Spit on your right hand! And wipe it on your left sleeve and hope
to die!" because if our parents had ever found out where we had
been, it could have been a side-oncer! (That's a very heavy clip
round the earhole; the rounds of the kitchen and up the dancers.)
Tommy was to become a life-saver for me in the distant future-
but that's a fair way off.

The Squadron is going to Summer Camp for a week. We are going to an airfield, east of York (Very hush, hush.). We will live and work alongside R.A.F. personnel and train with them.

First day at Camp; it's a Canadian Squadron. It reminds me of Beamsley Beacon: I hope they know how not to burn custard. Breakfast over, we are told to gather outside our Nissan Huts. "Squad 'shun! Fall in! Right dress! Eyes front! Stand at ease! Stand easy!"

"Right you Guys!" says a full Canadian accent to our rear. "Drop your trousers!" Some do; some don't. Some half do, or won't. "Come on Guys! Drop em! I want to see up your arses!" Nobody said anything about this carry-on. Bromide in drinks has been mentioned. "At last"!" says this voice. "Front rank! Bend over!" I am in the third rear rank so I can see all that is going on or what's coming off. Gum! I didn't think the wind was that cold or lazy! "Rear rank! Bend over." The timing is perfect: three lorry loads of W.A.A.F.S (Women's Auxillary Air Force.) pass our rear, or should I say, our rears.

My cheeks are hot; my bum is cold- but still hot. I bet every member of the rear rank had two sets of blushing cheeks that morning. To add insult to injury, this Canadian Doctor had a little lifting stick, which he used to check that we were clear at the front also.

Wednesday already! Today we are going to fly. The Squadron is equipped with Lancaster bombers. They are practicing circuits and bumps. That is: take off and fly in a circle round the Airfield. When Ground Control signals all clear; the plane touches down and flies off again- usually, three circuits and then a break and maybe an aircraft check.

I have collected my parachute harness and I proudly wear it. As we board the aircraft, the Gunner says to me, "I hope you don't have to bale out." "Why not?" says I. "Well! You're so thin, when the 'chute opens, you will slip straight out of the harness." "Nay! I am not that thin!" "Only joking!" says the grinning gunner. "You will be O.K." When I look back, the gear was much too large and slack around my body. I shudder to think what would have happened when the chute opened if I had had to bale out.

First flight ever then. The four Rolls-Royce Merlin engines are roaring and vibrating: eager to have their full power unleashed.

The whole plane is trembling; I am trembling. These four beasts are being held in check. They seem to be arguing their case to be given full power and escape from earthly bonds. They want to be up and away. I want to be up and away.

The crew sit either side of the fuselage, Jake and I with them. The engines increase to a crescendo: everything seems to be set free as the brakes are released; the wheels feel solid as we gain speed down the runway. Bump! Bump! Suddenly the vibration and trembling cease: we are airborne! Eventually the Lancaster levels- I would think at about one thousand feet. The engines settle back to a contented rhythm.

The Gunner shouts, "Do you want to go into the gun turret?" "Yes, please!" (The mid upper-turret is on top of the fuselage, roughly half way between nose and tail of the aircraft.) What a view! The farms, fields, and, there's a river gently passing by. We float on air. Well we couldn't float on 'owt else, could we? I am looking straight down the top of the fuselage. There's the tail and two big rudders. The engines are beating; I feel <u>my</u> heart pounding with excitement. I have a thought my Mother and Sister will never experience this wonderful feeling of elation and freedom mixed with a little bit of fear.

The Air Gunner is shouting something. I cannot hear because of the noise. As I look down, he seems to be telling me to touch something. I think I must have got it because he gives a thumbs-up. Right then! Let's see what's going on outside. Oh my God! Where's the plane gone? I am looking straight down to Mother Earth. What's happened? I think that was the longest three seconds of my life. 'Well! What happened?' You may well ask. What happened was this: the Gunner had showed me how to operate the gun turret and when I looked up, I had swung the turret ninety degrees to be at right angle to the fuselage.

It was wonderful to be able to operate the gun turret and get almost an all round view of the countryside. There's Jake in the Astrodome. The Astrodome is large enough to accommodate a man's head (Mind you! I know of one or two heads that it wouldn't fit!) It is situated behind the cockpit and it is used to navigate by the stars. He gives me a two-finger salute and he gets two back.

It was a brilliant week! We all hoped to have further flights. But alas! It was not to be.

"Hi, Mum! I'm home." "Are you?" Oops! Something's wrong. She's wearing that: 'Up the dancers' look. "I have had a wonderful week and I have flown in a Lancaster bomber with the Canadians." "Have you?" "Err yes, Mother!" Something's up but I can't put my finger on it. "Yes, Mother! We have had a busy week and we have done many things." "Oh! Have you!" "Yes, Mother!" This sound ominous. "When did you break your wrist then?" "My wrist, Mother?" "Yes! Your wrist! You know that thing holding your hand on to your arm." "But it's not broken, Mother!" "Are you sure?" "Sure! I'm sure! Here have a look!" What's she nagging on about my wrist for? "So you will be able to hold this then?" says Mum. She passes me a pencil. "Course I can!" What's up with her? Wrists and pencils? Is she going gaga? "When someone holds a pencil in their hand, what do they usually do?" "Why they write of course." "Of course they do and what do they write?" I wish she would pack it in, I am being a bit thick thinks I. "Well! They write lots of things: they write Grocery Orders and letters and... " "They write letters then?" "Yes, Mother!" "Like you didn't do last week!" "No! Err yes... Err no, Mother!" So that's it! Just because I hadn't written home. "But I said I would not write home." "So you did but I did not think you would keep your word." "But if I said I would not write and I did write, to write would have been wrong. You wouldn't want me to write a lie would you?" "I would just want you to write at least one letter." "Which letter would you have wanted me to write, Mum? There are twenty six to choose from?" "Ouch! That hurt Mum!" as she lands me one of her extra special side-oncers.

"Jake wrote two, and of all of the parents I have asked, you are the only, so-err-son who has not written home." "If I had written two letters like Jake, that would have been two wrongs, because I told you that I wouldn't write, and you always tell us that two wrongs don't make a right. It would be just like lying." "Don't try to blind me with science young man!" "Well, Mother! I am very sorry, but I bet I am the only one to bring a prez- zie home." "A present! What present?" "Close your eyes Mum! Right! Open the box!" "Good heavens! How many are there?" "About fifty boxes, I should think." "Where did you get them?" "Well! When the Canadians took over, they had been left behind by the British and none of the Canadians used 'Top Mill' snuff."

"Aye lad! Come here and have a cuddle! Thars not such a bad lad after all!" "Thanks Mum!"

As I have mentioned, Otley was a garrison town, full of soldiers: Tank Corps; Infantry- Yorks. and Lancs. and Scottish Regiments.

ANY VOLUNTEERS TO PLAY IN THE SQUADRON BAND.
PIPERS AND DRUMMERS REQUIRED.
We are privileged to have a King's Piper to teach Band Members.
Anybody interested – See the Band Master.

I read the notice; read it again. I would like to play the bagpipes but I can't read a note of music. I approach one of the veteran Pipers. "Hey Norman!" "Hey yourself! What's to do?" "Well! I would like to play the pipes but I can't read a note of music." "Join the Club!" says Norman. "You mean to tell me, you can't read music!" "Well! I remember I couldn't when I first started but I can now. If you join, I will help you. I should point out that the instruments were bought with donations from local businesses and individuals.

We learnt to play, first on a chanter: a reed instrument . They always reminded me of an Indian snake charmer and they worked because when anyone started to play, there were two individuals who would sway. I am progressing on the chanter. I am even play-ing the grace notes- a short flick of a finger or thumb in the right place of course.

"Hi, Mum!" "Hello, Peter! What have you got there in that box?" "These are my bagpipes Mum! I have to get used to balanc-ing them on my shoulder; squeezing the bag and playing." "What all at the same time?" "No, Mum! I balance on a Monday; squeeze on a Tuesday and play on a Wednesday." "Now then young man! Don't be cheeky!" "Sorry Mum! I couldn't resist it!" "You're for-given! Tell me how you play them."

"Well! First of all, I have to balance the drones…. err, the three pipes on my shoulder- like this, with the bag under my arm and play with the chanter held in front. Right, Mum?" "Yes, I see! So start playing then." "I can't!" "Why not?" "I can't play because I have no air in the bag." "Well! What do you do then?" "I bring the bag forward; hold it upright and fill it with air. When it's full, I thump it and the drones sound. Then I replace the thumped air and put the bag under my arm. The trick is not to squeeze too much air out of the bag, because squeezed out air has to be replaced." "Go on then! Have a go!" "Right, Mum! I will! It might be a bit difficult." "Why?" "Because the bag needs treating." "Well! How do you do that?" "Well! I am not sure but I think you put syrup or something into the bag to seal it and make it supple. I will have to check it out before I do owt to it."

Here we go then! It is my very first attempt. Each time I squeeze it, I lose too much air. Every note is forgotten as I try to play. "Whoa! Whoa! Oh stop!" shouts Mum with her ears covered. "That's the worst sound I have ever heard!" "Sorry, Mum! I need to practice." "You need a lot of practice. I am going out after tea and I won't be home until ten o'clock tonight. You will have the house to yourself." "Thanks Mum!" "You're welcome! But practice upstairs!" "Yes, Mother!"

"Good Morning, Mrs. Walker!" says Mum to our neighbour across the back gardens. "Good Morning, Mrs. Jackson! How are you?" "Oh, I am fine!" "Didn't you hear the Air Raid sirens last evening?" "No! I was out of town." "Well! They started about six o'clock and continuously sounded for about three hours or more. Percy was out with his binoculars all this time looking for Jerries but he didn't see a thing, and I will tell you another thing." "What other thing?" "Well, Mrs. Jackson! The All Clear never did sound!" My efforts caused the pipes to drone up and down- a pretty good imitation of the air raid warning in fact. I didn't manage to achieve a steady drone or moan which is akin to the All Clear. I was banned from practicing my bagpipes at home permanently. I was confined to playing on the chanter. I practiced hard at home using a pencil whenever I had some spare time and no chanter handy.

Today, Sunday morning, it is my first Church Parade as a Piper in the Band of the Fighting 279 Squadron. Here we go! The drums beat; the pipes wail into sound. "Quick March!" We're off! (Squeeze! Blow! Squeeze! Blow! 'How did you manage?' you may ask. No problem! All the holes are 'bunged up'. Once the bag is filled with air, it stays filled. All I have to do, is twiddle my fingers.)

So, here I am then marching in perfect step; head held high, bursting with pride and energetically twiddling my fingers and one thumb. I can conquer the world. Suddenly disaster! I must have squeezed the bag too hard when there was no need to do anything at all. At least two of the bungs must have popped out of the drones. Maybe it would have been better for me to have taken the reeds out of the drones, or left the bunging up to an expert, but I had had no advice, nobody had said owt. Here started the battle to keep the bag full of air, because if it emptied, there was nothing to grip under my arm. I am easily losing this fight. The result is a good imitation of a tired Air Raid siren.

I feel discomfort in my throat; my cheeks puff; lips start to tremble, a fit of giggles are imminent. I catch Ronnie's eye. He can play, but he has twigged. Another tired siren sounds, the pipes drone and fall silent. The drums sporadically cease to beat; we march along- accompanied by a deafening silence.

Oh, Lor! I wish I had stayed in bed, or died, or something! My eyes are blurred; cheeks are puffed; my throat is dry. Oh, Mother! How I wish I were at home with you even if I had been sent up the dancers. A single drum starts to beat the pace. I have been reading a book called 'Drums of the Dead." Now I know how that lot felt.

"Parade Halt!" "Fall out!" I have my eyes almost closed as if I can fall out unnoticed. A voice floats across the Parade: "Jackson! Just go home!" "Sir!" croaks I.

This was probably the most disappointing moment of my young life, because I had carefully planned this Sunday morning. As a practicing Catholic boy, I could not attend a Protestant Service as I would be damned to eternal Hell Fire. When the Parade disappeared into Church, I planned to take up my position on the wide footpath running along the front of the Church. Other Catholic boys, John, Paul and Richard, I had bribed with a napple each to disappear into Town. They would have gone to 'The Milk Bar' anyrode- but it pays to be sure.

"Attention!" "Eyes front!" "Pipes drooping!" I am here to guard my comrades, they don't know what I am up to and the people outside will think that I am under orders. Right turn! March twenty paces! Left turn! Attention! After a short while, march back to centre. Attention! Then a left turn and march twenty paces to the left point. This I would repeat for the duration of the Service- making sure I was nonchalant when my comrades appeared. Alas!

This was a shattered dream. I trudged home dejected: my head
and pipes drooping. It's a good mile home from the Church and
that day it seemed more like twenty.

Water passes under the bridge, as they say. I am a playing mem-
ber of the Band. I can play three Scottish tunes reasonably well:
'Highland Laddie'; 'Flowers of the Forest'; 'The Road to the Isles';
'God Save the King', and, 'On Ilkla Moor baht tat'- and with all
the grace notes. Would you like a translation of 'Ilkla Moor?' No?
Well! I will then! Here goes:

> Whar asta bin sin ah sor thee.
> Where had you been when I saw you.
> On Ilkla Moor baht tat.
> On Ilkley Moor without a hat.
> Thars barn ter catch thi death o cauld.
> You will catch a very bad cold.
> On Ilkla Moor Baht tat.
> On Ilkla Moor baht tat. On Ilkla Moor baht tat.
> 2nd verse.
> Then wi shall hav ter bury thee.
> Then we will have to bury you.
> On Ilkla Moor etc.
> 3rd verse.
> Then twermsle cum an eight thee up.
> Then the worms will come and eat you up
> On Ilkla Moor etc
> 4th verse.
> Thent ducks al cum an eight up twerms.
> Then the ducks will come and eat up the worms
> On Ilkla Moor etc
> 5th verse
> Then wi shall cum an eight up t ducks.
> Then we shall come and eat the ducks
> On Ilkla Moor etc.
> 6th verse.
> Then wi shall all have eten thee.
> Then we shall all have eaten you.
> On Ilkla Moor baht tat.
> On Ilkla Moor baht tat.

On Ilkla Moor baht tat.

Today I have received my Piper's emblem. I wear it on my arm with pride. It is a replica set of bagpipes, about 3 inches high, on a red velvety background. I have fastened it as close to the front as I dare, so that anyone coming the other way can't fail to see it, especially if I turn my arm inwards as I march along. If a photograph is taken, the badge is always to the fore, on the forearm as you might say.

The band is invited to various functions: Rural Shows; 'War Weapons'; 'Wings for Victory' and 'Buy a Gun for a Ship' etc. People are encouraged to save, or give monies towards the War effort. Some individuals have paid for a bomber or fighter. They must have had a lot of dosh.

Time passes quickly, especially since I left School. Tommy is in Engineering, of course; Freddy a Farmer; Jake is a Decorator and I am an Apprentice Joiner. The gang has fairly well broken up now that we are working for a living, but Tommy, Freddy, Jake and I seem to stick together and we are good mates.

"Oh! P... P... Peter," says George. "T... take... th... these c... clothes pr...props to Burley Wood... err Woodhead to M... Mrs. Wer... Williams." "Alright!" ("All... err alright B... Boss." th.. thinks I.) It's a nice day, I am looking forward to a pleasant walk. Mrs. Williams will give me a mug of cocoa, a big piece of fruit cake and probably a tanner (Two and a half new pence.) tip. As it turned out, I nearly got a bob (Five pence today.) and two pieces of cake.

"Bye Mrs. Williams!" "Goodbye Peter! Have a nice walk back." "I will!" So off I set. It's about a mile and a half back to the Workshop. As I approach the Village a voice calls, "I say young man! Who do you work for?" "Err, I am an Apprentice Joiner and I work for Manns." "Oh good! Manns do all my work. I have a job for you. Can you come and look and maybe measure it?" "Err right! Err, I suppose I could," says I nervously. This is the first job I have had to size up; it's a big responsibility: I might measure it wrong. "How will you measure it?" you may ask. I will use my two-foot ruler. "What's a two-foot ruler?" A two-foot rule, or ruler is made from boxwood. It consists of four lengths, six inch long and hinged to fold from each end to make it twelve inch long, this now swings on a pivot to close the ruler making it six inch long by double width. "Why not a three foot?" some of you may ask. Why not? I will tell you why not. A two foot can measure into smaller areas or spaces than a three foot. Happy now are we? Can you open a two-foot ruler in four movements, every movement to move away from you? Let me know how get on. "Come on young man!" says this lady. "Don't keep me waiting all day." "Err no Ma-am! I am coming!"

So I go into this house. I take a quick look round. An unmade bed on one wall with a dressing gown and nightdress draped over the bed. A big mantelpiece and range takes up most of another wall, various articles of clothing are hung across the mantle shelf being aired by a fire that glows bright red- a big kettle on a swivel metal shelf gently blows out steam. It is blackened really black from spending its life too near the glowing, smoking coke, coal, or whatever fire. There is a wooden scrub top table and one dining chair. An easy chair is drawn up to the fire- cosy like. My Mother spends a lot of her life doing the same thing as this kettle, but her legs tend to be red and wrinkled, not blackened. Everything seems tatty somehow as though it could do with a good going over, as Mum would say.

How different this lady is. She is quite bonny: not a hair out of place; she wears make up but not too much- just right in fact. The dress she wears reminds me of models in my mother's Mail Order Catalogue. Her slippers are quite striking: they are blood red with a gold pattern.

"Wha... What's the job Missus?" "Well! First of all would you like a drink?" I don't want a drink really, I have just had a bucket sized mug of cocoa at Mrs. Williams but the motto is: never refuse owt (Anything.) or you may get nowt (Nothing.) next time round.

"That will be fine! Can I have a drink of tea?" "Course you can." "What I want is a gate at the top of the steps to stop a baby falling down them." "I think I can manage that," thinks I. The cuppa duly arrives accompanied by ginger biscuits, so I am sat on the bed and my hostess is in the easy chair.

"My daughter has been to Paris and now she is paying the consequences." "Lucky girl!" thinks I, but how can she go to Paris when the Jerries are there and if she <u>has</u> managed to go, she must have gone on tick (credit) and now she is paying the consequences. "She has had to go to Hospital and I got up in such a rush that I haven't had time to put my knickers on." "Eh! err…" a ginger biscuit rests between my teeth. It should have been bitten by now but remains un bitten, everything freezes, except the mug spilling over gently in my trembling hand, leaving tiny hot spots on my leg as the liquid seeps through my trousers. "You don't believe me, do you?" "Of c… course I d…do." "No you don't!" "But! But! Missus, honestly I do!" "Well! I haven't got any knickers on! Look!" This most immaculate dress is lifted waist high; the easy chair is turned towards me. Oh, goodness gracious! Oh heck! I am seeing things that I have never seen before! Now everything is frozen, except those little hotspots are turning into tacky damp spots, I just can't move.

"Have you ever been to Paris, young Peter?" "No missus, I have only been as far as Blackpool." "Would you like to go to Paris with me?" "I couldn't afford it Missus and I wouldn't be able to get time off work." The missus gave a sigh; draped her dress where it should be draped and says: "You don't know what I am talking about do you? You haven't a clue, have you?" "No, Maam!" says I. "Well! Finish your drink and then you can go." "I think I had better go now, Mr. Mann will wonder where I am. I will tell him about the gate." "What gate?" "Th… the gate you don't now seem to want. Anyrode, I'm off!" And I shot out of the house. "Phew!"

"Did you have a good walk, Peter?" "Yes, Uncle Smith, it was very interesting. Oh! A lady asked me about a safety gate for her baby and then she seemed to change her mind." "Who was that?" "She lives on that Long Row." "I know who you mean. Don't take much notice of her, and if she ever tries to get you to go into her house, don't." "You can rely on that, Uncle Smith! You certainly can!"

"Hi, Tommy! How's things?" "Absolutely wonderful, couldn't be better! Life is really good." "What's got into you Mate?" "You'll never guess, not in a thousand years!" "Try me!" says I. "Go on then!" "You are…" "What?" "You are…" "Go on then!" "You are what I have been." "And what's that then." "You are hopelessly in love." "How did you guess?" "Well! I have been there a couple of times, haven't I?" "You sure have." "Well! Join the Club…" says I.

"Who is this vision of loveliness then?" "Her name is..." "Not Peggy?" says I. "No, Plug! I would never fall in love with a Peggy after what happened to you." "Well, come on then! Let's have it!" "Her name is 'Rose'." "Rose?" "Yes, Rose!" "She sounds prickly to me. She could be quite a thorn in your side or in a worse place." "Awe, come on Plug! Don't piss about! Rose is a beautiful name." "Sorry mate, only kidding! Rose is the best name in all the world. How did you meet her?" "Well! I haven't exactly met her." "Have you spoken to her?" "Well! Not really." "How do you mean, not really? Either you have or you haven't." "Well! It's like this. She works in the canteen and you have to tell her what grub you want." "I see! Well! You have spoken to her, haven't you?" "Well! I suppose so! But ordering grub isn't speaking: not speaking like speaking as if you are speaking to say something proper- if you see what I mean."

"Where does this Rose live then?" "Err up Bradford Road. I have followed her home and stood and watched her through the window having a meal, and it was siling it down (Heavy rain.) and I got pissing wet through but I didn't care. It felt like liquid sunshine." "You have got it bad mate!" says I. "No, Plug! I have got it good! Everything about Rose is good! So I may have got it bad, as you say, but I have got it very bad, which makes it very good, if you see what I mean." "Yes! I think I do." "Well! We have got to do something. I am getting headaches and stomach ache." "And what about the main ache?" "What's that, then Plug?" "Heartache, of course! It can cause many problems you know." "Well! It's probably my aching heart that's giving me this gut rot." (Stomachache). "Probably, Mate! probably!"

"What are we going to do then?" says Tommy wistfully. I tell you what we can do." "What's that then?" "We can do what we have done before." "What have we done before?" "You know." "No! I don't know and stop pissing me about." "Is this bloke bothering you?" "Ah, yes! I get it! You mean what we did with Peggy Stick?" "Exactly."

"Hello, Rose!" "Who are you and how do you know my name?" "Rose by another name would be almost as sweet," quotes I. "As sweet as what?" says this quite attractive young lady. "Well! Err as sweet as sugar or sweet pickles." "Thank you very much!" says this increasingly attractive lady. "Sorry!" says I. "You are far lovelier than any rose in full bloom and I am in love with you. Oh, Rose! Rose! You stand amongst the corn." "I think you have got that wrong, but it's a nice thought anyway. Thank you!" "You're very welcome! My sweet Rose!"

"Is this bloke bothering you?" "No! He isn't." "Eh! You what?" "No! He isn't bothering me at all." "Are you sure?" "Of course, I am sure!" "Are you sure sure? Because if he is I can get rid of him for you." "No! No! He is quite sweet! Leave him alone!" "Yes, Thomas! Leave me alone with Rose." We turn our backs on this bloke who was once my best mate. A tap on my shoulder; I turn and wham! A flash in my left eye; then pain; down I go.

Tommy had certainly clobbered me. I feel a bit faint as I lay on the ground. "You brute! Oh! You absolute brute!" says my beloved. "Oh! How could you be so brutish and cruel? Go away!" "Yes! Piss off!" mutters I. Tommy turns, his arms hang down. His head is dejected, and he slowly trudges away. If he had been a dog, his tail would have brushed the ground clean. My beloved is crouched by my side, one arm around my shoulders, the other gently stroking my hair. I press my head close to Rose. It was worth it after all, I have lost my best mate forever but I have got a sweetheart for the rest of my life.

Rose and I have been together for about a month. We have walked; talked; yes, we have even held hands. We have been on the rowing boats. I have kissed her twice but we both agree it was a waste of time and soppy. I am waiting on Kirkgate to take Rose to the flicks (Cinema.). Oh, flipping heck! Look who's here! It's my best ex-mate. Well! I won't look at, or talk to him. I am sure that he will ignore me. He looks different from a month ago. His head is high and the old jaunty step is there. I will look away and he will pass. "Hi, Plug!" "Err... Hi... Err hi, Tommy!" "Are you going to the flicks?" "Yes, Tommy! I am going with Rose." "Well! You will have a long wait, because she is queuing to go to Beech Hill flicks with Paul." "Paul! You don't mean our Paul?" "The very same mate, the very same!" "The traitor who makes our propellers and wheels." "Are you sure, Tommy?" "Sure, I'm sure! I have just seen them." "But, he is older than Rose!" "Well! It doesn't seem to bother her. He had his arm around her and they were having a gert big snog!" "Good!" says I. "How do you mean 'good'?" "Well, Tommy! I am getting brassed-off with

Rose." "Oh! She is wilting then?" "More like fallen off the bough mate. I am glad to be rid." "Well! I am glad to hear it. No hard feelings, mate?" "None at all Tommy! My goodness! How I've missed you!" "Me too, Mate!" "Do you mean to say that you have missed yourself then?" "No! I have missed you." "But you said when I said that I had missed you, that you had also." "What I said was that I had missed you, well that's what I meant anyrode." "So you really missed me then?" "Course I did! I have told you twice." "Once and a half times, I think, but thanks for missing me for once plus a half." "Your'e welcome Mate! Your'e welcome!"

"What went wrong then?" "Well, little things! My boots should have been shoes, but we only wear shoes for best. She wanted me to part my hair on the other side and wear deodorant." "What's deode... err dee... err what you just said?" "I haven't got a clue mate! It sounds like something to do with a dead body to me." "Aye lad! Tha (You.) could be reet but it could have been a lot worse tha naws (You know.)." "How worse?" "Well! She could have insisted that you should part it right down the middle." "Ye Gods!" "Yes! Ye Gods!" "I tell you mate! I bet it was like being engaged or something." "So! That's the end of Rose then?" "It sure is and you can tell that pillock at work, the contract is terminated." "I sure will!" says Tommy. "Tell you what! Let's both go to the flicks." "A good idea!" "What's on then?" asks Tommy, "You'll never guess," says I. "What's it called then?" "'Broken Hearts'," says I.

"That wasn't a bad film, but those two blokes got all they deserved." "How do you mean?" "Well, Plug!" says Tommy, "They trusted those two women with their lives and they paid the price: their lives were ruined- just as ours might have been." "That's true!" says I. "Well! I have been thinking." "Careful Tommy!" "No, Plug! Straight up! What I mean is, you meet a girl and she is everything, nay, more than the world to you and after a few weeks, it all changes. You couldn't care less and wonder what it was all about in the first place, It caused bad feelings; best mates fall out, some best mates even get whalloped." "Thanks a bunch mate!" "Your'e welcome Mate! Your'e welcome!" " People have been murdered in the name of love. I tell you mate! I am a bit frightened. When I thumped you, I hoped that you would not get up again. That's a terrible way to be, isn't it?" "Yes, Tommy,

it is! But do you think true love is like that?" "I don't know! I just
don't know." "Well Tommy! I will tell you what I think." "What
do you think then?" "Well! I think, that when you meet someone
and fall into true love, you will love her and do nothing to upset
her. It boils down to one word?" "What's that mate?" "Well! Not
one word but two words." "And what are these two words, Plug?"
"Self respect, Tommy! Self respect!" " Our parents have been married for umpteen years or so." "So what?" "Well! They haven't got
fed up with each other. They laugh, talk and cry together. They
seem very happy. They must still love each other, mustn't they?"
"Well Thomas! I may call you Thomas this once?" "Yes, Peter! Just
this once." "Well Thomas! You have answered your own question." "And what is the answer?" "We haven't found true love yet
and probably won't for a while yet." "Do you know Peter? I think
you're right." "Course I am!"

Uncle Smith is going to retire at the weekend. He says he
will pop in occasionally to keep an eye on me. We are working together in the Furniture Shop re-upholstering two easy
chairs. "Smith! Err Smith Mann! Are you there?" calls this oldish
sounding voice. "Through here Ben!" says my Uncle, "Come on
through." The door opens to show a smallish, elderly man, with
a flat cap, a cheeky round face with a silver gray moustache and
beard. He wears wire specs low down on his nose. Two clear blue
eyes peer over the top of the specs. An old charcoal coloured suit
with trousers too short: they reveal light blue socks and shiny, very
shiny, black boots. He stoops a little. He carries a black walking
stick. Everybody seemed to wear very shiny black boots in those
days. Well! All the blokes did.

"Peter!" "Yes, Uncle Smith!" "This gentleman is Ben Downe…
Err Mr. Ben Downe." "Err hello, Mr. Downe!" "Hello! What's
your name?" "Err Peter, Mr. Downe!" (It's a good name for him
because he is partly bent down already, thinks I.) "How are you
this fine morning?" "Oh, fair to midlin Smith! Fair to midlin!"
"What can we do for you?" "Well, Smith! I have come to order
a box." "You have come to the right place! Tell you what! Take
Peter here with you and see if he can fit you up. If you need any
help, just send Peter for me." "Right, Smith! I will do that! Come
on young Peter! Let's have you!"

So Mr. Downe and I troll out of the Furniture Shop into the

Yard and under the sheds. "These are our Box making timbers," says I. "We can spread them all out and you can pick which pieces you fancy." "Right young Peter! We will do that." "I will get my note book, and pencil, to take down the particulars. Then I will make us all a drink." says I. "Right young Peter! I will take a walk round the timber yard." The kettle has just boiled and after making three cocoa drinks, I am just about to open the door, when it is opened for me and Mr. Ben Downe is stood there, well almost stood up, he is wearing that stoop, which is the beginning of a bend down I suppose.

"How's it gone Ben?" "All done, Smith." "Well Ben! I must say that that was quick." "Yes, I have made my choice." "Come and have a cuppa." "Thanks." "And when we have had our drinks, Peter will take your measurements, if that's O.K.?" "Sure, that's fine!" Drinks duly over, notebook in one hand, two foot in the other, and a pencil balancing on my ear. I always had a problem balancing a pencil on my ear, once balanced, I had to incline my head to the left for the right ear or vice versa for the left ear. People would probably think that I had a round shoulder either the left one or the right depending on which ear that the pencil was balanced thereon at the time.

Job sorted out then, Mr. Downe has left. "What's the details then?" asks Uncle. "He wants a panel sided, oak coffin, with a raised lid, chrome fittings, suitable for a burial. It's got to have a raised lid with a wooden cross with his name etc. on it, and it's got to be as dark as we can stain and polish it." "And what's the measurements?" "Err they are five foot three and a half inches by a sixteen inch shoulder." "Is that five foot three and a half stood up or bent down then?" "Err stooping I suppose." "Well! We will make it five foot six with an eighteen inch shoulder and give it plenty of packing to make him comfortable." "He would like his walking stick to go with him in case they will let him go for a walk up there." "Right, Uncle Smith!" " Right!"

"Mr. Downe has given me five pound deposit. Can he come in for a fitting when it's ready?" "Of course, he can! Did you tell him if could be four weeks?" "Yes! He said that would be fine but could we make it at short notice, if we had to?" "Course, we could! No problem!" "Did you mark the set?" "Yes! I put the parts together and marked them MR. B.D. "A good job done then?"

"Yes, Uncle Smith! A job well done!" "Oh! Just one more thing, Uncle Smith! Mr. Downe wants to be laid on his left hand side because he says that he is more comfortable on his left side when he is going to sleep." "No problem Peter! Have you made a note of it?" "No! But I will do it right away." "Good lad! Let's have another cuppa." "Coming up, Uncle Smith!"

I was so happy at Manns but I was going to miss Uncle Smith terribly. He has promoted me Chief C.U.P. Second Class, (Reminds me of The Crescenters when I was promoted Full Gang Member, Second Class). C.U.P stands for Coffin maker, Upholsterer and Polisher. If there is anything that I can't cope with, I only have to ask.

Two months later and the coffin is ready for inspection. Why has it taken so long to make you may ask? Well dear reader! We make coffins that are ordered in between jobs or if we have any spare time. If a coffin is needed by a death, I pull out all the stops to have it made in time for a funeral. We never keep a dead customer waiting.

"Come in, Mr. Downe! Your coffin is prepared for your inspection." "Thank you Peter! I will!" He stops in mid stoop. His jaw drops: "Err is that... Err of course it is! It's my coffin, isn't it?" "It sure is Mr. Downe!" Mr. Downe is quite overcome: he hangs his walking stick on one of the trestles supporting the coffin; his hand caresses the lid. He walks all the way round the coffin touching and stroking and muttering, uses a handle like a doorknocker, and says, "Well! If I get any visitors after I am gone, I will at least know that they are there, and depending who, I could always turn on an extra deaf ear, couldn't I?" "By gum! That's funny! That is funny!" says I. "Of course it is young Pete! A good laugh is better than any bottle of medicine." "Course it is." says I. "Joking apart though, I think that you have done a wonderful job, a wonderful job." "Then he says, "Young man! You have made me a very happy man." "Thank you Mr. Downe," says I. "When I die, I want you to undertake my Funeral. Will you do that for me?" "Well! George usually does Funerals, but I am sure there will be no problem. Would you like to try it for size?" "And comfort, Peter! And comfort!" "Yes, of course, Mr. Downe!"

"We will lay it on these low blocks then you can get in easily. Mr, Downe takes off his old charcoal gray jacket and his shiny black boots. "Can I leave my socks on?" says he. "They are fresh washed." We lift the coffin on to the two blocks of wood. He climbs in and lays down. "This is <u>very</u> comfortable," says he. "Thank you kind Sir!" says I.

So I pull up a dining chair that's in for repair and Mr. Downe says "You know Peter, it may seem a bit strange to you, but I have always been a meticulous man." He sees the frown on my face. "'Meticulous' means to have everything just so: everything tidy and ordered." "Awe, right Mr. Downe! I see what you mean! Just like my Mum!" "Yes, I suppose so! I suppose so!" "So! I want everything to be in order at my Funeral. I have a feeling death is not far away. I am not afraid of death. I have tried to live a good life. I believe that there is a life hereafter. If there is I hope that I shall go to the right place; if there isn't, it just doesn't matter does it?" "No! I suppose not." "No! I am not afraid of death but I am afraid of dying." Another frown. "What I mean is that death comes to everyone: even a baby that is born today, could die at any time- so I don't fear that. It's the dying. I don't want to suffer or be a burden to anyone. Do you understand?" "Of course I do, Mr. Downe!"

"What's that bell, Peter?" "Oh! It's a customer. I will have to see what they want." "Off you go then! I will be alright here: it's so comfortable- I could go to sleep." "Righto, Mr. Downe! I will bring us a cuppa when I come back. I will lock the door for now, alright?" "Yes alright!" Mr. Downe closes his eyes with a contented sign and a gentle smile.

"Hello Mr. Dexter! What can I do for you?" "Good morning, young man! Has Ben Downe arrived yet?" "Err yes! He is in the Polishing Shop. I have worked for Mr. Dexter on several occasions. Mr. Bill Dexter is very smart: he is wearing a navy blue, pin stripe suit; a white, shadow stripe shirt; a blue tie with a gold and yellow motif. I think it may be a military tie. He is clean-shaven; he carries a cane with a gold handle and his trousers have a knife edge crease and are of a perfect length to reveal a pair of very shiny black shoes.

"Err! Can you hang on a sec. and I will tell Mr. Downe." "Yes, of course! But I know what he is here for." So I troll back to the Polishing Shop, unlock the door and let myself in. "Mr. Downe, err Mr. Dexter is here to see you. Err, Mr. Downe wake up! Mr. Dexter is here to see you." I bend down to awaken Mr. Ben

Downe. Ah! Err Mr. Downe isn't going to wake up: Mr Downe has died. He has died a happy contented man with the ghost of a smile on his face. I hope he is on his way to Heaven, and that he will enjoy his walks.

"Come in, Mr. Dexter! I have some sad news, Mr. Downe has passed away." "Well! He got that timing spot on didn't he?" "Yes! He did." Mr. Dexter stood by the coffin, bent his head and he said a silent prayer and then he stood to attention and saluted Mr. Downe.

"Er, young man, er, what is your name?" "Peter, Sir." "Well Peter, I think there is some mistake. Ben Downe is laying in my coffin." "Err what, er are you sure?" "Of course, I am sure. These are the special panels I discussed with George." "That can't be, that just can't be," says I. "Well, I think that coffin should be mine, but under the circumstances, there is not much that I can do, but I am disappointed." "Hang on Sir and I will check. What would you like to drink?" "A stiff whisky would be fine." He sees the look on my face and says, "Only joking, tea will be fine." "Will a mug be alright Sir?" "Yes, son, we had much worse than that in the War, Ben and I." What tales Bill and Ben could have told about the Boer War.

"Here's your tea, Mr. Dexter. I will now check." "Thank you young man." Off I shoot to check. No, none of the timbers are marked. What to do then: I will pick a set of oak and mark it and hope for the best. "And what are you doing young man?" "I am... Err I am... Well! I am marking this coffin set with your initials and I have just realized that you are known as 'Mr. William Bill Dexter'. The initials are the same as Mr. Downes, and somehow, there has been a mix-up and I was trying to sort it out." "Well, Peter! Full marks for trying! I will have the coffin set you are marking." "Well! It is one of our best sets." "I am sure it is." "And I will make a special job of it." "I am sure you will. Let's go back to Ben." Phew! That's sorted that then. Mr. Dexter and I troll back to the Polishing Shop. Mr. Dexter looks down and says, "You saved my life twice old chap, so sleep in peace." He slowly and quietly comes to attention and salutes his friend. There were two pairs of tearful eyes that day.

My war has been a quiet war so far. Bradford has been bombed but even Bradford was a long way off in those days. We had no call to travel to the cities, no reason at all. We would go on a day trip or whatever to the coast by train from Otley to Scarborough, Morecambe, or Blackpool- once in a blue moon if we were lucky.

February, l944. There's fighting in Italy. As far as we are concerned, it could be on another planet, it's so very far away. t I am seventeen years old. I can volunteer for the Services. I would have volunteered anyway but the alternative could be that I would be 'called-up' to be a 'Bevin Boy.' A 'Bevin Boy.' Some of you may wonder what's or what was a 'Bevin Boy.' Well! There was this bloke in the Government called Ernest Bevin. He was the Minister of Labour, or something, and any fit young man could be directed to work in the coalmines. The word 'directed' should probably read 'ordered'- anyway, if you were directed to work in the mines- that was it! That's where you went! (Jimmy Saville was a Bevin Boy.) Many young men volunteered to serve in the Forces rather than be a Bevin Boy.

DON'T GO DOWN THE MINE SON, THERE'S PLENTY OF COAL IN THE YARD.

I am very disappointed: the chances of being accepted for Air Crew are very slim. My education, or lack of it, will let me down. What to do then: after much thought and a little research, I have decided to volunteer for service in the Fleet Air Arm. The best of both worlds I think: working on aeroplanes (I might get some buckshee flights!), and with a bit of luck, I will get to see some of the wide, wide World.

Spick and span, shoes, yes shoes, shiny bright, even round the heels. Hair has been cut (No basin used!) and has an arrow straight parting down the left side. My best blue suit is from 'Weaver to Wearer' with trousers with knife-edge creases. Hand ironed by me, nobody else is allowed to press my trousers. I use a hot iron and a damp tea cloth. I wear a plain blue tie and a white handkerchief shows over my top left hand pocket. Wearing a tie isn't novel or new for me. When I met George Mann for the very first time, he took me to his house to meet his wife, Mary. As we talked about my Apprenticeship, George said, "You are a smart young fella! But there is just one thing missing." "What's missing Mr. Mann?" "A tie Peter! A tie!" says he as he lifts and flicks his with his right hand, just like Oliver Hardy. "A tie, Peter, makes all the difference." "Right, Mr. Mann! I..." He cuts me short. "Err call me George now that you are working for us." "Right Mr George, I will, and I will buy a tie, or borrow one of my Dad's till this weekend." "Haven't you got a tie of your own?" "No, George, err Mr. Mann, err George, I never hardly wear a tie." "Mary! Take Peter upstairs and let him pick a couple of ties out."

That day from being a no tie owner, I became a <u>two</u> tie owner. My father used to say things change and some times they change very quickly. How right he was. I have since worn a tie at all times during my life- except when abroad in hot countries. I would not feel correctly dressed without a tie.

Back to business then: on to the Bus Station; queue for and catch a 'Sammy Ledgard's' bus to Leeds; get off at the Headrow-near Lewis's Store. "Excuse me, Missus! Can you direct me to Lady Lane?" "Are you joining up, young man?" "Yes, I am!" "Well! It's down there on the right but if you want my advice, go home to your Mother." "Nay, Missus!" says I. "Ah can't do that!" "Why not?" "Well! I err… Well! I…" She cuts me short. "Listen son! My twin boys volunteered last year." "Good for them!" says I. "Whereabouts are they now. Are they together?" "No! One is abroad and the other boy is near home." "That's nice!" says I. "What are they in?" "They are both in a cemetery! They are both dead! So take my advice, lad, and get that same bus back home! Have you got a Mother?" "Err yes, Maam!" "Well! Catch that bus home. She will be very sad this morning. Go home and make her happy." "Nay, Missus! Ah can't do that! I'm sorry! I will have to be off." "Take care, Son! Take care!" "I will, Ma-am! I will!"

My Mum seemed alright when I left home this morning. Maybe she was quieter than usual, but I am sure that she was alright. Funny though! She gave me a hug and a kiss as she arranged my pocket-handkerchief. Surely she wasn't worrying about me getting killed. I won't die! It's always somebody else who 'Buys it.' No! It won't happen to me, and anyway, I have the St. Christopher's medal- my Mother bought for me when I was a baby. She had it blessed and it's always pinned on to my vest. I fumble under my tie and feel for the medal. Of course it's there. I give a little shiver and mentally pray: 'Hail Mary and St. Christopher protect me.' Course they will.

Here we are at the Recruiting Office at Lady Lane. The bloke on the door says, "Which Service are you volunteering for?" "Err the Fleet Air Arm, sir." "Up the stairs lad! Third door on the right." "Yes, Sir!" says I. I trundle up the steps and along the corridor, stop and knock. A very pleasant voice calls, "Do come in." A deep breath; a stifled cough and in we go. She of the very pleasant voice really is a vision of loveliness. She is sat at a big oak desk. She is wearing a Wren's (Women's Royal Naval Service) uniform. She has beautiful blue eyes and striking blond hair. Her make up is perfect. She reminds me of Lana Turner, the famous Hollywood star. "And what can we do for you, young man?" "Well, Misses! err Ma-am err Miss, I err... I have come to volunteer for the Fleet Air Arm." "And why do you want to join the Fleet Air Arm?" says this strong business like voice. Oh! There's a bloke in navy uniform sat there as well. I hadn't noticed him. "Because I err I like aeroplanes, err... and boats," says I as an afterthought. "That's as good a reason or reasons as any," says this chap, who I wish was not there if you see what I mean.

Well to cut a long story edgewise: they took my particulars and gave me a test to do. I sailed through it and then the naval chap says. "Congratulations! You have fulfilled the requirements." "Thank you, Sir!" "What do you do in Civi Street?" "I am a Joiner, Sir!" Whoops! They both stop writing; everything seemed to freeze. Time stands still for an eternity, well it felt like an eternity, The Lana Turner blond looks at me pen poised in mid air. The bloke's eyes open wide; a frown appears on his face. He gives a clear your throat cough and says, "A joiner?" "Yes, Sir, a Joiner!" "An apprentice joiner?" "Yes, an Apprentice Joiner." He slams his pen on to the papers on the desk, Lana delicately places hers alongside her notebook. "We can't take you lad." "Why not?" says I as I gaze appealingly into Lana's eyes. "We can't take you because you are an apprentice in the Building Trade. You will be called to rebuild the bombed cities." "B... but," I am cut short. "No B... buts, lad. That's it! There is nothing I can do." "Well! Why didn't you ask me what I did at the beginning and then I could have gone straight back home?" "Sorry lad! It's a new policy starting this week. We can't take you because you are an apprentice in the Building Trade. You are the first apprentice to volunteer. In future, I will check everybody at the start of proceedings. Sorry lad! Off you go." "Yes, Sir!" (Pillock! Thinks I.). A brief nod to Lana Loveliness; I turn, there's a tear in each eye and a lump in my throat.

As I travel back to Otley on the bus, my mind is in turmoil. Can I volunteer somewhere else and tell them that I am a wide boy, (A spiv, a black marketeer.) or surplus to requirements and of no use to my Country- apart from being in the forces? Will I be called up for the mines? Can I disappear until I am eighteen years old and then I would probably be 'called-up' to do my stint in the Forces?

"How have you gone on Son?" asks Mum. "I haven't got on, or into anything! I have been slung out before I got started!" I took particular notice of my Mother's reaction: the lady in Leeds was right; I have a very happy Mother this afternoon. She has given me a bob and a hug .<u>Another</u> reward for failure.

So they wouldn't take me even though I volunteered. I wasn't called-up and I didn't have to go down the coal-mines or build the bombed cities. I would come home every night hoping my 'call-up' papers would be waiting for me but- nowt happened! d I suppose with hindsight, I was very lucky. I had a quiet sort of war and a lonely one. Almost all my mates volunteered or were 'called-up'. Tommy went into the Fleet Air Arm, only Jake and I of our age were left at home.

The fact was, as I see it today, that the European War was almost won. The following year, two names hit the headlines: they were 'Hiroshima' and 'Nagasaki.'

"P... Peter." "Yes, George." "W... W...When y... you... g... get off the b... bus in the morning, will you go to Mrs. Rowbottom and shorten t... two doors?" "Yes, George!" "Yo... your t... tools will be waiting for you." "Righto George! I will do that." "G... good l... lad!"

It's a nice warm, sunny morning. Off the bus then; a twenty-minute walk to Mrs. Rowbottom's. It's about twenty past eight. Ring the bell; knock on the door. A key turns in the lock; three bolts are released: one at the top rail, one at the bottom rail and one down the door stile, about halfway up, or halfway down- take your pick. 'Ah! But how did you know how many bolts were on the door? And you seemed to know where they were.' Yes, dear reader, that's true! I fixed these bolts and the new lock a couple of weeks ago. I bet you thought you had caught me out there (Tha might be able ter beat a carpet but tha won't beat me.)

216   P.N. JACKSON

"Come in Peter! You're very early. Would you like a cup of coffee?" "Err yes, Mrs. Rowbottom! That will be fine." I was rarely offered coffee. In those days it was quite a novelty from tea or cocoa, or lemonade, and other unmentionables.

So I sort my tools out and mark the doors giving them three quarters of an inch clearance (About l9 mm.) to clear the new carpet and felt. Mrs. Rowbottom calls me to the kitchen with its almost obligatory whitewood, scrubbed tabletop. This is the life! A cup of coffee in my right hand; little finger extended (I'm learning.) and genteelly nibbling fruit cake, and biscuits.

Mrs. Rowbottom and I are discussing the end of the war in the Far East and about V.J. Celebrations (Victory In Japan Day.). I stand there at the table, enjoying the three C's: Coffee, Cake and Chat- and biscuits. The door opens from the Dining Room, I turn. It was a Digestive biscuit that froze in mid bite. My cup rattles and spills coffee into the saucer. It's still rattling.

Proudly stalking through the open door is young Miss Rowbottom. She has red hair and she is wearing red slippers. She is about sixteen years old and err and err… 'And what?' you may ask. And err, well and err that's it! There's nothing else. 'How do you mean 'nothing else'?' Well, Reader! That's it! Nothing else! The young lady stalked in as nature intended; saw me and without a sign, a frown, or a word, or a giggle, did an about turn that any squaddy (Soldier) would have been proud of and disappeared into the Dining Room.

Did I feel embarrassed then? No, not really. It happened very quickly. What were my impressions then? Well, reader! There was this red hair and, you know where, lot of curves, but the main impression was her cheeky, in more ways than one little bottom, as she strode away. In fact! Miss Rowbottom had a bottom not to be missed if you could manage to see it. 'You seemed to cope with this situation then.' Yes, reader! Apart from the initial shock, Mrs. Rowbottom and I carried on with our conversation as though nothing had happened. I finished my coffee, cake and chat, shortened the doors, packed by tools and left. Would you like to know how I coped as well as I did? Well, dear reader, Uncle Smith told me of his experiences and how he coped. We would rehearse situations and reactions but he never did a Tommy dress up (Good old Uncle Smith!). I must say that the veil between adolescence and adulthood was lifted a little that day. 'But wasn't the veil lifted with the ginger biscuit experience?' No, reader! That was more like the sacking dividing our workshop being riven down to reveal something nasty and a little bit evil- but today it was beautiful, as the Good Lord intended.

I had many more experiences during my years as a Journeyman Joiner. 'Go on then!' Sorry Reader, not on your Nelly! They are a closed-book.

So the War is over at last. We had street parties. It was a great feeling that we had won the War. I don't know about the older people but it never entered our heads that we would ever lose, everything had happened so far away. There was no T.V.; newspapers and the radio were censored. It could have been fought on another planet. I never saw a Jerry plane but I heard them; the only enemy that I was in contact with were the German prisoners and they were O.K.

'What's this 'V.J. Day' then?' some of you may ask. Well! 'V.J. Day' stands for 'Victory in Japan day'. 'V.E.' was 'Victory in Europe day'. We all had a couple of days off work- well I did! What did I do on V.E. day then? Do you know reader, believe it or not, I can't remember, but I do recall V.J. day.

One of the lads called Jack was home on leave. He was serving in the Navy. "I'm going to see my Grandma. How about coming with me? We can go on our bikes." "Yes, why not!" "Right then! I will call for you about seven in the morning." Five to seven, a knock on the door. "I'll get it Mum! It will be Jack." "Mornin, Jack!" "Mornin Plug! All ready?" "Yep!" "Bye Mum!" "Morning Jack! You're off to see your granny then?" "Yes, Mrs. Jackson!" "Where does she live?" Err in Newcastle." "In Newcastle? That's a long way off, it must be a hundred miles, Jack." "Is it, Mrs. Jackson. I didn't think it was so far." "Well! You will have to stop overnight." "That's no problem, Mum 'cos there's no work tomorrow, anyway!"

So Jack and I cycled to Newcastle. We were made very welcome and we returned home the following day. So that was my V.J.Day?" I remember it clearly because on the way up, we called in at a pub and the Landlord and Jack persuaded me to have a half pint of beer. It was my first and last drink ever. It tasted lousy. It reminded me of Morecambe. On a Sunday morning, it was a tradition to walk along the sea-front to Heysham and buy a glass of nettle beer. It tasted horrible. A few yards further on another stall sold soft drinks and a lot of people would buy a soft drink to kill the lousy taste of the first one. I bet the same bloke owned both stalls.

It's 1946. I am eighteen years old. 'You will be thinking of settling down with a nice young lady and getting married, or shacking up with someone.' No, younger reader! I know that you are not an older person- otherwise you wouldn't be asking these questions. Yes, I am eighteen years old; I have had many girl friends and probably kissed and cuddled them but engagement and marriage are a long way off- I think! Shacking up? Never! I am too busy for a permanent girl friend: Cycling, Fishing, Walking, Model-making, etc. I obviously haven't met the right girl yet and I would expect that when Miss Right comes along, I will fall in love, get engaged and marry, but not at this moment or many other moments.

Time passes: John Mann has retired; Ernest Mann has returned to the business. He has worked at AVRO. (A.V.Roe Aircraft Manufacturers.) producing aeroplanes: Lancasters, and Avro Ansons (Annies) during the War. In fact, he worked on an Annie for over two years, it was a gift to the Shah of Persia.

Young Mick has left school. He went with Mum to see this bloke about what he would like to do when he left. Michael told me the tale. He went with Mum for this interview and the bloke asked Mick what work he would like to do, so young Plug said "I want to be a Joiner." "That's very good." He was interrupted. "We have enough joiners in the family, so he can't be a joiner. He wants to be a Decorator." "No I don't! I want to be a Join-." Another interruption. "He doesn't know what he wants." "Yes, I do! I want to be a Bricklayer!" "Why not an Engineer?" "No, Mum! A Joiner or a Bricklayer." "You're not going to be a Joiner!" "Right, Mum! A Bricklayer it is." "You've chosen wisely Michael." "Yes, Missus he has". Next letter is "O"

So Michael started work as a Bricklayer. He stayed two days I think. Then he went to be an Engineering Apprentice. That didn't last long either. "You just don't know what you want, do you?" "Yes, I do!" "Well! What do you want to be?" "I want to be a Joiner." "Oh heck! Here we go again." "Yes, Mum! Here we go again!" So Mick has started work as an Apprentice Joiner at John Mann and Sons.

Mrs. Insole was a beautiful lady- just like a model or film star. She reminded me of Dorothy Lamour but she was better looking. She had a foreign accent; some said that she was German. Her husband was away most of the time. I think he held an important job in some Ministry or something. If she was a Foreign Alien, she was never interned during the War.

If there was any work to be done nobody wanted to know. Uncle Smith never went; George hadn't the patience- even John avoided Mrs. Insole when he could. So, it fell to yours truly to look after her. 'Why did the others shy away from her?' you may ask." "Well, reader! Mrs. Insole was the most meticulous, fussy, fastidious person, and other things I have ever come across but I have always had infinite patience- especially at my work or modelling. For instance, she would say in her very likeable accent, "Peeter, thare iss two knots in dis wood." "I would reply." "Well, Mrs. Insole! I think they give this piece of timber character." "Boot! I doon't warnt chaaracterr! I warnt a peece off wud with noo knots." "O.K, Mrs. Insole, I will select a good grained timber with noo knots, no knots." "Tank yoo, Peeter!" "You're welcome!"

"Peeter!" "Yes, Ma-am!" "Yoo haff poot tree scoows in dis woood." "Yes, it needs three screws to hold it up!" "Put I tink too scoows wud haf dun it." "Right, Mrs. Insole! Two screws it is then!" "Tank yoo Peeter!" "You're welcome Maa-am, you're welcome!"

So you can see why nobody wanted to know. I got on well with Mrs. Insole, it was a good C.C, and T, shop." (What's a good 'C, C, and T, Shop'? 'Coffee, Cake and Tips'.

"We have a ber... ber... big job for Mrs. Insole," says George one morning, "And Mrs. Insole w...wants you to do it for her." "Right George! What does she want?" "She wants a err...err S... Summer House b...building and s...sighting at the the... the t... top of her g... garden. Here are th... the dr...drawings."

I eye up the drawings, Mrs. Insole is certainly going to town. She wants a Summer House measuring twelve feet by ten feet with: cedar weather-board cladding; a hip-roof with cedar shingles and a dormer window in the roof (Well! It had to be in the roof otherwise it wouldn't be a dormer, would it?); glazed double doors- with stained glass; two stained glass windows and a veranda to the front. The building will have a fence all round, large enough for a play area to the right and a good space to the left. There will be a pair of gates to the front. The inside roof will be under drawn and the walls will be oak-panelled. There will be bunk beds; two electric heaters and a radio. The floor will be carpeted to a high standard. Oh I nearly forgot! A ladder had to be fitted to the wall opposite the front doors. 'What was the ladder for then?' The ladder was there for the inmates to climb up and look out of the dormer window.

This is a job that I can get my teeth into. Mrs. Insole looks after orphans and the like. She is certainly making them comfortable. She considers that the present accommodation is no longer suitable.

The job is progressing quite well. George comes in one day and says, "Mrs. Insole has had a bereavement. She wants you to make the c...coffin. It must be English Oak, st...stained and po...polished as d... dark as possible. Sh... she wa... ants four g... gold handles and a n... name pl... plate and it m... must b-be l...lead lined. These are th...the m...measurements. She w-wants Ernest and y...you t...to execute the f...funeral." "Right George! I will get on with it after lunch. When's the funeral?" "W... Wednesday."

The best figured oak is selected; small handles and name plate are ordered. The plumber lines it out with lead. Tuesday evening, Ernest collects the body and the coffin is sealed.

Wednesday, two o'clock, I am dressed in my dark 'Weaver to Wearer' suit, black tie and shoes- all supplied by Manns. Ernest is dressed in his Undertaker's rig-out. George drops us off at Mrs. Insole's gate. She is waiting dressed in black with a veil.

We proceed past the old summer house up to the top of the garden into the space, to the left of where the new building will be. A hole awaits. The gardener stands discretely in the background cap off head bowed, waiting to fill the hole in. He has a wooden cross with the deceased's, probably diseased, name on. There's no Minister or Priest; no Holy Water or prayers- just a gentle lowering of the coffin. Well! Even if Mrs. Insole <u>was</u> religious, I don't think she is, but <u>even</u> if she was, I don't think that even <u>she</u> wouldn't go any further just to bury a moggy (Cat.) would she?

Yes, reader, you may have cottoned-on: the new beautiful new Summer House is for any stray moggy that comes along. I think they must have passed the word around that it was a soft touch because there were always about a dozen or so permanent guests. Ah well!

It's Saturday afternoon. Tommy has called for me. We are going to walk into town. We are dressed 'Up to the nines.' as my Mum would say: sports jackets; gray flannels, with cut your finger creases; brown, yes brown shoes; yellow socks and a flashy tie each- even a pocket hankie peeping discreetly over the top of the top pocket, and a spare hankie in my trouser pocket- well I might want to polish my shoes if they get dusty or something, they must not let me down, they must be up to par. We will stand with any other lads outside Woolworths on Kirkgate then walk round the Store and congregate outside again, another troll round Woollies, looking for birds, and then across to the Milk Bar for a Milkshake or maybe a couple of shakes. There are two young ladies in the bar. Tommy and I know them slightly: one is called Rose and the other is Marie. No, straight up! They were called Rose and Marie (Nelson Eddy, and Janette Mc Donnell starred in the musical 'Rose Marie'- but I don't have to tell you mature people that do I?)

"Can we buy you two lovely ladies a milk shake or whatever?" gushes Thomas. I think that under the circumstances Thomas is in order for once. "What's the 'whatever' then?" asks Marie. "Yes! What's the 'whatever'?" parrots Rose. "Whatever you two visions of loveliness would like to drink." "What's your names?" asks Rose. "Thomas and Peter," says I. "I thought they called you Tommy and Plug?" "Well Rose! Our friends and mates do! But young ladies... Well I don't know!" "Well Tommy and Plug!" says Marie, "You can buy us a Milk Shake: one strawberry for Rose and a Vanilla for me." "Coming up ladies!" says I. "And you can take us to the First House of the Pictures, (Cinema) if you want to." "Oh, yes! That will be great!" say I. "Great!" echoes Thomas err Tommy. "But on one condition," says Marie. "What's that then?" "You can take us only if we pay our whack (Share.)." "Done!" says I. "Double done!" says Tommy. "We will go book four seats after our drinks and meet you here at five thirty."

"Which bird are you fancying then?" "Well!" says Tommy.

"They both seem O.K. I like Rose but remember the last Rose we tangled with?" "I sure do!" says I. "Tell you what, Plug! Let's toss for it." "O. K." Tommy tossed: I lost. Marie is mine.

"Let's go the Park way home!" says I. "We might pick a couple of birds up." "That's a good idea, Plug! We could take them to the flicks on Sunday night." "Come on then!" says I. "Coming on then!" almost quotes Tommy.

'But you already have two birds... err girl friends: err... Rose and Marie.' Well, reader! They are not really girl friends: just two girls. If they don't turn up, well: 'San Fairy Anne' ('San Fan' for short.)- it doesn't matter. We could probably find two more to fill the booked cinema seats. If they do turn up, we will share a choc-ice or whatever from the lady with the illuminated tray who patrols the aisles during the interval and spends the rest of the time, shining her torch on snogging couples. We will put our arms round them and probably steal a kiss and after the show, we may or may not, walk them home. It would probably depend on the weather.

Into the Park then, it looks like a wasted journey, not many birds about: two groups of girls and the odd singleton. "Not much doing," says I. "Nowt at all! Err... Hey up! Look yon (Yonder.) up the River! A rowing boat has just emerged from under the Bridge with two girls aboard. That looks interesting, Plug!" "Yes Tommy! Doesn't it?" Eventually, the boat docks at the steps. "May we help both you lovely voyagers ashore?" enquires Thomas (oops!). "Yes, you may," says the rower, a vision of loveliness. "Yes, you may," parrots the helmsman- err... girl.

Safely ashore Tommy says: "What are your names for two of the most more than beautiful creatures it has ever been by good fortune to meet? Truly ladies! You have made this a wonderful day." Two giggling girls ascend the steps holding our hands. We sit on a park bench overlooking the river. "You haven't much to say," says the taller of the two. "No" says I. "I am stood in awe. Well! Sat in awe of your beauty and radiance. I am spellbound!" "You have been to see two many flicks (films)!" says the shorter one, "Anyway, what are your names?" "Thomas and Peter," says I. "Please young, lovely ladies! Tell us your names, I cannot wait!" "I am Ruth and my friend is called Rubella. I am known as 'Ru', but Rubella likes to be called 'Bella'." " That's a wonderful combination of two very lovely names! Rubella for two very lovely ladies, we are enchanted, aren't we Plug, err Peter?" "Yes Tommy, err Thomas! We certainly are!" "'Rubella'! That sounds like Italian to me!" whispers Thomas. "It probably is," whispers I, but I think my Mum said that it was something to do with a German!" "I can't see that Plug." "No, neither can I." (My mum says 'Rubella' is the name for 'German Measles'. Whoops!)

"Can we take you ladies to the flicks tomorrow night?" "Why can't you take us tonight?" "Oh! Err, we are busy studying tonight. "Studying?" "What are you studying then?" "Well, Ru! I may call you 'Ru' mayn't I?" "Yes of course!" "And you can call me 'Bella' if you want." says Bella. "Well, Ru and Bella, we are studying to see if we are suitable material to go into the Priesthood." "What, you two?" "Yes, us two! Our Mothers, bless them, want us to be Priests." "So you are Roman Catholics then?" "Yes, we are!" says I "And we're proud to be Roman Catholics."

"What's the matter with being Roman Catholics then?" "Well!" says Ru, "My Mum says we Protestants shouldn't have anything to do with you, or to marry a Catholic." "Why not?" says I. "Well! She says that if you marry a Roman Catholic, you can become a drudge (Slave like.) and be burdened down with kids." "How does she make that out?" says I. "Well Peter! She says that Catholics breed like rabbits." "Where have we heard that before, Peter?" says Tommy. "Where indeed?" says I. "Well you can tell your Mother that we don't and I can prove it." "How?" says Ru. "Yes how?" parrots Bella. "Well! Bluebell err Rubella... err Ru and Bella, how many Catholic kids that you see running about have four legs and a tail?" "Well err... none!" "There you are then! Anyway, back to business. Are you coming tomorrow night to the flicks? It will have to be the second house." "Why?" "Well Ru! Peter and I go to Benediction for six o'clock, that's why." "What's 'Benediction' then?" "Well!" says Tommy, "The priest opens the Tabernacle and incenses the Blessed Sacrament and all true believ- ers received a blessing." "Awe right!" says Ru. "Right!" parrots, parrot Bella. "It sounds very interesting! Can we come?" "Err... Well err... I suppose..." "Oh go on Thomas! Let us come with you!" "Well! If you do come, you will have to wear a hat." "But we don't wear hats, how about head scarves?" "Well err, I suppose so, but come with something on your heads and then we can go to the flicks after Benediction."

So Ru and Bella came to Benediction. They seemed a bit over-awed. They were very quiet but they seemed to enjoy the hymns: 'O Salutaris Hostia.' (O saving victim opening wide.) and 'Quae coeli pandas ostium.' (The gate of heaven to man below.).

We went to the flicks together for about a month until, well we didn't stay in the cinema for a Month, but we all went once a week for about four weeks. Rose, Marie, Ruth and Bella, compared notes one day and we were dumped. Ah well san fairy an! One good thing did come out of this: Ruth converted to Catholicism; married a good Catholic boy and had two lovely twin girls. Well! There would have to be two if they were twins, wouldn't there? When I enquired if they had four legs and a tail, her husband who is still a very good friend of mine gave me a peculiar glance, be-cause he hadn't a Dolly Blue (Clue.) what I was talking about. I suppose Ruth filled him in. As a postscript, one thing I have forgotten until now is that when we walked young ladies home, maybe we would have a kiss and a cuddle, and would invariably swap girls. Ah well! Variety is the spice of life.

"Mornin Plug!" "Err... morning Tommy!" "What's up? You look like a bloke what is trying to give up smoking." "How can I want to give up smoking if I don't smoke?" "Well, you can't! But if you did smoke and wanted to give up, that's what you would look like." "I don't think you are making an ounce of sense." "Well, maybe not! But I was speaking hypothetically." "Speaking hyper... err hypo... err hype...?" "Hype-oh-thet-i-cally that's what I said." "Well! I have never heard of 'hypothetically'." "By George, he's got it! I think he's got it!" "Course I have now! But what does it mean?" "What does it mean?" "I just said that parrot!" "Well Plug! It refers to something that isn't there and may never happen." "If you ask me, it sounds like a 'Charlie Chuck': a bloke spending a heck of time busy looking at nowt." "Well! let's forget about hy-pothetical nowts and talk about sensible summats! O.K?"

"So Plug! Tell me what's the matter?" "What's the matter? I will tell you what the matter is: our lass has decided that she wants to learn to ride a bike and I am under strict orders to teach her. Can you imagine me running behind, and balancing a girl?" "No, I can't." "No and neither can I. It didn't go too well last night." "Well! Perhaps when she has found her feet, she will be O.K." "If she has lost her feet and can't find them, she will not be able to walk, let alone be able to pedal a bike, idiot!" "Well! It takes one to know one." "Well! If she gets cold feet, she might not try again and chuck it in." "Tommy, you have lost me! If she has lost her feet and can't find them, how can she feel them to know whether they are cold or hot feet?" "Well! I will explain: 'To find one's feet.' is 'to be able to do whatever'- dost see? (Do you see?)" "Dost?" "And 'To have cold feet.' means that 'you can't go through with whatever'- dost see?" "Double dost?" says I. I will ask Sheila Wheeler to teach her and you could pay her in apples couldn't you Tommy?" "Thank you very much!" "You're welcome!" "I will tell you what! With a name like Sheila Wheeler, she should make a good teacher of the bicycle. My Mum says that she is a bit of a lass, in fact, Mum says that she is foot loose and fancy free and she thinks there is something afoot there." "What's 'afoot' then, there, Tommy?" "About twelve inches I would think! Gotcha Plug!" "Awe Tommy! Pack it in! Pack it in!"

> Mary had a little lamb.
> It had sooty foot.
> And every where that Mary went,
> Its sooty foot it put.

"Well! You will have to ask your Dad, you know!" says Mum. "Yes, I know that!" "Are you sure you want to do this?" "Yes, I think so! Err yes, I am sure!" "Well! If you want my advice, you won't do it: it won't do you any good." "Awe Mum! Some of my mates have started." "And what about you?" "Well, sort of! But I would like it to be official." "Well! If you must do it, you must get your father's permission." "Yes Mother."

"Err Dad." "Yes, Son." "Err... I have something to ask you." "What's that then?" "Err... Well Dad... I err... would like to start smoking." "Start if you want son, but you'll never have owt in your pocket." How right he was! For the few years that I did smoke any spare cash went on cigs- and I must say that I enjoyed a fag.

'But you're eighteen years old, surely you could have smoked without your Father's permission.' Yes, reader, I could have but I would never have smoked in my Father's company, or if there was

a chance of meeting him with a fag in my mouth. It boiled down
to respect for my parents and family. But how did young Mick go
on then you might ask. Well he had a crafty Woodbine or Craven
"A" now and again, but I seem to remember that things changed
very quickly after the war, not always for the better may I add, so
Mick probably never got round to asking for permission. I suppose
that it just happened.

'By the way, how is young Mick getting on at Manns?' Well
reader, he is doing very well. He is a quick learner and enthusiastic. He will make a good joiner. 'And where are you working
today?' Mick and I are going to replace some wooden spouting
(Rain-gutters.) that have rotted. We are going to a house up Hag
Farm Road. The handcart is loaded with two sets of wooden extension ladders. The lengths of spouts are laid inverted on the ladders. They make a platform for the paraphernalia required for the
job: cans of paint, creosote and tar hang on hooks. They swing
and clatter when we move. Reminds me of dear old 'Herlloww
Albert.' ('Mothballs.')

A handcart must be carefully loaded so that it is balanced just
heavy at the opposite end to the shaft. The shaft is used to <u>push</u>
the cart. If the balance is heavy at the shaft end, it takes a lot of
holding up, but if it is too heavy to the front end, and an obstacle
is encountered such as a pothole, or somebody laid dead in the
road, whoever is holding the shaft can end up air borne into mid
air as the cart tips up, sheds its load, and hurls the shaft man into
space. Hag Farm Road is full of potholes not many bodies though,
so we have to get it right.

Here we are then! We have arrived at Mrs. Faddy's big wrought
iron gates. We are greeted by an overfed Scottie-dog. It wheezes
and snuffles as it shuffles along it pushes its nose through the bars.
It is called 'Jasper'. It should have been called 'Gasper' I reckon.
Mick opens the gates: "Come on Jasper! Let's have you!" says Mick
as he scoops Jasper up into his arms. "Let's go for a little walkies
shall we?" Off they troll for about fifty yards up the lane. I am
sure Jasper likes his little bit of freedom, it's obvious that the canine is spoilt rotten. Mick puts him down and off Jasper trundles,
grunting, wheezing, gasping and sniffing in the hedgerows. He's
probably got the wind of a rabbit, but if he sets one up, he hasn't a
cat in ★★ll's chance, or should I say dog in ★★lls chance of catch-

ing it.

In we go, gates closed behind us, Jasper is happy in his freedom. We trundle the handcart up the drive and into the backyard. Mick rings the doorbell. Eventually, Mrs. Faddy appears. She is very tall and very thin; she stoops slightly- giving the impression that she is about to fall over. Her face is sad, but that is deceiving, when Mrs. Faddy speaks, it's a pleasant voice and she invariably gives a gentle smile. She wears a white apron that starts from just below her neck all the way down to almost touching the ground, from neck nearly to deck you could say.

She greets us with, "Would you like a cup of coffee and cake before you start?" "Yes! That would be fine Mrs. Faddy! (I have noticed that coffee is becoming quite popular.)." Coffee over; down to business. First, we have to pull down the lengths of rotting gutter. The new lengths are pre-tarred on the inside and paint primed on the outside. They will be halved. An area of about six inch long and about one inch thick will be cut away from underneath one length. The next length is cut away from the top leaving a tongue an inch thick to replace the cut out in the first piece. The lengths are screwed together and then unscrewed. A recess is cut away about an inch and a half long and about a quarter of an inch deep at the end of each length, any bare timbers are painted with primer.

The gutter is offered up, fixed by nailing through from the inside into the spar feet making sure that it is falling down towards a down pipe, not 'falling down' as in 'falling down', but dropping from a high to a low at the down pipe end . At a corner, the gutter is mitred and jointed to the correct length from the last new piece to the short point of the mitre. This measurement usually taken by marking a measuring stick, this being a length of timber about an inch square, to the correct length.

The gutter is then screwed together. Paint and putty are applied to the recesses; a piece of lead (Pre-fitted on the deck.) is painted on the underneath and nailed into the recess with galvanised felt nails. Any surplus, gooey painted putty, is trimmed off with a putty knife. (Well! You wouldn't use a carving knife would you?) To complete the work, the joints and the nail heads are tarred, putty is used to cover tiny sins and flaws in the joinery work.

In brains and skill, we put our trust
If that won't do, then putty must

The job is going well: the old gutter is down on the deck and we are jointing the lengths- using three or four saw stocks (Trestles.). Mrs. Faddy appears with a tray. It's a darned good C.C. and some C shop! "Here you are," says she. "Thank you Mrs. Faddy! It's most welcome!" says I. "How is the work going then Peter?" "Oh, very good! We should have the new gutter fixed today." "Oh good! By the way! Have you seen Jasper! I can't find him anywhere. I am a little bit worried. He is not used to being out all alone." "I haven't seen him anywhere in the garden, since we arrived," says Mick. Which was quite true, (More or less.). "Oh dear!" says a steadily becoming distraught tall thin lady. "Don't worry, Mrs. Faddy! I will find Jasper for you." "Oh, thank you Michael! You're a treasure!" "I will go now before I have my cuppa," and off he trots. We both know that Jasper will be either just up the lane or at the gates, wheezing and snuffling to get in. Mick locates Jasper, picks him up and walks up the lane to kill a bit of time. How do I know this, when you cannot see him you may ask? Well reader! Jasper and Mick have done this many times before. But why did Michael do this? If you hang on a few minutes you will find out.

"Here they come," says I. perched like a sparrow on top of the ladder. "Oh, thank goodness!" says she. "Where was he Michael?" "Up the lane Mrs. Faddy! But he seems to be alright now." Mrs. Faddy takes Jasper from Mick, gives him a kiss and a cuddle, Jasper that is, not Michael and disappears into the house.

But you <u>still</u> don't see why Michael did this. Just hang on. "Michael!" calls Mrs. Faddy from the ground. "Yes, Mrs. Faddy!" says Mick from the top of the other ladder. "Can you come down?" I give him the nod; he winks and down he goes. The words float up to me. "Thank you very much for searching for and rescuing Jasper. Here you are, please take this. I will tell Mr. Mann what a good lad you are." "Thank you Mrs. Faddy! It's been a pleasure." Mick climbs his ladder; looks at me; raises his eyes towards heaven and with a wry smile, gently rocks his head from side to side. "How much then young Plug?" "The going rate," says he. "What's the going rate at present then?" "A dollar (five shillings old money,

or 25p today's money) a Jasper." says he. Seeing Mick was earn-
ing about fifteen shillings a week (75p) a dollar (25p) wasn't a bad
little pick up. Mrs. Faddy never seemed to cotton that Jasper went
missing every time that Mick called. If she did ever cotton-on, she
never let on, may be she was playing a game, because she was not
one of the idle thoughtless rich, she knew the carry on of some of
us workers. So Mick and I had many a gasper (fag/cigarette} cour-
tesy of Jasper the gasper.

November, l946 and I have celebrated my birthday. I am nineteen years old. No! We didn't have a booze-up or a wild party: a
couple of drinks at the Milk Bar; a card and a new tie from my
parents, and a card from my sister, Maureen.

We have experienced a spell of very cold weather. The River
Wharfe is frozen. It has not been pronounced as being safe officially, but some idiots are chancing it. A couple of inch of overnight snow blankets everything with a covering so clean and
white. Most chimneys are spewing smoke vigorously as domes-
ticity moves into gear to cope with a new day. Snow melts on
some roofs, slides and shutters to the ground. The gritters have
done their work: the roads and footpaths are beginning to thaw.
Tommy and I are serving at Mass. We have arranged to have a
walk down Wharfe Meadows to see if it is safe to go on the ice.

Sunday afternoon in the Park; the warning notices are still in
place. About half a dozen blokes and a couple of girls, either can't
read, or they are just plain stupid. They could be dead stupid or
stupid dead! I know that two of the blokes can read because they
are ex-classmates of mine- so they are definitely stupid.

There's a snowball fight in full swing near the Weir. About
a dozen lads and half a dozen lasses are having a fair old battle.
Everybody is hurling snowballs at anybody else. Tommy and I
look at each other; spread our palms forward; shrug our shoulders
and without a word join in. Wham! I have taken a hit on my right
cheek. "Where did that come from?" As I turn another missile
hits my right shoulder. There he is! Sorry the he is a she! "Duck!"
Another missile is launched from this lass with a grin a mile wide.
She is about five feet two; wearing a blue head-square; a white
mac with a belt and galoshes (Water-proof boots.) "I'll have you
for that!" says I as I scoop up some snow and give chase. By gum!
She can't half run! I will have to pack in smoking fags.

"When I catch you, I will rub your face in the snow." "You will have to catch me first!" laughs she. Did I catch her and rub her in the snow? No reader! It was like Mrs. Faddy's dog trying to catch a rabbit. If I had caught her, I wouldn't have rubbed her- or any other lass. I would do nothing to cause a girl distress. Now, if it had been a bloke, things would have been different.

The battle fought itself to a standstill; we all had a good laugh and dispersed. I saw Dorothy a few days later, skating, (not very well) on the River. A right little wobbler and faller but I'll say this: each time she fell, she came bouncing back. 'Oh! You know her name then?' Yes, reader, I asked one of her mates. 'Did you join her on the ice?' 'Not on your nelly!

Christmas is approaching. Tommy and I are invited to a party at the 'Toby Jug.' Café in Bridge Street- opposite the Catholic Church. After a nice Buffet, we gather in the Party Room upstairs. 'You will never guess who was there, reader.' 'Go on! Try me!' 'Alright then! Tell me!' 'Well! I reckon it was a tiny accurate snow-baller called Dorothy.' 'You're right, reader! How did you guess?' 'Nay lad! It didn't take Rocket Science to work that one out.'

We played games, most involved kisses and cuddles. I found myself with Dorothy during one game and I said, "Can I take you home after the Party." She whispered," Yes." I don't know why I committed myself to walking her home because it was a lousy night: the wind was blowing and the snow snowing- anyway, I did and asked her if we could meet again. Thank goodness this little lass said Yes!

"Hi Tommy!" "Hiya Plug!" (Yes, I am still called Plug.) "How did you get on last night?" "Well Plug! I took Jean home." "Are you seeing her again then?" "No! I don't think so but I bet you are seeing that Dorothy again." "Yes, I am! What makes you so sure?" "I don't know really! But I will tell you one thing: you're going to marry that girl!" "Nay, Tommy! We've only just met!" "Well, mark my words! That's the girl for you!"

So Dorothy and I started courting. After a couple of years, we became engaged and married on the 12th May, 1951. We are both 23 years old and have courted for four years. We honeymooned in Southport and during this holiday, Dorothy and I committed ourselves to each other. The last letter is "N", but I cannot believe that you need it.

Tommy started courting about six months after the Christmas Party. Inevitably, we drifted apart but were always mates. We would go to the flicks now and again. Eventually, he went abroad to work and we didn't see each other for several years. In fact, I was to see Tommy on one last occasion when I reckon he saved my life.

Dorothy and I are settling down into married bliss. We have a son Christopher, we are very happy. We didn't know it at this time, but Christopher was to be our only child. Dorothy suffered several miscarriages. At one time, we considered adoption, but they made it so difficult that we never got around to it.

I am working very hard at Manns: long hours; brain work, and sometimes, very heavy physical effort is required. Ernest Mann is running the business and we have a couple of apprentices- apart from Mick. It seems to be my lot to face the flak from customers and to try and placate them. I think Ernest was a Joiner because he was expected to follow his Grandfather and Father (Uncle Smith) into the business. I think he would have made an Accountant or the like. Mick used to say that he would have made a good snooker player rather than a joiner but he trained to be a Joiner because it was expected of him.

The very first sign that something was amiss happened one Saturday afternoon about four weeks before Christmas. I was working alone and as I bent to start the circular saw, the right hand side of my face twitched. As I straightened up, I felt a little bit dizzy. I thought nothing of it at the time but the twitching persisted and I sort of felt peculiar.

Christmas Holiday, a couple of days off work. By gum! I feel tired! I can't keep awake and I have aches and pains, but it was Christmas. Dorothy and Christopher, now aged ten, and I had a happy break. Back to work then I feel a bit better. The rest has done me good.

It is the Feast of the Epiphany, celebrating the coming of the Magi bearing gifts for the infant Jesus It is a Holy Day of obligation. All practising Catholics must attend Mass under pain of Mortal Sin: it is like a Sunday. Mass is at eight-o-clock in the evening but typical of the 'carry on' at Manns: I didn't catch the ten past five bus to Otley- the same as Mick. No! I worked until seven-o-clock; got the ten past seven bus; dashed home; rushed

my meal; changed; raced to Church and managed it with a couple
of minutes to spare.

The Church is packed. I will probably find a seat at the front. I
walk down the aisle. Ye Gods! I feel peculiar! In fact, I feel lousy!
Anyway there's a space in the second pew from the front. Mick is
sat in the third row. I give him a nod and thank goodness, I am
sat down.

The Priest and Servers come on to the Altar; the congregation
stands, but I don't, I can't- I am frozen! The walls of the Church
seem to be moving forwards and backwards. A steel like band
clamps round my head. I close my eyes; I am sweating profusely.
'Calm down Peter!' thinks I, 'Take a few deep breathes.' A touch
on my shoulder: "Are you alright, mate?" whispers Michael. "No
Mick! I feel lousy! Can you get me home?" "Course I can, come
on!"

The next thing I half remember was Michael ringing the
doorbell. Dorothy answering. I blurted out, "I can't go on any
longer." I brushed past her and crawled upstairs. I was having a
breakdown.

"What just like that?" you may ask. No! Not just like that! I had
worked very hard- sometimes seventy hours a week. Ironically,
it wasn't really for the money, but we were so busy and trying to
please all our customers, my mind and body had said: 'Enough is
enough.' and everything stopped like a clapped-out car engine.

The Doctor prescribed some tablets called 'Purple Hearts.'- so
called because they were purple and were heart shaped. They offered a temporary cure. I felt that I could hold the world about
my head like 'Atlas' but after a short period of time they lost their
effectiveness and to cut a long story edgeways, I went as a vol-
untary patient to Scalebor Park Mental Hospital, at Burley in
Wharfedale.

I was in Neverneverland: everything was unreal- the clamp
round my head prevented me from thinking clearly. Dorothy
and Chris visited. Dorothy came every day but I was on another
planet. There was no passing of time, in fact, 'nowt happened.'
They told me afterwards that I was just like a zombie. Dorothy
and Christopher apparently tried to make conversation, I could
hear them but it could have been Japanese or Greek, as my Mum
would say.

I was several weeks in Hospital. They tried many treatments and drugs. The Doctors concluded that there was nothing medically or mentally wrong with me. I had succumbed to excessive mental and physical work, total rest was the answer.

"I can't drink this milk: it's too cold!" Now where have I heard that before? My eyes are closed, I furrow my brow that's the first normal action I remember. I must be dreaming. "I reckon we should have our <u>own</u> competition: we will have a piss-up." "We can't do that Tommy; we are too young to drink." This is the first time that I have spoken as far as I can recall. "No, Plug! We will have a piss up in the bogs." "Is that you, Tommy?" "Well, old pal! If you open your blinkers, you will see it's me."

I must be dreaming! I am thirty-five years old and here I am talking to a young Tommy! Now I <u>am</u> going ga-ga! A touch on my shoulder: "Come on mate! Waken up! We are going up Giants arse to Weston Wood to rip up any snickles. Right then! Let's be off!" I open my eyes and… Oh my God! <u>It is</u> Tommy! Same shock of hair; same toothy grin: "Welcome back Mate!" "Oh! Oh! Glad to be back!" "Come here! Let's have a hug!"

Tommy had heard of my plight; he was living in South Africa. He had immediately come to England and had visited me almost every evening. He had sat for hours quietly talking to me. Eventually, he made a breakthrough and brought me back to reality. I reckon he saved my life, because although I never told anyone at the time, the only lucid thoughts that I had during my stay in Hospital were suicide.

Tommy stayed around until I was well on the way to recovery. I was never to see him again. He died abroad many years later.

So life goes on, Dorothy and I have been married fifty two years. Chris is a bachelor with his own pad in Lancashire. He lives at home during the week as he is a mature student at Bradford University studying for an Advanced Nursing Diploma, however, he decided that a career in nursing was not for him, so now he is a Teaching Assistant involved with youngsters who have learning difficulties. He is as happy as Larry, who ever Larry is.

From the day we met, Dorothy and I have never had a <u>real</u> barney: just little ones; we have had our differences but have always made up. We have loved and trusted each other and have never had a moment's anxiety over our total commitment to each other.

These words are Dorothy's dear reader and mine also.

I am privileged to have had two loving parents who did not push religion down my throat but they taught me self-respect and respect for others and honesty.

My Mother used to say: "There's enough misery in this World without adding to it."

It's a nice Friday afternoon. I am walking along Kirkgate towards the Jubilee Clock. It's Market Day. The young man about ten yards in front of me has thrown something into the gutter. 'Litter lout!' thinks I. Let's see what he has chucked down. I will give it back to him and tell him to take it home. 'Ah!' as I retrieve the litter I look up, a very frantic young man is searching his pockets, he turns to search the ground. "Have you lost something young sir?" "Yes! I have lost some money." "How much?" "A hundred quid." "Well you are a lucky lad! I saw you drop it and I thought it was litter. Here you are!" A shaken young man gasped: "Thank you! Oh bless you!" It's a pleasure!" says I.

I rejected the proffered ten-pound note and I say, "It's made my day young sir!"

I take no credit for my action. It was perfectly normal, that's how I had been brought up. Thanks Mum! Thanks Dad!

A few weeks later, I was conned out of a twenty-pound note by a bloke who wanted change for the Car Park, or so he said. Ah well! That's life!

So here we are Marie, this is a tale of my childhood, adolescence and growing into manhood. This story ends with Tommy's demise.

I have had a good life with many happy memories and some sad ones. Perhaps I may write another book sometime but this book was inspired by Thomas (Oops!) Tommy. I am not afraid of death but maybe how I die. I pray for a happy exit. Now where have I heard that before? Was it Bill or Ben or maybe both? Being old certainly does not bother me. I have no regrets, I think the World was far happier and content when I made my entrance than it is today. I feel a certain sadness for the youngsters: 'Gimme! Gimme! I want! I want!'. Television and the abuse of this wonderful invention has a lot to answer for. Hey ho!

When my time comes and if I make it to the Big Gates, I suppose St. Peter will be there to welcome me. I guess it could go something like this. "Hello Sir!" "Hello yourself, young Plug!" "Err, I think that you have got that wrong! Young Plug is still living! Err well! He's living at his home I mean!" "No mistake, Son! You're all young uns to me! Coom on in an mek thisen at ome!" "Oh, you can speak Yorkshire English then?" "Of course! It's part of the job. I can teach you to speak in any language." "Now where have I heard something like that before?" thinks I. Oh yes! I remember it was that rotten British sniper and his penny whistle. He said that he could teach Kaiser Bill to play in any language.

"There are lots of your family and relatives waiting to greet you and some other people: Sir. Bill (My first gang leader); Uncle Smith; Willi, Mr. Ben Downe and Bill Dexter." "Oh! It's Ben and Bill! Not Bill and Ben then?." "It's nice to see that you have still got your sense of humour." "Yes! I have always had a good sense of humour! Probably because I was an Undertaker, and an Embalmer." "Probably! Oh, I nearly forgot! Luther wants to see you." "Luther? Not Luther, Luther?" "Yes, the same Luther!" "But I must say that I am a bit surprised! There must have been a cockup... err a mistake." "No mistake lad! When he came back from the War, without a scratch I may add, he was so pleased that he vowed to mend his ways." "Well! I am still surprised." "He was sorry for all the bullying, and the twilts he handed out, also for all the twilts that he promised, and never got round to handing out."

"Well!" says I. "It takes some believing but there we are." "It's never too late! It's never too late, Son! Anyrode! What have you done with your life?" "Well! It's been a longish one! I found time to write this little book." "I hope that it's not full of sex, porn or filthy language?" "No, it isn't! If it was, I don't think that I would be here talking to you." "Your'e reet there son!" "It's mainly about my best mate." "Ah, of course! You mean Tommy?" "That's right! Spot on!" "Come and sit down here! I will take a look at your little book, and whilst we wait, I will send for Tommy." "Good!" says I. "Now we can finally settle that argument we had about space, and I have a gut feeling that I am going to lose it."

Printed in the United States
By Bookmasters